# CENTER C

# HEALING, MAGIC AND

# SELF-KNOWLEDGE

### ORIGINAL ARTICLES & AUDIO TRANSCRIPTS

◆ THE CENTER OF STILLNESS MEDITATION ◆
◆ THE SELF-HEALING ARCHAEOUS ◆
◆ THE MAGIC OF IHVH-ADNI ◆
◆ KNOW THYSELF ◆

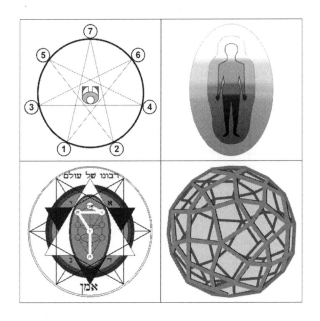

## RAWN CLARK
2012

# CENTER OF STILLNESS, HEALING, MAGIC AND SELF-KNOWLEDGE
## Original Articles & Audio Transcripts
By Rawn Clark

◄──────────────────────►

For more of Rawn Clark's work online, please visit —
www.ABardonCompanion.com
www.RawnMade.com

◄──────────────────────►

# CONTENTS

PREFACE ... 5

## THE CENTER OF STILLNESS MEDITATION
ORIGINAL ARTICLE (1995) ... 11
AUDIO RECORDING TRANSCRIPT (2003) ... 25

## RAWN'S SELF-HEALING ARCHAEOUS
ORIGINAL ARTICLE (1997) ... 37
AUDIO LESSON TRANSCRIPTS (2002)
  LESSON ONE: Awareness and Integration of the Physical Body ... 51
  LESSON TWO: Awareness and Integration of the Astral Body ... 56
  LESSON THREE: Awareness and Integration of the Mental Body ... 62
  LESSON FOUR: Passive Separation of the Astra-Mental Body ... 68
  LESSON FIVE: Passive Separation of the Solitary Mental Body ... 78
  LESSON SIX: Elemental Balancing and Re-integration ... 86
  LESSON SEVEN: Astra-Mental Wandering ... 90
  LESSON EIGHT: Techniques of Mental Wandering ... 95
  LESSON NINE: The Fine Art of Integration ... 100

## THE MAGIC OF IHVH-ADNI
ORIGINAL ARTICLE (1998) "ATTENDING THE UNITY" ... 113
AUDIO LESSON TRANSCRIPTS (2002)
  LESSON ONE: Pronunciation, Tonality and Rhythm ... 123
  LESSON TWO: Three-Part Magical Speech ... 126
  LESSON THREE: Energetics ... 129
  LESSON FOUR: Applications ... 135
  LESSON FIVE: Creating a Triple Shield ... 142
  LESSON SIX: Consciousness Raising ... 148
  LESSON SEVEN: Setting the Tone of the Temporal Moment ... 155
  LESSON EIGHT: Healing From Afar ... 167
  LESSON NINE: The Blessing of IHVH-ADNI ... 173
FURTHER DEVELOPMENTS (2003-2004)
  THE FINAL FORM ... 183
  TMO AND THE ARCHAEOUS ... 187
  THE PATH OF BRILLIANCE ... 192

## KNOW THYSELF
AUDIO SERIES TRANSCRIPTS (2006)
  INTRODUCTION ... 203
  ONE: PHYSICAL PERCEPTION ... 208
  TWO: ASTRAL PERCEPTION ... 217
  THREE: MENTAL PERCEPTION ... 223

## APPENDIX
SOWANTHA: A Mystical Journey ... 233

# PREFACE

Whilst awaiting the arrival of several crystals for a magical Tool I've been commissioned to make, I decided to fill the otherwise empty work days by putting this book together. This latest volume in my recent barrage of books is a compilation of four past works originally created during the period from 1995 through 2006.

There are four aspects that link each of these pieces together. First is that each was born when I was living a solitary, rustic life in the countryside of Northern California and in some way reflects the inspiration of my natural surroundings. Second is that each is an original creation — neither repetition of another's work nor commentary upon another's work — simply my own work, drawn from within my own Self. Third is that the intent of each piece is the empowerment of the reader, the setting out of technique capable of enabling and liberating the reader's own direct personal experience. And fourth is the fact that I recorded audio versions of each piece.

I guess a fifth connection must be admitted as well — until the publication of this book, each existed only in digital format online, on CD and on personal computers. And while that's lovely and makes them widely and freely available to those with access to computers and audio players, it is also a bit foolish — what happens when the electricity goes out??? What happens when the internet crashes and all those bits of data go poof??? So, this then is my bid for an existence beyond the inevitable cyber-collapse for my creations!

**The Center of Stillness Meditation** was written not too long after my first direct experience of merging with my Greater Self in Binah and is based upon the spontaneous journey I took at that time. In the original 1995 article, I translated my spontaneous experience into a method or technique that would enable others to pursue a similar journey of Self discovery.

In the later 1990s, the CSM article was published as a small pamphlet and appeared in a very obscure journal. It wasn't until I first posted it on my website ABardonCompanion.com in 2001 that it garnered a wider audience and popularity. A year later I wrote and then recorded an abbreviated audio version in which I guided the listener through the core technique. This was revised and improved and in 2003 it was posted for free download on my website and for sale as an audio CD.

In this book I reproduce the original 1995 article and a transcript of the 2003 audio recording.

**Rawn's Self-Healing Archaeous** describes a self-healing technique that evolved over a number of years and which I personally have found extremely beneficial.

Although written a couple of years after the CSM, it shares much the same history — pamphlet, very obscure journal and then posting online in 2001 and recording in 2002. With the Archaeous however, the recording was broken down into a series of nine "Lessons" which progressively guide the listener deeper and deeper into various applications of the core technique. The Self-Healing Archaeous techniques have become very popular in the past decade!

Here I present the original 1997 article and transcripts of all nine audio "Lessons".

**The Magic of IHVH-ADNI**, known commonly as **TMO**, is very close to my heart and feels to me to be my most important contribution. Of all my work thusfar, TMO has certainly had the greatest impact globally with thousands of practitioners worldwide and more engaging with it every day that passes.

I was first introduced to TMO (in a somewhat more rudimentary form than I present here) in the late 1980s under circumstances I will not describe due to their very personal nature. Over the decade that followed, I practiced incessantly and gradually refined the technique. In 1998 I finally found voice to share TMO through an article titled "Attending The Unity". This too was published as a pamphlet and appeared in the same very obscure journal. And as with the CSM and the Archaeous, it was posted on my website for the first time in 2001, however instead of garnering practitioners at the time, it generated a huge amount of curiosity and questions all of which prompted me to create a series of audio "Lessons" in the TMO practice. The nine TMO audio "Lessons" are my most popular recordings.

Shortly after the release of the audio "Lessons" the *TMO Working Group* was formed to explore the possibilities of using TMO in a group context. The *TMO-WG* is still going strong with members from across the globe engaged in regular group work. As it turned out, TMO is ideal for group work!

Here I present the original 1998 article and transcripts of all nine audio "Lessons". Additionally, I have included three more recent articles which describe further developments in TMO.

If TMO interests you, then I strongly recommend that you download the free audio files by visiting my website ABardonCompanion.com or tmo-wg.net.

**Know ThySelf** was created in 2006 in an effort to clarify experientially (instead of just intellectually) the meaning of the term "self" in an Hermetic context, specifically a Bardonian context. It was presented as a series of three audio files in which the listener is guided through a process of self-recognition. It too has proved quite popular and I'm always receiving requests to continue the audio series! Here I present transcripts of the audio files.

And just for good measure I've tagged on an Appendix that contains a piece I wrote in 1996 titled, **SOWANTHA: A MYSTICAL JOURNEY**. I've included it because it is referenced in the Archaeous text and it is also quite relevant to much of the material in all four sections of this book.

Well, I hope you enjoy the read and find some valuable techniques to experiment with! And if you are reading this *after* the cyber-collapse and there are no more audio recordings to refer to, then I hope that what you read here will be sufficient to re-ignite the practice of these techniques. As I was for myself in the creating of these techniques, you will have to be your own guide. Let experimentation and experience lead you!

My best to you!
  Rawn Clark
  Berlin, Germany
  12 June 2012

# THE
# CENTER OF
# STILLNESS
# MEDITATION

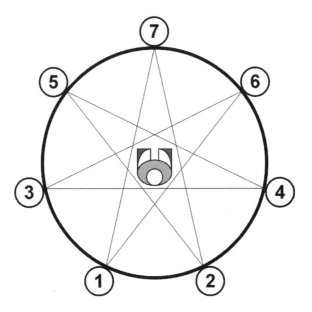

## THE ORIGINAL ARTICLE
1995

# INTRODUCTION

There is, in the nature of human consciousness, the need to take apart, particularize, define and limit a thing in order to come to an understanding of it. In the name of science, we dissect the frog of experience in the hopes of learning how it works, ignoring the fact that we have killed it in the process and are examining a dead thing. The error we fall into is that we neglect to re-integrate our nascent understanding back into the organic whole from which we have plucked it.

Instead of removing the frog to our laboratory, we also have the option of taking our laboratory to the frog, and observing our subject in its natural environment, with its livelihood still intact.

Our natural environment is the Infinite Universe, within which we humans exist across a broad spectrum of vibration. We experience one end of this continuum through our most sublime thoughts; and the other end, through the physical reality of our bodies. The realm between these two poles, that which personalizes and binds our thoughts to our physical bodies, is our emotional field of experience. These levels of human vibration have been defined as "spirit" (mental body, the realm of thought), "soul" (astral body, the realm of emotion), and "physical" (physical body, the realm of sensation). However, it must be realized that these divisions are arbitrary, human constructs, for there is no point at which one degree of vibration is separate from that next to it.

Our experience at the physical level is one of aloneness. We live as separate beings, within a Universe filled with other separate beings. Yet laying behind these levels of vibration, is That which is vibrated, or vibrates -- the One Self of which we are all an expression. It is this base fabric which calls to us in our physical aloneness and reminds us of the core truth that we are all somehow connected.

The whole of human existence is a dance between our experience of separateness and our primal need for connectedness. One of the great paradoxes of the Universe, is that it is the very fact of our physical existence that blinds us to the level at which we are connected. The physical world so captivates our conscious awareness that we are seldom cognizant of what lies beyond it; yet, it is only by casting our awareness beyond it, only by tearing our attention from it and turning within, that we come to experience the deeper levels of Self and touch upon our primal Unity.

The main barrier then, to a conscious experience of our shared inner Self, is that our bodily senses gobble up the majority of our attention. This is a natural consequence of a physical existence, and cannot really be judged in terms of good or bad. It simply is. The senses can be viewed as either a wondrous Gift from a Benign Universe, whose only purpose is to give us the faculties needed for physical life; or, as an onus of evil, which we are doomed to suffer and battle. The meditation technique which follows is based upon the former and stresses a non-judgmental control over the senses.

We each have an inherent ability to negate the senses. While you have been reading this, have not your senses of hearing, smell, taste, and touch been diminished as your attention turned to seeing, emotionally feeling, and rationally thinking about these words? This is but one example of how we sub-consciously select one or two sensory inputs over the others. The active ingredient here is attention, or conscious awareness, and it is this key which the Center of Stillness Meditation (CSM) technique employs in its training of the conscious negation of the senses. By building upon what we each do a million times a day un-consciously, the CSM brings it to the level of a conscious faculty.

The ability to negate the senses at will, takes effort and persistence to attain; especially with any consistency. But even with the first brief moment of separation from the senses, comes a re-acquaintance with the Center of Stillness, that Primal Quiet we all know in our bones. Once this Stillness has been experienced, the question of effort becomes irrelevant in light of the exciting possibilities perceived within. The further refining of one's control over the senses passes quickly thereafter, and the inner realms unfold.

The first realm to open is that of the personality. In the CSM, this is visualized as a web of light-fibers, which we each spin within the stream of time-space. This is the level at which we place our Selves within the context of where and when we are, and bind ourselves to a physical expression. The personality is our creation -- one which we usually create un-consciously and feel little power with.

As with our power to negate the senses, we also have an inherent ability to craft our personality. Remember back to your adolescence, when "peer-pressure" was the weather-vane of who you chose to be (at least to some extent); a time of trying on several different masks and choosing ones that felt "safe", or hopefully, "right" for you. As you grew into your adulthood, did you not discard certain masks for new ones? We each have experiences of changing "bad habits", or annoying little idiosyncrasies, to better fit into our lives. The muscles we use in our un-conscious, selective negation of the senses, are the same ones we use in the unconscious crafting of our personalities. The CSM exercises these muscles upon the personality, and you learn to consciously craft it, weaving it anew into a clearer expression of who you are and want to be.

The experiences with the personality invariably lead to the awareness that there is a Self who is experiencing -- a core which is the Doer, the Crafter. This is the next level to unfold, the level of Individual Self, the Self-Who-Acts. We most often experience this aspect of Self through very strong feelings, or intuitions, that a certain course is the one we must follow. Probably the most dramatic experiences of your life have been accompanied by the clear knowledge of who you are at the core. This is your Individuality; your Self perceiving itself as an autonomous, unique Individual. It is the Individuality which projects and crafts the web of the personality, and consequently manifests physically in a body; or to put it another way, the personality and the physical body are the vehicles of the Individual Self.

In the CSM, the level of Individual Self is visualized as a Sun with the aspects of the personality and physical body orbiting as it's solar system. This Sun exists in an Infinite Universe, filled with other Individual Selves, other solar systems, other stars populating the night sky. From the perspective of Individual Self, one looks "down" to the personality and body, wielding them as magical tools in the clear expression of the Individuality's purpose. As with the senses and the personality, the CSM takes this otherwise un-consciously natural process and makes of it a consciously integrated faculty. One learns to act powerfully and directly in the Universe as an equally important Individual.

As the Individual Self matures and learns to express itself more clearly, the power of its essential purpose asserts itself. The knowledge, and more importantly, the experience, that all is interconnected and of One Source, begins to crystallize. Slowly, one is lead to the Great Transformation, which comes with the opening of the next level of Self, that of the Greater Self.

The Greater Self is the first level at which we truly experience an interconnectedness. The Greater Self exists beyond space-time-meaning (that which is the foundation of space-time), manifesting countless Individualities (and consequently, personalities and physical bodies) within its stream. Since words are space-time constructs, it becomes impossible to clearly describe such a realm -- only poetry and mysticism can approach an expression of it -- so my words must be taken as symbols, filled-to-brimming with meaning. That said, I would describe it as a womb, from which we emerge as Individual foci of conscious awareness. Yet, there are several (an infinite number of?) Greater Selves, casting their progeny into the river of existence; so this is clearly not the Ultimate Connectedness which calls to us. Such a connection comes only with the awareness of The One Self, the Self of which we are all equal centers of expression. This is the Ultimate Union with All, the ultimate goal of the CSM.

# CSM PRACTICE

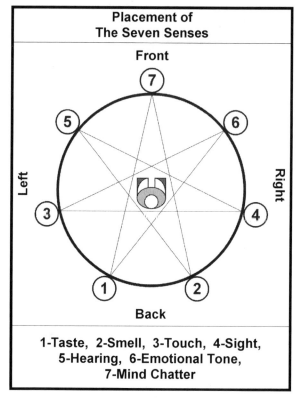

**Placement of
The Seven Senses**

**Front**

**Left**

**Right**

**Back**

1-Taste, 2-Smell, 3-Touch, 4-Sight,
5-Hearing, 6-Emotional Tone,
7-Mind Chatter

### #10 - MALKUTH: Body
Acknowledgment of, and separation from, the seven senses
(taste, smell, touch, sight, hearing, emotional tone, and mind chatter).

The CSM begins with the physical body; its comfort and relaxation. Find for yourself a comfortable position, one that you can remain comfortable in for at least half an hour. For some this will be achieved best by sitting upright in a cushioned chair; for others, by laying down flat on the back, or through the assumption of a chosen yogic asana.

Once you are settled, close your eyes, calm yourself and take note of your breath. Count out your inhale and your exhale, and for a few moments, breathe to this steady rhythm.

Shift your awareness to your feet, and gently relax each of their muscles. Release all the tension from your feet. Follow by gently relaxing and releasing the tension from your ankles, then calves, knees, thighs, hips, buttocks, groin, stomach, lower-back, upper-back, chest, shoulders, upper-arms, elbows, forearms, wrists, hands, neck, throat, mouth, cheeks, nose, eyes, forehead, scalp, ears, and rectum. Release all the tension from your Body.

Turn your attention to the taste in your mouth. Note it closely and experience it as clearly, and thoroughly, as you can. Willfully and abruptly, let it go. Consciously release it, just as you did with the tension in your body -- as if you were opening your hands and letting go of something which you had grasped. Willfully separate the sense of taste from your Self. Make of it a sphere of whatever color seems appropriate, and place it behind you, to the left.

You are now separate from the sense of taste. To reconnect with it, simply reach behind you and touch the sphere. This brings taste back to you as a usable sensory organ; it re-unites you with taste, re-involves your attention. Disengage from taste once again, by first taking close note of its input of information, and then by consciously separating it from your Self. Let it go, and place it external to your Self, behind you, to the left.

Willfully turn your attention **AWAY** from the sphere of taste and **TO** your sense of smell. As before, delve deeply into your experience of this sense's input. Smell all there is to be smelled. Note all the thoughts and emotions that these smells bring up, and let them go -- try to focus on smell alone, try to isolate this one sense -- let smell happen without judgment, or extraneous thought. Then abruptly, and willfully, let smell go. Separate it from your Self, placing it as a colored sphere, behind you, to the right. Picture it clearly, suspended next to the sphere of taste. Both are external to you and do not involve your attention.

Willfully turn your mind's eye **AWAY** from the spheres of taste and smell, and **TO** your sense of touch. Clearly feel all that your nerves relay to you... delve into each sensation, trying always to isolate the sense of touch. Let it go as before, and place its sphere directly to your left, next to that of taste.

To your right, you will place the sphere of your sense of sight, following the same process used with the previous senses. In front of you, slightly to the left, place the sphere of your sense of hearing, next to that of touch.

This completes the separation from the five physical senses. Laying behind these physical senses are those of the astral and mental bodies. The senses of the astral body manifest in the physical matrix through the Emotional Tone, and those of the mental body, through the Mind Chatter. Though the Emotional Tone and Mind Chatter have their source in subtler realms than the physical, they nonetheless, impact our physical experience in the same ways that the five physical senses do. Consequently, they too must be let go of.

With the five physical senses separate from you, and surrounding you, look within and experience your Emotional Tone. Try to isolate it even from "thought"...FEEL it, know it...and let it go. Separate it from your Self, and place its sphere in front of you, slightly to the right, next to that of sight. Each time that it, or any of the senses, reaches out and grabs your awareness, note it, and then return it to its separateness.

Willfully turn your attention **AWAY** from your Emotional Tone, and **TO** your Mind's Chatter. As with the other senses, delve into your Mind's Chatter, experiencing it as fully as possible. Isolate it, and let it flow of its own, without your involvement, or attachment to certain threads of its progression. Each time you are drawn into it, note the fact and then separate from it. Externalize it, make of it a beautifully radiant sphere, and place it directly in front of you.

The experience of Self, with all seven senses separate and external, is the Center of Stillness. At first, this Center of Stillness may be elusive, but as your ability to separate the senses increases, your presence within it will extend from moments to minutes, then to tens of minutes, and so on.

Of all the seven senses, Mind Chatter is the most subtle and the one to which we have the strongest attraction. So, do not be discouraged by the brevity of your initial successes with its separation. Each time you exercise your separating-muscle, the effort required becomes less and the result greater. Before you know it, your ability will have grown to the point of absolute control over all seven of the senses, and quick access to the Center of Stillness.

### #9 - YESOD: Personality (instinct)
Complete control over the Senses.
Attention turns to the "Web" of one's life.

Once you have broken through the barrier of the seven senses, build upon your skill at negating the senses, and concentrate on attaining the Center of Stillness. Visualize yourself sitting in the Center of infinite space, with the spheres of the senses surrounding you -- separate, yet at your beck and call. All about you is a quiet darkness. Spend a good amount of time coming to know and feeling comfortable with this Center. Drink heartily from this cup of silence.

Directly below you, begin visualizing the web of your personality; the tapestry you weave of your life. Let each light-fiber of its structure be made from some aspect of who you are in the world. Be absolutely honest with your self about your good points as well as your bad points. Look at your life and reflect its meaning in your web. Each and every aspect of who you are and how you express your Self, must be carefully gathered, acknowledged and woven into your web. Craft a web that truly and completely reflects the totality of your personality.

As you weave, you will be faced with making value judgments about the strands of your personality. You will be sorely tempted to deny their place in your work of Art, but please do not. The first goal is to get a picture of your personality exactly as it exists now, without getting caught up in value judgments and consequent self-change. Do not try to craft your personality into something new at this stage, merely diagram it and in that way, come to know its every wrinkle, blemish, and beauty.

Return repeatedly to the Center of Stillness and craft this symbol of your personality until you feel it to be complete. Then ask yourself if you're really sure it's thorough enough. Keep asking until you're sure that you're sure.

### #8 - HOD: Personality (rational mind)
Study of the "Web" and beginning of conscious activity within it.

The web, when complete, is a thing of rare beauty. It is totally unique to each individual: a one-of-a-kind work of Art. Now that you have come to know the ins and outs of the personality you currently manifest, you can begin to change it and shape it into a clearer expression of your Self.

We each carry within us a sensory organ which will guide us in self-change -- our conscience. Our conscience, above all other factors, speaks to us of what is personally right or wrong. It can override all other "laws", or it can be ignored and denied, but it *always* speaks to our inner ear.

Examine your web with the search-light of your conscience and note what aspects of it, what patterns of reactive, instinctive behavior, emerge into your field of view. Begin actively making those value judgments you tried to avoid earlier. Look closely at your web and judge it honestly, with self-love and acceptance. Judge its good parts as well as its bad parts. Make note of what you desire to transform and the parts you wish to preserve.

Once you have a solid image of what you wish to accomplish in terms of self-change, then and only then, should you begin making changes. Choose one item at a time and work with it till you have achieved the transformation you desire. I use the word "transformation" quite intentionally, because I wish to stress that this is not a "getting rid of"; but rather, a shifting of an already present energy-substance to a new focus. Your task is to transform the light-fiber of your chosen item into the new aspect you desire.

Self-change however, requires more than mere visualization. As with all the aspects of the CSM, the process of self-change must be integrated into one's physical life. The transformations you cause in the web of your personality must be reflected in who you are in the world, they must be evident in your consequent actions and patterns of thought.

Work at transforming your chosen item with every faculty at your disposal and do not rest until you have met with success. When your life and the light-fiber of your chosen item match each other, reflecting the reality of your successful transformation, only then should you move on to another item.

### #7 - NETZACH: Personality (lower emotions)
Mastery over the "Web". Attention turns to separation
from the "Web" and toward Individual Self.

Keep returning to the Center of Stillness and the web of your personality, continuing relentlessly in your work of self-change. Gradually, your web and your life will reflect the personality you have chosen to self-craft. Let it be an image of unique and great beauty, clearly expressive of your core nature.

The work with the personality never really reaches an end. Life experiences will always show you parts of yourself that need improvement, parts you were unaware of previously, or that suddenly no longer serve you well. "Perfection" is an elusive and fluid thing at this level of self expression. So, over the years, you will need to return periodically to your web with the critical eye of your conscience, and make new adjustments.

At a certain point (you will know when it arrives) you must say "enough for now", and move on from involvement with your web. If you can look at the tapestry of light-fibers and feel proud of who you have become, then you have truly reached this turning point and are ready to move on.

Sitting in the Center of Stillness, look down at the web of your personality. Experience it as fully as you can, listening closely to its input, to what it tells you of your core nature. Now, let it go. Separate it from your Self just as you did with the seven senses. It lies below you, separate from you. To re-involve yourself with it, merely touch it and you are reunited. Note its input, and then carefully return it to its separateness.

In this state of separateness from the senses and the web, spend time meditating upon the Self-Who-Acts. Strive to identify with that part of you which crafted the web so carefully. This is your Individuality, the aspect of Self which is expressed through the web of your personality.

Return often to this meditation.

### #6 - TIPHARETH: Individuality (core)
Separation from the "Web" and the achievement of
the perspective of Individual-Self.

At some point, there will occur a shift in your perspective, and you will find your Self looking down at the personality and body, as you would look down at your feet. They are still an integral part of you, a part required for physical existence and expression; yet, they are somehow separate in a totally new way.

This shift in perspective is very difficult to describe with words. Suffice it to say that it will be a transformative revelation; a cathartic experience of coming to know and experience your Self as a powerful, autonomous Individual.

Once this new perspective has been achieved, visualize your Self as an Individual Sun, with the aspects of your personality, the seven senses, and your body, orbiting about you. Stand as the center of gravity in the solar system of your life. All around you, in the darkness of infinite space, the night sky is populated with countless other solar systems. Each bright point of light is a Star like your Self.

Keep returning to this experience of Individual Self, building upon your initial revelation until it is easily attained and comfortable.

### #5 - GEBURAH: Individuality (will)
Study of the Individual-Self and beginning of its
conscious activity in the external Universe.

Your task now is to become consciously and directly active as an Individual. Look down at your web and your physical existence. How clearly is your Individual Self expressed through their agency? As you come to know and identify with your Individual Self, project your essential nature into your web and your physical life.

Let each breath, each thought and action, express clearly the goals and tasks of your Individuality. As you move throughout your life, see to it that each moment reflects who you are. Shape and craft your life to this end. It is after all, the vehicle of your Individuality's physical expression.

Come to know, experience, and exercise your Individual power in the Universe.

### #4 - GEDULAH: Individuality (higher emotions)
Mastery of the Individual-Self. Attention turns to separation from
Individual-Self and toward Greater-Self.

Look now to those other Stars which fill the Universe. Reach out and communicate with your neighbors, as one Individual to another. Over time, become active within this community of Individuals, contributing your own unique talents and perspectives to the Universal culture.

As you travel and experience the Universe, you will encounter other Individuals who seem completely familiar, as if they were parts of your Self. Gradually, the awareness of a deep level of connection with these others will emerge. This is the initial perception and experience of the Greater Self, the level of Self at which many of us are One.

This level of connection appears to be hidden by a veil. While it is only with the blessing of Divine Providence that this veil can be truly penetrated, it still requires a concomitant personal effort to lift. So, spend time meditating upon this barrier. Study it thoroughly. Approach it and try your best to pass through it. When the time is ripe, you will succeed in separating from your Individuality and uniting with your Greater Self.

### #3 - BINAH: Greater Self (Understanding)
Separation from Individual-Self and the achievement of the
perspective of Greater-Self.

When you have, with the grace of the Divine, penetrated the veil, you will no longer be the person you were before that moment. Your experience of the Self and its role will be totally and dramatically transformed. This can be a very unsettling time for your physical life, so treat yourself well throughout.

Come to know your Greater Self, returning to this perspective often as you strive to integrate its awareness into your life. Look down to your Individuality, personality, and physical body, and note how clearly they manifest the purpose of your Greater Self. This is to be a time of Self-discovery.

### #2 - CHOKMAH: Greater Self (Wisdom)
Mastery as Greater-Self and its activity in the external Universe.
Attention turns to separation from the Greater-Self
and toward The One Self.

When you are comfortable with the experience of Greater Self, begin crafting the Individuality to better express the Greater Self's goals. See to it that the Greater Self is fully integrated at the levels of Individuality, personality, and physical body. Then, reach out, and communicate with the other Greater Selves that you perceive. Much like the experience of your Individuality joining the larger community of the Universe, exert the power of your Greater Self within this new, subtler Universe.

These experiences will lead you to the realization of The One Self, the level at which even the various Greater Selves are united. Though the veil between the Greater Self and The One Self is very ephemeral, it still requires conscious effort (and, of course, the blessings of Divine Providence) to breach. Guidance for this task must come from within.

### #1 - KETHER: The One Self
Separation from the Greater-Self and Unity with The One Self.

Ultimately, one separates from even the Greater Self, and merges completely with The One Self. This is the true experience of Unity.

May we all be so Blest!

# THE
# CENTER OF
# STILLNESS
# MEDITATION

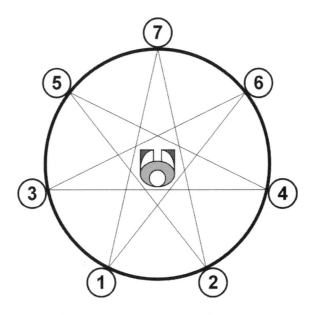

# THE AUDIO RECORDING
2003

# INTRODUCTION

There is, in the nature of human consciousness, the need to take apart, particularize, define and limit a thing in order to come to an understanding of it. In the name of science, we dissect the frog of experience in the hopes of learning how it works, ignoring the fact that we have killed it in the process and are examining a dead thing. The error we fall into is that we neglect to re-integrate our nascent understanding back into the organic whole from which we have plucked it.

Instead of removing the frog to our laboratory, we also have the option of taking our laboratory to the frog, and observing our subject in its natural environment, with its livelihood still intact.

Our natural environment is the Infinite Universe, within which we humans exist across a broad spectrum of vibration. We experience one end of this continuum through our most sublime thoughts; and the other end, through the physical reality of our bodies. The realm between these two poles, that which personalizes and binds our thoughts to our physical bodies, is our emotional field of experience. In Hermetics, these three primary levels of human vibration have been defined as "spirit", our mental body and the realm of thought; as "soul", our astral body and the realm of emotion; and as "material", our physical body and the realm of sensation.

Our experience at the physical level is basically one of aloneness. We live as separate beings, within a Universe filled with other separate beings. Yet lying behind these levels of vibration, is That which vibrates -- the One Self of which we are all an expression. It is this base fabric which calls to us in our experience of physical aloneness and reminds us of the core truth that we are all somehow connected.

The whole of human existence is a dance between our experience of separateness and our primal need for connectedness. One of the great paradoxes of the Universe, is that it's our physical existence with its experience of separation, that blinds us to the level at which we are connected. The physical world so captivates our conscious awareness that we are seldom cognizant of what lies beyond it. Yet it is only by casting our awareness beyond it, only by tearing our attention away from it and turning within, that we come to experience the deeper levels of Self and touch upon our primal Unity.

The main barrier then, to a conscious experience of our shared inner Self, is that our bodily senses gobble up the majority of our attention. This is a natural consequence of a physical existence, and cannot really be judged in terms of good or bad. It simply is.

We each have an inherent ability to negate the senses. While you have been listening to my voice, have not your senses of sight, smell, taste, and touch been diminished as your attention turned to hearing, emotionally feeling, and rationally thinking about these words? This is but one example of how we sub-consciously select one or two sensory inputs over the others. The active ingredient here is attention, or conscious awareness, and it is this key which the Center of Stillness Meditation technique employs in its training of the conscious negation of the senses. By building upon what we each do a million times a day un-consciously, the CSM brings it to the level of a conscious faculty.

The CSM defines seven senses. In addition to the traditional five physical senses, the CSM takes into account those of the astral and mental bodies. The reason for this is because these subtle senses impact our physical experience and, even if we aren't cognizant of it, their input affects our lives and our experience just as significantly as do sight, hearing, smell, taste and touch.

The basic technique is really very simple. We begin by focusing our whole attention upon the input from one sense. Having isolated this particular bit of sensory information, we willfully move our attention away from that sense and turn it toward the input from the next sense. In other words, we ignore one sense at a time until we've reached a point when all of the input from the senses is being ignored.

In the CSM, the senses are addressed in a sequence designed to accommodate the average person's sensory preferences. We begin with the sense of taste, which for most is the sense we pay least attention to while listening and thinking. Then we move on to smelling, touch, sight and hearing.

Each sense is visualized as a sphere of specifically colored light which you are instructed to willfully separate from yourself. These spheres are arranged around you in a specific sequence, based upon their relative importance and overall ability to distract you.

Once the traditional five senses have been separated and ignored, attention turns to the sensory input of the astral and mental senses.

The senses of the astral body manifest in the physical matrix through our emotional tone or mood. The important impact that one's emotional state has upon one's thought process and upon one's physical perceptions is well known. But while the impact that the five traditional senses have upon one's ability to reach deep levels of meditation is generally dealt with in meditational techniques, the impact of one's emotional state is rarely even mentioned, let alone addressed effectively. With the CSM however, emotional tone is treated in the same manner as the five physical senses are. We observe the present state of our emotions within and then willfully separate our awareness from the input of this astral sense.

Similarly, the senses of the mental body manifest in the physical matrix through the mind's chatter. Mental chatter is the result of the physical brain's processing of the input from the subtle senses resident in one's mental body. This chatter takes up a significant amount of the brain's attention, therefore dulling the depth and quality of our perceptual ability and obscuring the deeper levels of Mind and thought that are available to us. When the brain's chatter is quieted, the deeper Mind is revealed and the CSM takes direct advantage of this fact as you are directed to willfully separate from the input of this mental sense.

The ability to negate the senses at will, takes effort and persistence to attain; especially with any consistency. But even with the first brief moment of separation from the senses, comes a re-acquaintance with the Center of Stillness, that Primal Quiet we all know in our bones. Once this Stillness has been experienced, the question of effort becomes irrelevant in light of the exciting possibilities perceived within. The further refining of one's control over the senses passes quickly thereafter, and the inner realms unfold.

In the audio rendition of the CSM, we will briefly explore a few of the options open to us.

The first realm to open is that of the personality. In the CSM, this is visualized as a web of light-fibers, which we each spin within the stream of time-space. This is the level at which we place our Selves within the context of where and when we are, and bind ourselves to a physical expression. The personality is our creation -- one which we usually create un-consciously and feel little power with.

As with our power to negate the senses, we also have an inherent ability to craft our personality. Remember back to your adolescence, when "peer-pressure" was the weather-vane of who you chose to be; a time of trying on several different masks and choosing ones that felt "safe", or hopefully, "right" for you. As you grew into your adulthood, did you not discard certain masks for new ones? We each have experiences of changing "bad habits", or annoying little idiosyncrasies, to better fit into our lives. The muscles we use in our un-conscious, selective negation of the senses, are the same ones we use in the un-conscious crafting of our personalities. The CSM exercises these muscles upon the personality, and you learn to consciously craft it, weaving it anew into a clearer expression of who you are and want to be.

As we let go of our focus upon the personality, we are invariably led to the awareness that there is a Self who is experiencing -- a core which is the Doer, the Crafter. This is the next level to unfold, the level of Individual Self, the Self-Who-Acts. This is your Individuality; your Self perceiving itself as an autonomous, unique Individual. It is the Individuality which projects and crafts the web of the personality, and consequently manifests physically in a body; or to put it another way, the personality and the physical body are the vehicles of the Individual Self.

In the CSM, the level of Individual Self is visualized as a Sun with the aspects of the personality and physical body orbiting as its solar system. This Sun exists in an Infinite Universe, filled with other Individual Selves, other solar systems, other stars populating the night sky.

We expand our Individual Self awareness until we touch the metaphorical edges of the infinite universe and then we let go of Individuality and universe and simply exist as a still center of BEing.

Then we consciously re-integrate our awareness of the universe, of the Individual and personal selves, and then of the seven senses which bind us to physical life.

While the audio rendition of the CSM lasts for only about 20 minutes, the Center of Stillness itself is a far richer territory, deserving of lengthy investigation. My hope is that this brief recording will serve as an introduction to this inner universe of possibilities and will inspire you to deeper and more extensive self-directed exploration.

So, let's move on to the practice itself.


## PRACTICE

The Center of Stillness Meditation, begins with the comfort and relaxation of your physical body. I suggest that you either sit in a comfortable chair, lie down or assume your favorite asana.

Once you are settled comfortably, close your eyes and observe your breathing. Focus entirely upon your breathing and relax. Let go of all other concerns for this short span of time.

Shift your awareness to your feet and gently relax all the muscles in your feet. Now begin moving up your body, relaxing each set of muscles as you go. Relax your calves; your thighs; your hips and buttocks; relax your abdomen and lower back; relax your chest and upper back; relax your shoulders; relax your upper-arms, forearms and hands; relax your neck, mouth, cheeks, eyes, forehead and scalp. Let every bit of tension drain from your body and pass downward, into the earth.

Focus again on your breathing. Let it flow naturally.

Now shift your attention to the taste in your mouth. Explore the input of this sense. What does it taste like? What does it make you think of? Delve deeply into all that this sense has to tell you in this moment.

Now separate the sense of taste itself, from the thoughts and emotions that arise with it. Isolate taste and taste alone. Recognize it as simply a sensation without any special significance.

Now let go of this sense's input just as you let go of all the tension in your body. Separate the sense of taste from yourself and shape it into a sphere, giving it a dull green color. Willfully separate this sphere of taste from yourself and place it behind you, to the left.

With your mind's eye, look back at it. See it floating there. It is separate from you and no longer registers as a sensation.

Now reach out mentally and bring it back into yourself. Reconnect with your sense of taste. This is all you have to do to again receive its input.

Now separate taste from yourself once more and return it to its status as a separate, dull green sphere, behind you, to the left.

Now willfully turn your attention away from the sphere of taste and focus upon your sense of smell. Delve deeply into whatever you smell at this moment. As before, isolate just smell and smell alone. Separate your smelling from your thinking and your feeling. Recognize it as simply a sensation without any special significance.

Now abruptly and willfully, separate yourself from your sense of smell. Shape it into a sphere of dull yellow and place it behind you, to the right. Clearly see it floating next to your green sphere of taste. You are separate from its input.

Now willfully turn your attention away from the spheres of taste and smell and focus upon your sense of touch. Clearly feel everything that your nerves relay to you in this moment. Delve into each sensation and isolate the sense of touch. Separate it from your thinking and from your emotional feelings. Recognize it as simply a sensation without any special significance.

Now abruptly and willfully, separate yourself from your sense of touch. Shape it into a sphere of pale violet and place it directly to your left, next to the green sphere of taste. You are separate from its input.

Now willfully turn your attention away from the sphere of touch and focus upon your sense of sight. Clearly see everything that your eyes relay to you in this moment. Delve into each visual sensation and isolate the sense of sight. Separate it from your thinking and from your emotional feelings. Recognize it as simply a sensation without any special significance.

Now abruptly and willfully, separate yourself from your sense of sight. Shape it into a sphere of soft red and place it directly to your right, next to the yellow sphere of smell. You are separate from its input.

Now willfully turn your attention away from the sphere of sight and focus upon your sense of hearing. Clearly hear everything that your ears relay to you in this moment. Delve into each sensation and isolate the sense of hearing. Separate it from your thinking and from your emotional feelings. Recognize it as simply a sensation without any special significance.

Ordinarily, you will let everything you hear go, just as you have with your other senses, but since you are listening to my guiding voice, this will not be possible. So this time, you must let go of every auditory sensation EXCEPT my voice..

Now abruptly and willfully, separate yourself from your sense of hearing. Shape it into a sphere of pale blue and place it in front of you, slightly to the left, next to the violet sphere of touch. You are separate from its input.

With the five physical senses separate and surrounding you, look within and experience your emotional tone. Take very careful note of the emotions you are feeling in this moment. Isolate your ambient emotions from your mind's chatter and all other sensory input. Recognize that this too is simply a sensation without any special significance.

Now abruptly and willfully, separate yourself from your emotional tone. Shape it into a sphere of pure silver and place it in front of you, slightly to the right, next to the red sphere of sight. You are separate from its input.

Now willfully turn your attention away from the sphere of your emotional tone and focus upon your mind's chatter. As with the other senses, delve into your mind's chatter, experiencing it as fully as possible. Isolate it and let it flow of its own accord, without your involvement or attachment to certain threads of its progression. Recognize it as simply a sensation without any special significance.

Now abruptly and willfully, separate yourself from your mind's chatter. Shape it into a beautiful sphere of radiant gold and place it directly in front of you. You are separate from its input.

Each time any of these seven senses reaches out and grabs your attention, note it and then return it to its separateness.

Visualize yourself sitting in the center of infinite space with the spheres of the senses surrounding you -- separate yet at your beck and call. All about you is a quiet darkness. Drink heartily from this cup of silent stillness.

> Pause <

And now, gently focus your attention on my voice once again. I will be your guide on a journey of exploration. Let's see what lies beyond this Center of Stillness.

Look below you. The senses are separate and surround you, but below you is the web of your personality; the tapestry you weave of your life. Each light-fiber of its structure is made from some aspect of who you are in the world. It perfectly reflects your good points as well as your bad points.

The web is a thing of rare beauty. It is totally unique to each individual: a one-of-a-kind work of Art. Examine this tapestry of your personality. How well does it reflect your Central Stillness?

> Pause <

With your mind, reshape your web. Remake it into a clear expression of your true Self. Let it be an image of unique and great beauty, clearly expressive of your core nature.

> Pause <

Now, let it go. Separate it from your Self just as you did with the Seven Senses. It lies below you, separate from you.

In this state of separateness from the senses and the web, spend a moment meditating upon the Self-Who-Acts. Strive to identify with that part of you which crafted the web so carefully. This is your Individuality, the aspect of Self expressed through the web of your personality.

> Pause <

Now look down at the web and senses, as you would look down at your feet. They are still an integral part of you, a part required for physical existence and expression; yet, they are somehow separate in a totally new way.

Now visualize your Self as an Individual Sun, with the web of your personality and the spheres of the seven senses orbiting about you. Stand as the center of gravity in the solar system of your life.

Now look upward to the rest of the universe, outward, beyond your senses and beneath the web of your life -- there lies the infinite universe, filled with other Suns just like you. You are at its exact Center. The Still Center of yourself *is* the Still Center of the infinite universe.

The Still Center of this infinity exists every where, every when and every why. Time and space are no longer barriers to you. You are free, free to explore the infinite universe.

Briefly brush your awareness against the very edges of the infinite universe.

> Pause <

Now let the universe go as well. Turn your attention inward once again to the Center of Self.

Simply BE... Quiet... Still...

> Pause <

Now gently become aware of the universe surrounding you. Reconnect with it. Fill it with your Central Stillness and let it fill you.

And now turn to the web of your life below you. Reconnect with it as well and fill it with your Central Stillness.

And now become aware of the seven spheres of the senses surrounding you. Reach out with your awareness directly in front of you and touch the golden sphere of Mind Chatter. Reconnect with it. Bring it back into yourself.

In front of you, slightly to the right, is the silver sphere of your Emotions. Draw it back into yourself.

In front of you, slightly to the left, is the blue sphere of Hearing. Draw it back into yourself.

Directly to your right is the red sphere of Sight. Draw it back into yourself.

Directly to your left is the violet sphere of Tactile Sensations. Draw it back into yourself.

Behind you, slightly to the right, is the yellow sphere of Smell. Draw it back into yourself.

And finally, behind you, slightly to the left, is the green sphere of Taste. Draw it back into yourself.

You are now reunited with your full array of physical senses. Fill them with your Central Stillness.

Now sense your physical body. Notice your breath and breathe consciously. Fill your entire body with your Central Stillness.

Now begin moving your hands gently over your body. Move your hands up along your thighs and up your abdomen and chest, up to your face and back down again, awakening your body to normal sensation. Ground your awareness firmly in your body!

Now gently open your eyes. Just sit quietly for a moment and reorient yourself. Bring your Central Stillness into this moment. Into this place. Here. Now.

Now get up and go about your business. Carry your Central Stillness within you and express it through every thought, every word and every deed.

# RAWN'S
# SELF-HEALING
# ARCHAEOUS

# THE ORIGINAL ARTICLE

Completed March 23, 1997, at 8:45pm, PST. At this very moment, rising in the East, the ruddy disk of the partially eclipsed full Moon, with its small, crowning crescent of brilliant white, lies counterpoint in the sky to Comet Hale-Bopp, whose star-like core and twin tails fill the north-western horizon. Mars stands directly above the Moon, having already cast his redness into her pool of unveiled earth-shadow.

Awestruck by this magnificent celestial display, I am moved to offer this Archaeous as a humble gift of thanks to so generous a Universe!

# INTRODUCTION

Until fairly recently, the most common philosophy underlying the treatment of disease was the idea that healing could be best accomplished by strengthening the body's own natural mechanisms of self-repair. The vision of today's western medicine however, has shifted focus from strengthening the human body, to artificially regulating it; and from healing the human body itself, to destroying the bodies of specific invading organisms. Perhaps in moderation this is a wise and appropriate tactic for our times -- times in which it seems the human immune-system faces insurmountable challenges -- but dare we head so recklessly and with so little forethought, toward completely writing-off our bodies' own natural powers?

I for one, say "no". I think we must cherish and nurture these powers. If we combine them with our western medical approach, perhaps *then* we will find the ability to transform apace with our changing environment. This at least, has been my particular approach to healing, and it is a bias which you will find echoed throughout this Archaeous.

Healing is a topic which concerns me both practically and philosophically. For example, I do not equate "healing" with "cure", though I really like it when they coincide! I see that struggle, pain, and death, are each as healing in their own ways as are ease, pleasure, and re-birth.

They are all inevitable in life, so for "health" to really mean anything, I believe it must encompass them all and empower one to creatively adapt to them all. To me, "health" does not equal "living forever". My personal sense of health, is defined by the quality of my life, not by its duration.

Self-healing is a part of my magical practice. As such, my approach to self-healing is as varied as the magical Traditions I have practiced -- multiplied, of course, by my unleashed imagination. The specific techniques of the Self-Healing Archaeous, stem directly from my work with Franz Bardon's excellent book, "Initiation Into Hermetics".

Like Bardon, the Archaeous defines three "bodies" which correspond to three "realms": Mental, Astral, and Physical. The healing effects of the Archaeous are achieved through the conscious manipulation of these three bodies, and *most especially*, through their integration.

At every step in the Archaeous, one works in conscious cooperation with the pathways of influence and power which Nature herself provides. The technique mimics one of Nature's most essential processes: Integration + Separation + Re-integration . . . the rhythm of life itself. To this fundamental equation, is added the practitioner's own magical will, along with the focus of healing.

Prerequisite to beginning work with this Self-Healing Archaeous, I recommend that you undergo a sincere process of self-discovery. We each come to know ourselves by our own unique paths -- some with concentrated effort, some with apparent ease, some only by graduation from the "School of Hard Knocks", etc. -- so I won't presume to dictate how you specifically should go about this task. It is imperative that you understand however, that for healing effects to reliably result from the Archaeous practice, you must have first healed (by whatever means) the most basic wounds which frighten you away from self-knowledge. If these wounds are still raw within you, then please address them prior to pursuing the Archaeous. Otherwise, the Archaeous may prove distressing to you, and you will risk manifesting only the negative pole of the healing continuum.

When approached from a well grounded and honest knowledge of one's self, the healing effects of the Archaeous will be affirmative of one's inner health, and will directly externalize it. As is Nature's way, what you sow, will determine what you eventually reap.

# Rawn's Self-Healing Archaeous

**Stage #1)  Healing through discerning and integrating your three bodies --**

### Integrating the Physical:

Situate yourself comfortably.

Turn your attention to your feet and relax them completely. Intimately experience every physical sensation that your feet relay to you at this moment.

Slowly move your attention up your legs, relaxing and connecting with each vein, muscle, bone, organ and patch of skin. Continue upward in this manner till you have established a clear and relaxed awareness of your entire physical body.

Though certainly healing in its own right, this primary step of connecting closely with your physical body, is a common one and therefore is not counted among the Archaeous' thirteen enumerated "levels" of healing. In effect, this step corresponds to zero and, quite appropriately, it is where the Archaeous both begins *and* ends.

### Integrating the Astral:

With your awareness thus spread evenly throughout your physical body, expand your focus outward a few inches till you sense your astral body's vibrant energy. Though difficult to adequately describe, once it is encountered and experienced, the feeling of the astral body's "bright" energy will be unmistakable.

Generally, it is physically stimulating -- for some people, it is dangerously so. Therefore, it is best to approach a conscious sensorial contact with your astral body, in controlled and small increments. Begin with just a few brief moments of contact with this energy, and then immediately restrict the focus of your awareness back down to the dimensions of your physical body.

Whatever energy you feel stimulating your physical body, must then be consciously integrated into your physical muscles, bones, organs, skin, etc. By mentally guiding this bright astral energy into your physical body, into your very cellular structure itself, you effect the first level of healing in the Archaeous.

Acclimate your physical body to your astral energy slowly. Your goal over time, is to be able to comfortably sense your entire astral body and consciously integrate it into your physical body. Your focus at this point is not to be upon "astral travel" or the *separation* of your astral form from your physical; rather, it is to be exclusively upon the *integration* of the two.

Again, a note of caution is in order: The astral body acts as a matrix for the physical body. Its bright energy is the medium through which the mental body determines the nature of its physical vehicle. The character of the astral energy, is that it is shaped by the mental level (thought and will); and in its own turn, it shapes the physical level.

Therefore, when you consciously (mentally) connect with your physical body and then expand that awareness to include your astral body, you will have opened nature's own pathways of healing. Consciously integrating your astral matrix into your physical body, grounds this bright energy into physical manifestation, bringing your physical body into closer accord with your astral matrix.

At this level of work, your magical will substitutes for nature's unaided will. If you have not performed the preliminary work of self-discovery and have not crafted an intimate knowledge of your inner self, you may find nature's power to be more than your will can manage. The danger is that nature's power, when mishandled, can easily become the relentless cause of unexpected side-effects. In this Archaeous process, whatever your mental body has expressed -- consciously *and* unconsciously -- through your astral matrix, will be powerfully impressed upon your physical structure. If you are at peace within yourself, then the Archaeous will be immediately healing and will bring your inner peace outward. But if you are filled with inner turmoil, the Archaeous' healing will be very painful as your inner turmoil progresses outward.

### Integrating the Mental:

Having reached the stage at which you comfortably experience your physical body, simultaneously permeated with the bright energy of your astral body, turn your attention inward upon your conscious awareness itself. This is your mental body. You have, in fact, been directing this whole exercise with your mental body.

When you first turned your attention to your feet, it represented a movement of the focus of your conscious awareness. You contracted, shifted, and then expanded this focus, eventually including your entire physical and astral bodies within its purview. These are the actions of one's mental body, and are representative of its fluidity, adaptability and subtleness.

At first, its dimensions are difficult to discern, but this is only because our mental bodies are an utterly integral part of our experience of self and of our mechanisms of perception. In sensing the dimensions of your mental body, you must strive to see the forest from amidst the trees, so to speak.

Hold these thoughts in mind now as you consciously shape and shift the focus of your awareness, working up from your feet till you have reached the point where you are aware of your entire, relaxed physical body. Spend some time in this state, actively meditating with the idea that the parameters of your awareness, are also the parameters of your mental body. Learn to sense those parameters first; and then once they are known, work toward *conscious* control of them.

Now expand those mental parameters till they include your astral body, keeping in mind the following two points: #1) It is your mental body which is expanding. #2) Your mental body experiences this expansion through the sensoria of your astral and physical bodies.

Consciously permeate every bit of your astral body's energy, and carefully integrate your mental body into your astral form. When you have intimately joined your mental and astral forms, turn to integrating them thus united, into your physical body. Spend some time in this state, meditating on the awareness of your three bodies joined together.

This is the second level of healing in the Archaeous, and completes the first and most important stage of the Archaeous -- *conscious integration*.

## Stage #2) Healing through separating and resting your three bodies --

### Vacating the Physical:

Sit comfortably or lay down in a place where you are certain you will not be disturbed. I advise that you also cast a magic circle of protection around your body.

With the full awareness of your three bodies well integrated, restrict your metal body's focus and concentrate on the feel of your bright astral energy. Now attempt to slowly and gently stand up with only your astral and mental bodies, leaving your physical body seated (or lying down).

This may (or may not) take many hours of repeated experiments to accomplish. If you have difficulties at first, then begin by trying to move only your astral-mental arm, and slowly work your way to a whole body movement.

You will find that your astral-mental body feels very, very like your physical body. This is so because it is really your astral body which houses your senses . . . the physical organs of sense, are merely the apparatus through which the astral body perceives the physical world. So, whether a stimulus is generated in the physical *or* the astral realm, the mental body still perceives it through the sensoria of the astral body.

At the same time, you will find your astral-mental body to have very different abilities than your physical body. At first you may want to fly off in celebration of the sense of freedom which the separation of your astral-mental body generates. For the purposes of this Archaeous however, you must fight this tendency for the moment and not stray more than a foot or two from your physical body. Your focus here, should be upon a gentle, controlled separation and not upon "travel".

When you have succeeded in standing up with your astral-mental body, turn around and examine your physical body. Concentrate intently upon the separation of your sensoria from your physical body. Transfer the control of your physical body's breathing to the rise and fall of your astral-mental body's chest. Concentrate upon the sensations throughout your astral-mental body, and let go of those you may still be receiving from your physical body.

Only in death is the astral-mental completely severed from the physical. While you live, no matter how advanced your magical skills, there will always remain a thread-like connection between your three bodies upon their separation. This thread of connection is a very real thing and is injured in very real ways by "snapping" -- either back into your physical body, or abruptly out of your physical body. To prevent trauma to your astral-mental umbilicus, take great care to: a) make sure you will not be physically disturbed while you work; and b), always separate your bodies gently and slowly.

This thread of connection also means that you cannot *completely* separate your astral-mental sensoria from perception of (at least the stronger) physical stimuli. These are simply Nature's ways. Nonetheless, you can isolate your awareness and then, even though some physical sensations may still impose themselves upon your astral-mental sensoria, you can limit the extent to which they draw your attention back into your physical body. By turning and examining your physical body, you increase the reality of your separation. This increases further as you shift your full awareness of sensation from your physical body to your astral-mental.

If you are comfortable standing still in your astral-mental form, then slowly walk around, straying no more than a few feet from your physical body. Concentrate on all the astral-mental sensations of walking, feeling the movement of your astral-mental limbs and the touch of your astral-mental feet upon the floor.

Now turn again to your physical body. Observe that its rhythm is slowing and that every part of it is completely relaxed. This is the resting of your physical body and is the third level of healing in the Archaeous.

## Vacating the Astral:

Turn your attention now as completely away from your resting physical body as you can. Concentrate again, upon the feel of your astral-mental form alone. Lay down on the floor, making sure to feel each movement of your astral-mental body.

Slowly, and this will take control since your impulse will be to fly off, arise from your astral body, with your mental body alone. Disconnect your mental body from all astral sensations as thoroughly as you can. Observe your astral body from directly above and watch as it too slows and rests. This is the fourth level of healing in the Archaeous.

## Resting the Mental:

Still your mental body and turn its focus inward and away from your astral and physical bodies. Enter into a passive meditation for several minutes and rest your mental body. Note how it slows and clarifies. This resting of your mental body is the fifth level of healing in the Archaeous and completes the second stage -- *conscious separation.*

As each of your bodies rest, they naturally revert to a more pristine and healthful state, very similar to the physical effects of sleep. The act of letting them rest separately, decreases the input from one level to the next, thus increasing the *depth* of their rest. Without the active impress of the astral energy, your physical body rests more calmly and completely than even in sleep since it is undisturbed by dreaming. Likewise, your astral body, separated from both physical *and* mental input, rests as it rarely does in the course of a normal human life. And freed from both astral and physical restraints, your mental body can be led to a very deep state of restful calm.

Allow at least five minutes of rest for your mental body. Adding in your working time, this will equal about ten minutes of rest for your astral body, and at least fifteen minutes for your physical body. If you have worked through the separations in less than ten minutes, then extend your mental body's rest until your physical and astral bodies will have rested at least these approximate amounts of time.

## Stage #3) Healing through re-integration of your three bodies --

### Re-integration of the Astral-Mental:

Arouse your well rested mental body and turn your attention to your reclining astral body. Gently and willfully re-join your mental and astral forms. Re-integrate them, thoroughly permeating every aspect of your bright astral energy with your conscious awareness. Stand up with your astral-mental body, paying very close attention to the sensorial details of your astral-mental movements.

The re-integration of your well rested astral and mental forms, is the sixth level of healing in the Archaeous.

### Re-integration of the Physical:

Turn your attention now to your rested physical body. Gently and willfully re-join your astral-mental form with your physical body. Consciously lead the bright astral-mental energy into each and every cell of your physical structure, re-integrating your three bodies completely. Perform this final re-integration with careful attention to its thoroughness.

While it is important to not return too *abruptly* to normal waking consciousness and to the animation of your physical body; it is nevertheless of equal importance that you *do* return to this state, and that you return as *completely* as possible. Once you have re-inhabited your physical body, gently increase your connection with it, and slowly work your way to its full re-possession. Finalize your grounding back into normal waking consciousness with a gentle physical movement such as running your hands lightly over your entire body -- from the top of your head, down to your toes.

Under no circumstances should you transit directly from the re-joining of your astral-mental with your physical, to standing up and physically moving around. The conscious *integration* of your three bodies is the most healing aspect of the Archaeous practice, so if your re-integration is only partial, the healing benefits will likewise be only partial (i.e., non-existent, or at best unpredictable).

Having first integrated, then separated, rested, and now finally re-integrated your three bodies, you will have reached the seventh level of healing in the Archaeous. This marks the completion of its third stage -- *conscious re-integration.*

These seven levels of healing constitute the basic formula of the Self-Healing Archaeous. This equation is based upon the number 3 and is expressed as a three-fold process (integration+separation+re-integration), enacted upon a three-fold being (mental+astral+physical). Another way of putting it would be: $(3/1)\times 3$.

When you have mastered this triple-triple process, the next step will be to turn to the inclusion of the number 4. This is done by factoring in the four universal Elements: Fire, Air, Water and Earth. Harmonizing the Elements in each of your three bodies, opens you to still further levels of healing possible with the Archaeous: viz., $(3\times 4)\times 3$.

**Stage #4)   Healing through the Elemental balancing of your three bodies --**

### Mental Equilibrium of the Elements:

Work  through the first two stages of the Archaeous, up to the point where you have separated and rested your three bodies.  The following will replace the third stage of the Archaeous proper:

Arouse your rested mental body and fill it with equal portions of the four pristine, universal Elements.  Follow the sequence of: Earth-Water-Air-Fire, starting with Earth at the "foot" of your mental form, working upwards and ending with Fire at the "top".  Balance the Elements in your mental body and rid yourself of any excess you may have accumulated. Bask joyously in this re-vivifying Equilibrium!

The Elements thus balanced in your mental body, is the eighth level of healing in the Archaeous.

### Astral-Mental Equilibrium of the Elements:

Turn your attention now to your reclining and fully rested astral body. Gently sink down into it and regain full awareness of it.  Consciously permeate it as before, linking your astral and mental bodies intimately together.  When you are ready, stand up with your astral-mental body, paying close attention to reconnecting with all of the astral sensations. Stand still and closely integrate your astral and mental bodies.

Consciously vitalize your astral body with the Elemental Equilibrium of your mental body.  Bring the balancing influence of your re-vivified mental body firmly into all aspects of your rested astral energy.

Now fill your astral-mental body with equal portions of the four pristine, universal Elements: your astral-mental legs with the Earth; your gut with the Water; your chest with the Air; and your head with the Fire. Balance the Elements in your astral-mental body and rid yourself of any excess you may have accumulated.  Bask anew in the re-vivifying Elemental Equilibrium!

This marks the ninth level of healing in the Archaeous.

### Physical-Astral-Mental Equilibrium of the Elements:

Look now to your well rested physical body, and gently re-enter it. Extend yourself into its every cell, reconnecting fully with the awareness of your three bodies together.  Animate it carefully and thoroughly with the balancing influence of your astral-mental Equilibrium.

Now fill your physical-astral-mental body with equal portions of the four Elements as before.  Balance them, and then rid yourself of any excess. Concentrate upon the sensations caused by this re-vivifying Equilibrium of your three bodies united. Integrate every bit of astral-mental energy you can into your physical structure, consciously guiding it into every cell of your physical body. Release whatever excess energy remains.

Visualize your mental body as actively brightening and willfully giving direction to, the astral. Also visualize the physical conforming its structure into agreement with this renewed astral template. This final integration and balancing should be pursued with the utmost care and concentration.

This is the tenth (and a truly profound!) level of healing in the Archaeous. Inculcating the Elemental Equilibrium throughout your three bodies in this direct manner is "advanced" work and should be approached with due reverence. Attainment of the integrated physical-astral-mental Elemental Equilibrium, marks the completion of the fourth stage of the Archaeous -- *conscious balancing*.

Only now, at this stage, do we turn to astral and mental "travel". Such travel, when entertained without a prerequisite Equilibrium of the Elements, can easily do harm to your health. This is not to say that one must first pass through the specific process of this Archaeous to safely approach astral-mental travel. Equilibrium of the Elements comes to one by any number of routes. I cannot count the number of people I have encountered who possess this Equilibrium unknowingly, having attained it simply through the "school of life"! For many of these people, astral travel is an easy matter with no ill effects. Whatever your perception of the state of your internal Equilibrium is at this moment, be sure to pause before continuing and honestly evaluate the *reality* of its status. If you find imbalance, then for the sake of your health, please attend to the correction of this imbalance *before* you engage in astral-mental travel.


**Stage #5)  Healing through mental and astral travel --**

**Mental Travel:**

Proceed as in #4 up to the point where your mental body has attained an Equilibrium of the Elements. Instead of turning your attention back to your astral body, you will turn your awareness outward. Travel beyond your circle with your balanced mental body, leaving both your astral and physical bodies behind; and, in your own unique way, seek out experiences which will augment your healing and clarify your Equilibrium. Try not to lose track of your focus upon *healing* during your travel.

When your travel has reached its natural conclusion, return to the circle containing your astral and physical bodies. Focus your awareness firmly back into your circle and examine your astral body. Proceed as in #4 with the process of balancing and re-integrating your astral-mental body and then your physical-astral-mental body. Pay close attention to incorporating what you have gleaned from your mental travels, into your astral and then physical bodies.

Often times, specific physical acts are required to fully ground the healing lessons of your mental travel into your physical body. Always follow through with the accomplishment of these tasks, or as noted in the re-integration of #3, your final results may be only partial.

Mental travel is common to our everyday experience, though perhaps as I have outlined it in this Archaeous it is not recognizable as such. Essentially, mental travel is any projection of your thoughts towards a focus other than your astral-physical sensoria. Intense thinking is a form of mental travel, as are daydreaming, meditation, etc. The focus of our conscious awareness (what we generally experience of our mental body) is a very subtle vehicle, capable of whatever our imagination contrives for it to do.

The mental travel of the Archaeous differs from common mental travel such as a daydream, because it is here made a conscious act of self-will and given the specific focus of healing. Furthermore, the Archaeous always ends with the thorough re-integration of your mental body and the lessons of your travel, into your physical-astral-mental unit. In common mental travel however, we rarely take thought of re-integrating our attention thoroughly back into our physical awareness . . . consequently we spend a certain part of our time engaged in only partial contact with our physical realities.

When the lessons gleaned from your mental travel have been consciously integrated into your united physical-astral-mental body, you will have attained the eleventh level of healing in the Archaeous.

### Astral-Mental Travel:

The difference between mental travel and astral-mental travel is comparable to the difference between a daydream and a genuine dream. The greatest difference is that in astral-mental travel, like in dreaming, we have a full sensorial experience; whilst in a daydream or mental travel, we rarely have any sensory impressions other than sight and a mental form of "hearing".

By consciously uniting your mental and astral bodies, you access a fuller sensorial experience for your travels. This integrates your otherwise strictly mental lessons, at the astral and mental levels *simultaneously*; consequently, the subsequent physical integration is more complete and more readily achieved.

Along with expanding your mental experience into a sensorial one, the inclusion of your astral form will also tend to limit your travel possibilities. In other words, you will find that there are places you can reach with your naked mental body, but which you will find impossible to reach with your denser astral-mental body.

Consider these factors well, and plan your astral-mental travel before you begin.

Proceed as in #4 up to the point where your astral-mental body has attained an Equilibrium of the Elements. Now venture outward with your fully integrated astral-mental body and seek your healing experience.

Under no circumstances should you separate from your astral form during your astral-mental travel . . . it is unwise to leave your astral form un-attended in any place other than within the confines of your protective circle. If your healing takes you beyond the limits of your astral form, then plan ahead and divide your journey into mental and astral components. Accomplish your mental travel first; return to your circle and re-integrate your astral-mental body; and *then*, accomplish your astral tasks.

When your astral-mental travel is complete, return to your circle, orient yourself, and then follow the usual process of thoroughly balancing and re-integrating your physical-astral-mental body. This is the twelfth level of healing in the Archaeous and marks the completion of its fifth stage -- *conscious travel*.


### Stage #6) Healing through integrated self-expression --

When you have mastered the foregoing, turn your will toward the prolonging of your integrated physical-astral-mental awareness.

Upon completing your final re-integration, focus upon the triplicity of your physical-astral-mental body. As you arise and begin physical movement, do so with the full awareness that your three bodies are working in unison. Sense the intimate details of your physical, astral and mental bodies *simultaneously*, and extend this awareness for as long as you are able. Work to make each moment and the actions which fill it, a fully conscious and intentional physical, astral and mental experience.

At first, the maintenance of this intensely focused awareness will be possible only for a few brief moments. With perseverance, you can willfully teach yourself how to expand those moments into seconds, then minutes, and eventually into hours.

Self-expression of your integrated physical-astral-mental being, is the thirteenth, and ultimate, level of healing in the Archaeous and concludes its sixth stage -- *conscious being*.

# RAWN'S
# SELF-HEALING
# ARCHAEOUS

# THE AUDIO LESSONS

In 2002 I recorded a series of nine guided audio "Lessons" in the Self-Healing Archaeous technique. What follows are the scripts of those recordings.

# ~ Lesson One ~
# The Complete Awareness and Integration
# of the Physical Body

## Introduction:

I call this technique an archaeous because it's patterned after an Al-chemical work known as the archaeous of water. In this Alchemical work, one takes a volume of water and separates it into its Elements through a process of distillation. Once the parts are separated and puri-fied, they are recombined or re-integrated, resulting in empowered water that has faculties it didn't possess before. The self-healing archaeous fol-lows this same Alchemical pattern of separation, purification and subse-quent re-integration, but instead of water, our subject is the three part hu-man body.

Like Bardon, the Archaeous defines three "bodies" which correspond to three "realms": Mental, Astral, and Physical. The healing effects of the Archaeous are achieved through the conscious manipulation of these three bodies, and *most especially*, through their integration.

At every step in the Archaeous, one works in conscious cooperation with the pathways of influence and power which Nature herself provides. The technique mimics one of Nature's most essential processes: Integra-tion + Separation + Re-integration . . . the rhythm of life itself. To this fundamental equation, is added the practitioner's own magical will, along with the focus of healing.

Lessons one, two and three, are concerned with the complete aware-ness of each body and their integration with each of the others. Lesson one with the complete awareness, relaxation and integration of the physi-cal body; lesson two with the complete awareness of the astral body and its conscious integration with the physical body; and, lesson three with the complete awareness of the mental body and its conscious integration with the astral and physical bodies.

Lessons four and five are concerned with the passive separation of these bodies, one from the other, and with their subsequent re-integration. During the period of separation, each body naturally achieves a degree of rest unknown to it by any other means. The ar-chaeous takes full advantage of this healing by-product of their restful solitude.

Lesson six is concerned with the purification and balancing of each solitary body and the subsequent re-integration of these balanced bodies. This is achieved through the loading of each body with the four Elements in their appropriate regions.

Lessons seven and eight concern astral– and mental-wandering respectively.

The final lesson, nine, is concerned with a higher form of integration -- that of integrated self-expression through your consciously unified and Elementally balanced physical-astral-mental body.

The Archaeous is designed to be pursued in conjunction with the work of Initiation Into Hermetics. Lessons one, two and three, which are focused upon integration, are suitable at any of Bardon's Steps.

Lessons four and five however, which are focused upon separation, should only be pursued after the completion of Step Two and the attainment of the rudimentary Elemental Equilibrium.

Lesson six, which pertains to manipulation of the Four Elements, should only be pursued after good progress has been achieved with Step Four and the work of accumulating the Elements.

And finally, lesson seven should not be undertaken until the work of Step Six is begun.

So, let's move on to the practice of lesson one and the complete awareness, relaxation and integration of the physical body.

**Practice:**

Close your eyes and situate yourself comfortably. It is best is if you sit upright, with your hands resting gently on your thighs, as this will help you resist the temptation to fall asleep during the relaxation phase.

Clear your mind of all unwanted, mundane concerns and thoughts. Now focus your attention upon your feet. Become aware of how your feet feel. Sense the toes and the arches and the tops of your feet. Now relax all the tension in your feet.

Move your awareness upwards to your calves. Similarly, become aware of how your calves feel and relax away all of the tension stored in their musculature.

Now move your awareness to your thighs. Note how they feel and relax their muscles.

Now move to your buttocks and groin and relax all of the muscles in this area.

Relax all the tension from your abdomen and gut.

From your lower back.

Your upper back.

Release all the tension from your chest.

Relax your shoulders, arms and hands.

Relax all the muscles in your neck.

Relax your jaw and mouth.

Relax your nose.

Your eyes.

Your cheeks.

Your ears.

Now relax your scalp.

Focus on how relaxed your entire body is at this moment.

Now focus your awareness in the Fire region of your head, from the base of your neck to the top of your scalp. Sense all of the various parts that compose this region. Sense the skin that covers your head and face. Sense your eyes, right and left; your nose and sinuses; your ears, right and left; your tongue, teeth and lips. Sense your neck and throat. Now sense all the parts of your head region at once. Put all of these sensations together and sense your whole head region as a single unit.

Now move your awareness down to the Air region of your chest, from the tops of your shoulders down to your solar plexus, plus your upper arms, right and left, down to your elbows. Sense all of the various parts that compose this region. Sense the skin that covers your torso. Sense the skin, muscle and bone of your right upper arm and shoulder. Sense the skin, muscle and bone of your left upper arm and shoulder. Sense your breathing lungs and your beating heart. Sense your upper spine, your ribs and your breast. Now sense all parts of your chest region at once. Put all of these sensations together and sense your chest region as a single unit.

Now move your awareness down to the Water region of your abdomen, from the bottom of your sternum down to just above your genitalia, plus your forearms, right and left, from elbows to wrists. Sense all the various parts that compose this region. Sense the skin that covers your abdomen and lower back. Sense the skin, muscle and bone of your right elbow and forearm. Sense the skin, muscle and bone of your left elbow and forearm. Sense your stomach, your intestines, your kidneys and the all other organs that fill your abdomen. Sense your lower spine and all the musculature that supports your abdomen. Now sense all the parts of your abdominal region at once. Put all of these sensations together and sense your abdominal region as a single unit.

Now move your awareness down to the Earth region of your legs, from the top of your hips down to the soles of your feet, plus your wrists and hands, right and left. Sense all the various parts that compose this region. Sense the skin, muscle and bone of your right wrist and hand. Sense the skin, muscle and bone of your left wrist and hand. Sense the skin and muscle of your buttocks and the bone of your pelvis. Sense your genetalia. Sense the skin, muscle and bone of your right thigh, your right calf, and your right foot. Sense the skin, muscle and bone of your left thigh, your left calf, and your left foot. Now sense all the parts of your leg region at once. Put all of these sensations together and sense your leg region as a single unit.

Sense the solid, supportive, Earth nature of this region as a whole. It is the solid foundation upon which you stand.

Now, retain your awareness of the Earthy leg region and add the Watery region of your abdomen to this awareness. Sense your leg region and your abdominal region simultaneously. Sense the fluid, digestive Water nature of your abdominal region and let it float atop the solid Earth region of your legs. Sense how the Water nature of your abdominal region penetrates the uppermost layer of the Earth nature of your leg region, binding the two regions together.

Now retain this awareness of the conjoined Earth and Water regions, stretching from the bottoms of your feet up to your sternum, and add the Air region of your chest to this awareness. Sense your leg region, your abdominal region and your chest region simultaneously. Sense the respiring, light Air nature of your chest region and let it hover over the fluid Water region of your abdomen, which floats atop the solid Earth region of your legs. Sense how the Air nature of your chest region mingles with the uppermost layer of the Water nature of your abdominal region, binding the two regions together. Sense how these three regions connect, one to the other and form a conjoined whole.

Now retain this awareness of the conjoined Earth, Water and Air regions, stretching from the soles of your feet up to the tops of your shoulders, and add the Fire region of your head to this awareness. Sense your leg region, your abdominal region, your chest region and your head region simultaneously. Sense the active, expressive Fire nature of your head region and let it dance upon the Airy nature of your chest region, which hovers over the Watery nature of your abdominal region, which in turn, floats atop the solid Earthy nature of your leg region. Sense how the Fire nature of your head region consumes the uppermost layer of the Air nature of your chest region, binding these two regions together. Sense how these four regions connect, one with the other, to form a single body.

Sense your entire body as a single unified whole.

Now visualize roots growing downward from the base of your spine, the palms of your hands and the soles of your feet. Cause them to burrow deep into the soil below your feet. From the soil below you, draw whatever energetic nutrients your body needs, up into the Earth region of your body. Sense how the Water region passes these energetic nutrients to the Air region and how the Air feeds them to the Fire region. Sense how the Fire region, thus nourished, sends a return energy downward into the Air region, which in turn is passed by the Air to the Water region. Sense how this energy flows from the Water region, down into the Earth region and back, through your roots, to the soil below your feet.

Release any excess energy you may sense within your body, through your roots and into the soil below. Release any negativity you may harbor, through your roots and into the soil below.

Now turn your awareness away from your roots and return to sensing your whole body. Sense the unification of the four regions.

Now begin your return to normal awareness. Before opening your eyes or moving your body, take a moment to listen to the noises around you, to smell the air, etc. Now take a deep breath and exhale it gently. Now move your hands up along your thighs and up your abdomen and chest, up to your face and back down again, awakening your body to normal sensation. Now gently open your eyes and slowly begin to physically move about.

When this technique becomes easy for you to perform, you may move on to lesson two and the complete awareness and integration of the astral body.

# ~ Lesson Two ~
## The Complete Awareness and Integration of the Astral Body

**Introduction:**

The astral body is composed of emotional-energy, as opposed to physical-energy. Unlike physical energy, emotional-energy is not measurable with scientific instruments. Therefore the astral body should not be confused with the aura since the aura, which can be measured, is composed of physical-energy, albeit of a highly rarified nature. An aura is naturally generated by a living physical body and while it reflects the nature of the astral body, it is not the astral body itself.

The astral body is an intermediary body caused by the descent of the mental body, into the physical plane and is dependant upon this connection between mental and physical for its existence. If the mental influx is cut off or if the physical vessel is destroyed, the astral body begins to disintegrate. The raw astral substance is crystallized into an astral body only when there is a descent of the mental into the physical.

Each astral body reflects the descending mental influx that forms it, thus your own natural astral body is just as unique as your physical body. No two are exactly alike.

An astral body acts as a two-way connector between the mental and physical bodies. Whatever transpires in your mental body is reflected in your astral body and passes through your astral body to effect your physical body. Conversely, whatever happens to your physical body effects your astral body and, by extension, your mental body.

The seat of perception is the mental body but the seat of sensation is the astral body. When you experience a sensation you perceive it initially with your mental senses. This is a perception of the essential meaning that underlies the sensation. This essential meaning is then personalized by your astral body and the sensation is given significance.

Significance is a matter of the emotional content that we associate with a particular thing, idea, event, etc. Which emotions we associate with which thing depends upon our upbringing, just as much as it depends upon our self-developed thoughts and experiences. This attribution of emotional significance to our perceptions is a very complex and primarily unconscious, process. The habitual pattern that a person follows in their attribution of emotional significance is know as their personality. This is why the astral body is generally equated with the personality. However, the astral body is more than just a complex of emotional responses. It's also our link to the astral realm.

The first work in Hermetic initiation is the analysis and subsequent transformation of the personality. Understanding the dynamics of one's own personality allows the initiate to more clearly perceive the essential meaning that underlies each sensation, event, thing or idea. When you can see through your instinctual emotional interpretations and understand why you are reacting in that particular manner, you are then in a position to *consciously* respond, instead of reacting out of unconscious habit. This reformation of the personality removes it from the realm of pure unconscious, habitual reaction and turns it into a conscious tool of self-expression. With this tool in hand, the initiate seeks to clearly express their own essential meaning through the medium of conscious emotions.

One task of this lesson of the Archaeous is the sensing of your astral body. This adds a new dimension to the work of analyzing and transforming the personality by providing a sensory point of reference to a process that is primarily intellectual.

The astral body feels very similar to the physical body but has a vibrancy to it that physical sensation does not. The feeling is very much like the physical sensation of goose bumps or that other-worldly tingling sensation that arises when you encounter something deeply significant.

Since the astral body is so intimately connected to the physical body, the sensing of the astral body feels to the physical nerves like you're hooked up to a mild current of electricity. It's as if you feel the tips of each hair on your body as the electric current forces them to stand straight out. But this is only how your brain naturally interprets the conscious sensing of the astral body.

As I said previously, the astral body is not composed of physical energy, so what you feel of it with your physical body, is not the astral body itself. Instead, it is a physical sensation caused by your brain's habit of translating the conscious awareness of significance into physical sensation. Since your brain is receiving an input of significance and essential meaning that it naturally associates with physical sensation, it is responding by firing off a few neurons that create the physical sensations I've described.

This fact can lead to a great amount of confusion as many will conclude that the astral body is an energetic or etheric body. So please remember as you're sensing your astral body that what you feel as a physical sensation is only an effect of becoming conscious of your astral body. Do not identify it as the astral body itself, but rather, look beyond the physical sensation and try to perceive the significance underlying the sensation. That is where you will find the true astral body.

The physical body corresponds to the Earth Element and the astral body, to the Water Element. The astral body is very fluidic and rhythmic in nature and tends to adapt itself to any vibration it encounters. For this reason, all things perceived through hearing have an especially direct impact upon your astral body. A really moving song, for example, directly manipulates your astral body, evoking specific, predictable emotional responses through sound and rhythm.

Since music is probably the best example of the effect that sound and rhythm have upon your astral or emotional body, I will be using snippets of a few appropriate musical passages as an aid during the exercise itself.

So, let's move on to the practice of lesson two and the complete awareness and integration of the astral body.


**Practice:**

Each lesson of the archaeous begins with the relaxation and awareness of the physical body. Assuming that you have mastered lesson one, we will move through the initial relaxation phase fairly quickly.

Situate yourself comfortably, sitting upright, with your hands resting gently on your thighs, and clear your mind of all unwanted, mundane concerns and thoughts.

Now focus your awareness in the Earth region of your physical body and quickly relax all of the muscles in this region. Release every bit of tension.

Now move your awareness upwards to your Water region and relax all of the muscles in this region. Release every bit of tension.

Now move your awareness upwards to your Air region and relax all of the muscles in this region. Release every bit of tension.

Now move your awareness upwards to your Fire region and relax all of the muscles in this region. Release every bit of tension.

Now sense your entire head region as a whole.

Add to this your chest region and sense both together.

Add to this your abdominal region and sense all three together.

And finally, add your leg region and sense your entire physical body as a whole.

Project your roots down into the soil below you and release every bit of negativity you might be holding.

Now return your focus to sensing your entire physical body as a whole. Feel the solidity of the Earth region, the fluidity of the Water region, the lightness of the Air region and the electricity of the head region. Sense how these four regions penetrate each other and are a single, inseparable whole.

Now focus your awareness in the skin that covers your entire body. Sense the surface of your entire physical body.

Now push your awareness outward just a couple of inches or about 5 centimeters. Sense the vibrant energy that exists when you push your awareness ever so slightly outward.

Hold onto the sensation of this energy. Focus your mind exclusively upon sensing this energy. This is your astral body.

Now focus your awareness in the area surrounding your physical body's Earth region. Sense the energetic solidity of this area of your astral body. Here are your foundational emotions. The rudimentary emotions and beliefs from which all the rest of your emotions spring. Sense their solid energy pulsating within the Earth region of your astral body.

**[Earth Music]**

Now focus your awareness in the area surrounding your physical body's Water region. Sense the energetic fluidity of this area of your astral body. Here are your emotions that adapt your foundational emotions so that they fit with the outside world. The emotions and beliefs that translate your foundation into action. Sense their fluid energy pulsating within the Water region of your astral body.

**[Water Music]**

Now focus your awareness in the area surrounding your physical body's Air region. Sense the energetic lightness of this area of your astral body. Here are your emotions that communicate your foundational emotions to the outside world. The surface emotions and beliefs that you express every day. Sense their changeable energy pulsating within the Air region of your astral body.

**[Air Music]**

Now focus your awareness in the area surrounding your physical body's Fire region. Sense the energetic expansiveness of this area of your astral body. Here are your most fleeting and most passionate emotions. The powerful emotions whose expression is transformative. Sense their radiant energy pulsating within the Fire region of your astral body.

**[Fire Music]**

Now add the awareness of the Air region of your astral body to that of the Fire region. Sense how the energy of these two regions blend, one with the other. Sense these two regions as a single unit.

Now add the awareness of the Water region of your astral body to that of the combined Air and Fire. Sense how the energy of the Water region blends with the energy of the combined Air and Fire and form a single unit. Sense the unity of these three regions of your astral body.

Now add the awareness of the Earth region of your astral body to that of the combined Water, Air and Fire. Sense how the energy of the Earth region blends with the combined energy of Water, Air and Fire. Sense how the Earth region solidifies your astral body, holding it all together as a single unit.

Focus on the vibrant energy of your entire astral body.

Now shrink your awareness back down to your skin and sense the skin that covers your entire physical body. Draw the energy of your astral body inward still further and let it permeate your entire physical body to its core. Draw the energy of your astral body down into the very marrow of your bones.

Sense the bright energy that fills your entire physical body. Sense the Fiery energy permeating the head region of your physical body. The Airy energy permeating the chest region of your physical body. The Watery energy permeating the abdominal region of your physical body. And the Earthy energy permeating the leg region of your physical body.

Now project your roots deep into the soil below you and release all of the excess energy you feel. Just release what ever needs to flow down into the earth. Don't force it, just let it flow. Your physical body knows how much to retain and how much to release, so trust its wisdom.

Now return your awareness to sensing your physical body. Sense the solidity of your leg region, the fluidity of your abdominal region, the lightness of your chest region and the electricity of your head region.

Sense all four regions simultaneously as a unified whole.
Now begin your return to normal awareness. Before opening your eyes or moving your body, take a moment to listen to the noises around you, to smell the air, etc.

Now take a deep breath and exhale it gently.

Now move your hands up along your thighs and up your abdomen and chest, up to your face and back down again, awakening your body to normal sensation.

Now gently open your eyes and slowly begin to physically move about.

When this technique becomes easy for you to perform, you may move on to lesson three and the complete awareness and integration of the mental body.

# ~ Lesson Three ~
## The Complete Awareness and Integration of the Mental Body

**Introduction:**

The physical body senses things and the astral body feels them, but it is the mental body that perceives these sensations and feelings. Your mental body is your conscious awareness. Wherever your awareness is focused is where your mental body is. For example when your awareness is focused in your feet, your mental body is concentrated around your feet. When your awareness is spread throughout your entire body, your mental body is likewise spread throughout your entire body. In the preceding two lessons, it was your mental body that was directing the entire exercise.

The mental body is the most pliable and fluid of our three bodies. It alone can assume any shape, size, color, or tone and can transfer itself to any place or time. It can even be all of these things simultaneously and exist every where and every when, simultaneously. The mental body or conscious awareness, is our link to higher levels of Self and to the Unity of all Self.

The mental body has two aspects, one temporal and one eternal. Our temporal mental body is what we use here and now, within the realm of time and space. This is the mental body that incarnates and which, through repeated incarnation, evolves. In its purest form, this is the Individual Self or Solar, Tiphareth Self. It's this level of Self that descends into the physical realm and is the causal agent behind the formation of the astral body. In other words, our conscious awareness or mental body, permeates our physical body and our astral body simultaneously. The temporal mental body is what gives life to our astral and physical bodies.

The eternal mental body, on the other hand, is what gives life to our temporal mental body. This is the Greater Self or Binah Self which exists within the eternal or supernal realm. There are an infinite number of these Greater Selves, each one of which projects countless temporal mental bodies into the temporal realm. This projection of Individual Selves or temporal mental bodies into the temporal realm is what continuously creates our temporal reality.

Our temporal mental body is continuously fed and sustained by an influx descending from our own Greater Self. This is most readily perceived as the inner voice of one's conscience. In occult literature, the conscious awareness of this influx is often called the Holy Guardian Angel. Its counsel is always with us whether we recognize it as such or not.

Paul Foster Case best described this relationship between the eternal Binah, or Greater Self and the temporal, Individual Self, in his Pattern On The Trestleboard statement for number three, corresponding to Binah. Quote: "Three. Filled with Understanding of its perfect law, I am guided, moment by moment, along the path of liberation."

Since this lesson of the Archaeous concerns only the temporal mental body, I will not go further into this complex subject of the eternal mental body. If you wish to learn more about this, then I invite you to read a piece I wrote several years ago, titled, "Sowantha". [Which I have included as an Appendix (page 233).]

So, getting back to the main subject of this lesson of the Archaeous -- our temporal mental body. This is our conscious awareness.

Our conscious awareness is composed of the four Elements, just like our astral and physical bodies. The four Elemental regions of the physical body, correspond to the physical functions and sensations of those areas of our physical body. The leg region supports us, our abdominal region is where the rhythmic and fluid processes of digestion occur, the chest where the airy respiration occurs, and the head where the finer senses and brain reside. With the astral body, on the other hand, the regions correspond to the quality of emotional energy and to the significance we attach to physical sensory perceptions.

The division of the mental body into Elemental regions is even more subtle than emotional significance. Here, the Elemental regions correspond to the quality of awareness and perception. As I said at the outset, it is the mental body that perceives sensation. Without perception, sensation means nothing. The point being, that each perception by our senses *means* something. The perception of meaning that is hidden within sensation, occurs at four essential levels and this is what defines the Elemental regions of the mental body.

Corresponding to the Fire region is the direct perception of essential meaning. This is perception of the universal, objective and impersonal meaning behind each sensation.

Corresponding to the Air region is the perception of ideas and thoughts. This is the first layer of clothing given to essential meaning by our cognitive process. It is the beginning of our subjectification and personalization of essential meaning.

Corresponding to the Water region is the perception of personal significance or emotion. This is the heart of our personalization of essential meaning and is the most subjectifying component of our mechanism of perception. Here also is the sub-conscious aspect of the psyche, a realm where essential meaning is densely clothed with highly personalized symbols.

And finally, corresponding to the Earth region is the mundane awareness. This level of awareness is the active combination of the Fire, Air and Water aspects, processed through the physical brain, seated firmly in time and space. Its focus is primarily the physical realm. Here also is the influence of the rudimentary biologic consciousness of the physical body itself -- the inherited, cellular memory of human instinct.

In the practice of lesson three, we will explore the Elemental regions of our mental bodies in a unique way. We will begin as usual with the relaxation and complete awareness of the physical body, firmly planting us in the Earth region of our mental body. Here we will focus upon perceiving the emotional significance hidden within our perception of physical sensation.

Next we will extend our awareness outward and sense our astral bodies, planting ourselves firmly in the Water region of our mental body. Here we will focus upon perceiving the thoughts and ideas hidden within our perception of emotional significance.

This will lead us to the Air region of thoughts and ideas, independent of the astral and physical sensations. Here we will focus upon perceiving the essential meaning hidden within our perception of thoughts.

This will lead to the Fire region of our mental bodies where we will focus upon the direct perception of the naked, unfiltered essential meaning. This will be a form of the emptiness or vacancy of mind exercise from Step One of IIH.

So, let's turn now to the practice of lesson three, the complete awareness and integration of the mental body.


**Practice:**

Situate yourself comfortably, sitting upright, with your hands resting gently on your thighs, and clear your mind of all unwanted, mundane concerns and thoughts.

Now focus your awareness in the Earth region of your physical body and quickly relax all of the muscles in this region. Release every bit of tension.

Now move your awareness upwards to your Water region and relax all of the muscles in this region. Release every bit of tension.

Now move your awareness upwards to your Air region and relax all of the muscles in this region. Release every bit of tension.

Now move your awareness upwards to your Fire region and relax all of the muscles in this region. Release every bit of tension.

Now sense your entire head region as a whole.

Add to this your chest region and sense both together.

Add to this your abdominal region and sense all three together.

And finally, add your leg region and sense your entire physical body as a whole.

Project your roots down into the soil below you and release every bit of negativity you might be holding.

Now return your focus to sensing your entire physical body as a whole. Feel the solidity of the Earth region, the fluidity of the Water region, the lightness of the Air region and the electricity of the head region. Sense how these four regions penetrate each other and are a single, inseparable whole.

Focus intently upon the physical sensation of your entire body. This perception of pure physical sensation is the Earth region of your mental body.

Now let go of your perception of physical sensation itself and focus upon the emotional significance communicated to your consciousness by these sensations. How do these sensations make you feel? Happy? Sad? Neutral? Energized? Tired?

**2 minutes silence**

Now shift your awareness to your astral body. Sense the Earth region of your astral body. Its Water region, Air region and Fire region. Sense your astral body as a whole. Focus your awareness upon the direct perception of emotional significance. This perception of pure emotional significance is the Water region of your mental body.

Now let go of your perception of emotional significance and focus upon the thoughts and ideas that compose that significance. What thoughts and ideas serve as the building blocks of the emotional significance you perceive?

**2 minutes silence**

Now shift your awareness entirely away from the perception of sensations of any kind. Isolate just the thoughts and ideas that fill your awareness and perceive them directly. This perception of pure thought and idea is the Air region of your mental body.

Now let go of your perception of thoughts and ideas and focus upon the essential meaning they express. Look beyond the clothing of thought and seek the pearl of essential meaning that gives birth to thought and idea.

**2 minutes silence**

Now release all thoughts from your mind and submerse your awareness in the essential meaning itself. This direct perception of essential meaning is the Fire region of your mental body.

**3 minutes silence**

Now gently allow your perception of essential meaning to take form as thought. Perceive how the Air region of your mental body unites with the Fire region, giving it its first degree of substance.

**1 minute silence**

Now gently allow the thoughts which express your perception of essential meaning to take form as emotional significance. Perceive how the Water region of your mental body naturally adheres to the combined Fire and Air, uniting to give personal significance to your perception of essential meaning.

**1 minute silence**

Sense your entire astral body and gently allow the emotional significance you perceive to sink down into the sensation of your entire physical body. Perceive how the Earth region of your mental body is a natural consequence of the unification of Fire, Air and Water.

**1 minute silence**

Sense your entire physical body.

Spread your awareness to encompass your astral body and your physical body simultaneously.

Spread your awareness to encompass your perception of essential meaning in its three forms of thought, emotional significance and physical sensation. Perceive the common link of essential meaning which unites your three bodies.

**2 minutes silence**

Now restrict your awareness to just the sensing of your physical body. Sense the Fire region of your physical body. Its Air region, Water region and Earth region. Sense the unification of these four regions.

Now send your roots deep down into the soil below and release any excess of energy that you may feel.

Turn your attention away from your roots and back to the sensing of your physical body.

Now begin your return to normal awareness. Before opening your eyes or moving your body, take a moment to listen to the noises around you, to smell the air, etc.

Now take a deep breath and exhale it gently.

Now move your hands up along your thighs and up your abdomen and chest, up to your face and back down again, awakening your body to normal sensation.

Now gently open your eyes and slowly begin to physically move about.

When this technique becomes easy for you to perform, you may move on to lesson four.

# ~ Lesson Four ~
# The Passive Separation and Resting
# of the Astra-Mental Body

## Introduction:

This Lesson is suitable only for those who have successfully completed Step Two of IIH. The primary reason for this prerequisite is because a rudimentary Elemental balance is essential for accomplishing a passive separation of the astra-mental body from the physical body. In the absence of a rudimentary Elemental balance, this separation requires an accumulation of significant amounts of energy in order to overcome the natural resistance encountered when one tries to separate an imbalanced astral body from its physical shell.

A secondary reason for this prerequisite is because by the completion of Step Two your mental will has reached a level of great strength due to the sensory concentration exercises. The passive separation of your three bodies is entirely directed by your mental body and requires sufficient will power and focus to achieve.

One benefit of the passive separation of the astra-mental body from its physical shell is that it affords a deep degree of rest for the physical shell itself. This has a very healing effect that is rarely achieved in the course of a normal life. The effect is similar to sleeping yet deeper due to the fact that during normal sleep the astra-mental body does not actually leave the physical shell.

You will note that I've been referring to the astra-mental body instead of just an astral body. The reason I use this specific term is to emphasize the fact that without the mental body, the astral body is unconscious, inert and incapable of activity of any sort. All astral wandering of any kind is accomplished by the conjoined astral and mental bodies and since they act in unison, I call this conjoined body an astra-mental body.

The first step in separation of the astra-mental body from its physical shell is a conscious act of withdrawing the mental body from the Earth region of itself. Awareness is turned away from the direct perception of physical sensation and fixed upon the Water region of the mental body and the direct perception of emotional significance.

When conscious awareness is withdrawn from the Earth region of the mental body there ceases to be a conscious awareness of physical sensation. Without the ingredient of our conscious attention, the Earth region of the mental body fades into the far background of awareness. By simultaneously focusing the whole of our attention upon the Water region, we increase the strength of our astral body and bring it to the forefront of our conscious awareness.

These two simultaneous acts constrict and condense the mental body into its Water, Air and Fire regions and place the mental body's focus within the astral body. This conjunction of the astral and mental bodies wherein the mental body is focused upon its astral shell instead of its physical shell, is the true astra-mental body.

So our first step in the passive separation will be a one-pointedness meditation wherein we focus our conscious awareness exclusively upon the experience of our astral body.

The second step is a spatial one. Here we must willfully move our astra-mental body slightly away from the same space occupied by our physical shell. The ease with which this is accomplished depends upon how completely you have focused your conscious awareness within your astral body. If you are expecting *only* the physical sensations of move-ment or are conceptualizing it in those terms, then this may be very diffi-cult for you at first. Just remember that the only thing that can hinder this separation is your mind so if you have difficulty, work at letting go of your preconceptions of what it *should* feel like... Be present and in the moment instead of off exploring the no-time zone of speculation and expectation.

In the Archaeous, I will have you stand upright, right next to your physical shell. At first you will focus exclusively upon the astral sensa-tions of separation and of standing. You will examine your astral body from its Earth region upwards. Once your astra-mental body is firmly and wholly separated, I will turn your attention toward an examination of your empty physical shell. Here you will have an opportunity to directly perceive the emotional significance of your own physical form and to further increase the completeness of your separation from it.

We will let the physical shell rest for several minutes total before re-turning our astra-mental body to it. The process of return is one of gentle descent and fully conscious reintegration.

The first step of reintegration is to reoccupy the same space as our physical shell. This is done slowly and requires self-control to avoid the inclination to just snap back.

The second step is to reintegrate the Earth region of the mental body. This is accomplished by shifting the conscious awareness away from di-rect perception of the astral body and focusing it upon the direct percep-tion of physical sensation. This too is done slowly and gently and, as usual, will involve the four Elemental regions of the physical body.

During the experience of observing your physical shell from the per-spective of your separate astra-mental body, you will be instructed to no-tice a silver cord or thread that connects your astra-mental body to your physical shell. This is all that remains of the Earth region of your mental body when your conscious attention is focused exclusively within your astra-mental body and when your astra-mental body occupies a different space than its physical shell. The Earth region remains rooted in the physical shell and this is what keeps the physical body functioning enough to sustain its life. This is your physical shell's lifeline, so to speak.

While this cord is eventually capable of nearly infinite elasticity, it is at first a fairly fragile thing which can easily be harmed. It's therefore important to treat your physical shell's lifeline with care and respect. After all, you have to return to that physical shell and suffer through any negative consequences your actions might cause.

The things that harm this lifeline and which you must avoid are, number one, snapping back into your physical shell. This violent return stresses the cord and bypasses the process of conscious reintegration, both of which will leave you feeling out of sorts. So when you do return, it's wise to return gently and with full awareness of the entire process of reintegration.

To avoid this snapping back effect, I suggest that you make sure you will not be disturbed while you're performing the Archaeous. Tell your housemates not to disturb you under any circumstances, lock your door, unplug your phone and turn off the lights. This becomes less important once you are proficient at the process of separation and reintegration. With practice, you will be able to effectively reintegrate your astra-mental body with your physical shell in an instant, with full awareness and no detrimental after-effects. So if someone does disturb you, your return will remain under *your* control and not be harmful.

The number two thing to avoid is wandering too far away from the location of your physical shell too soon. Since this is only the Earth region of your mental body it is the most rigid part and therefore the most prone to breaking. Imagine if you will, a plastic, clay-like substance that is at first hard, but as you handle it and work it with your fingers, it begins to loosen and become more and more pliable. With patience, it will stretch as far as you can stretch your arms without breaking. But if you were to immediately try stretching it or try stretching it all the way when it's only just starting to loosen, it would snap in two.

Your silver cord, the lifeline between yourself and your physical shell, has these same properties. It *can* be broken. 99% of the time that this happens, the astra-mental body will immediately snap back into the physical shell. This is an almost insurmountable manifestation of the instinct of self-preservation. Nature's way of making sure we don't kill ourselves. But the consequences are still quite unpleasant, albeit usually not terminal.

The primary effect of a cord break is that the astra-mental body cannot fully reintegrate with the physical shell until the cord itself has healed. In other words, the Fire, Air and Water regions of the mental body are not fully integrated with the Earth region. A very mild example of this would be a strong sense of feeling disconnected from events and your own life, mentally and emotionally disoriented. Physical effects would be exhaustion and the exacerbation of any present ailments.

In other words, take good care of your silver cord! If you always treat it conscientiously and with gentle care then you will have absolutely nothing to fear.

Lesson four of the Archaeous demands that you already possess a strong will and are in control of yourself to such a degree that if you are tempted to wander too far or are lured by other actions that would harm your physical shell's lifeline, you *will* be capable of refusing the temptation and sticking to the task at hand. If, in absolute honesty with yourself, you do not yet possess this ability of self-direction in the face of temptation, then I *very* strongly suggest that you proceed no further with the Archaeous until you have developed it. The first three lessons will greatly help your progress in achieving that ability, so please focus yourself on them for now and return to lesson four at a future date.

A final issue I want to raise before moving on to the practice is what you should do if you have difficulty at first with the actual separation act of moving away from your physical shell. Since the recording may progress at a speed that doesn't match your own, I suggest that if you can't separate apace with the recording, then spend the time while I'm talking about what to do after you've separated, focused instead upon the sensations of your astral body and the direct perception of emotional significance. Use that time to deepen your sense of separation from the Earth region of your mental body. This will help prepare you for the next time you perform the lesson.

So, let's turn now to the practice itself.


**Practice:**

Before we begin, make sure that you will not be disturbed. If you haven't done so already, then put the recording on pause and take a moment now to lock the door, turn off the phone and turn out the lights.

Situate yourself comfortably, either sitting upright, with your hands resting gently on your thighs, or lying down on your back. Clear your mind of all unwanted, mundane concerns and thoughts.

Now focus your awareness in the Earth region of your physical body and quickly relax all of the muscles in this region. Release every bit of tension.

Now move your awareness upwards to your Water region and relax all of the muscles in this region. Release every bit of tension.

Now move your awareness upwards to your Air region and relax all of the muscles in this region. Release every bit of tension.

Now move your awareness upwards to your Fire region and relax all of the muscles in this region. Release every bit of tension.

Now sense your entire head region as a whole.

Add to this your chest region and sense both together.

Add to this your abdominal region and sense all three together.

And finally, add your leg region and sense your entire physical body as a whole.

Project your roots down into the soil below you and release every bit of negativity you might be holding.

Now return your focus to sensing your entire physical body as a whole. Feel the solidity of the Earth region, the fluidity of the Water region, the lightness of the Air region and the electricity of the head region. Sense how these four regions penetrate each other and are a single, inseparable whole.

Focus intently upon the physical sensation of your entire body. This perception of pure physical sensation is the Earth region of your mental body.

Now push your awareness outward slightly until you feel the vibrant energy of your astral body. Focus just upon your astral body and the direct perception of emotional significance. Willfully turn your attention away from the Earth region of your mental body and focus exclusively upon the Water region of your mental body.

Focus upon the emotional significance of the solid energy you perceive within the Earth region of your astral body.

Now move your awareness upward to the Water region of your astral body and sense the significance of the fluid energy you perceive there.

Now move your awareness upward to the Air region of your astral body and sense the significance of the light energy you perceive there.

Now move your awareness upward to the Fire region of your astral body and sense the significance of the radiant energy you perceive there.

Hold this awareness of your astral body's Fire region and add to it the awareness of the Air region. Sense these two regions of your astral body as a unified whole.

Hold this awareness of your astral body's conjoined Fire and Air regions and add to it the awareness of the Water region. Sense these three regions of your astral body as a unified whole.

Hold this awareness of your astral body's conjoined Fire, Air and Water regions and add to it the awareness of the Earth region. Sense these four regions of your astral body as a unified whole.

Focus all of your awareness upon the sensations of your entire astral body. Focus upon the direct perception of emotional significance.

Hold this awareness of the Water region of your mental body and add to it the awareness of the Air region of your mental body. Incorporate the direct perception of thoughts and ideas into your direct perception of emotional significance and sense these two regions of your mental body as a unified whole.

Hold this awareness of your mental body's conjoined Water and Air regions and add to it the awareness of the Fire region of your mental body. Incorporate the direct perception of essential meaning into your direct perceptions of thoughts, ideas and emotional significance and sense these three regions of your mental body as a unified whole.

Focus all of your awareness upon the sensations and perceptions of your entire astra-mental body. Sense the fluidic emotional energy of the Water region, the light thought energy of the Air region and the radiant energy of essential meaning in the Fire region. Sense how these three qualities of perception interpenetrate each other and form a unified whole.

Now sense the parameters of your astra-mental body and imagine that this is your astra-mental skin. Your astra-mental skin is independent of your physical skin and you are able to move your astral-mental body independently of your physical shell. Without moving your physical body, raise the right hand and arm of your astra-mental body so that it is fully extended in front of you..

Now lower it back into alignment with your physical position.

Focus again upon the sensations and perception of your entire astra-mental body. Sense the astra-mental skin that defines the shape and size of your astra-mental body.

Now, without moving your physical body at all, slowly stand upright with your astra-mental body. If you were sitting in a chair, you should now be standing immediately in front of the chair with your back to your physical shell. If you were lying down, then you should now be standing immediately at the feet of, and facing away from your reclining physical shell.

Stand perfectly still within your astra-mental body and focus your awareness upon the sensations you perceive. Sense the solid energy of the Earth region of your astral body, the fluid energy of its Water region, the light energy of its Air region and the radiant energy of its Fire region. Sense all four regions of your astral body as a unified whole, standing upright, independent of your physical shell.

Hold this awareness of the Water region of your mental body and add to it the awareness of the Air region of your mental body. Sense their union.

Hold this awareness of your mental body's conjoined Water and Air regions and add to it the awareness of the Fire region of your mental body. Sense the unification of your entire astra-mental body.

Now look through your astra-mental eyes and directly perceive the emotional significance of whatever lies directly in front of you in the room where you're standing. As you examine with your astra-mental eyes, also perceive the current of thoughts and ideas that underlie this direct perception of emotional significance. Now look still deeper and perceive the essential meaning that these thoughts and emotional significance give shape to.

Now slowly turn to your right until you are looking directly at your empty physical shell. Examine your physical shell with your astra-mental eyes and directly perceive the emotional significance of its form. Resist any inclination to re-enter your physical shell with all of your mental will power.

Take a moment now to sense your astra-mental skin once again and reaffirm your separateness and independence from your physical shell.

Now return to your examination of your physical shell. Once again, directly perceive the emotional significance expressed by your physical form with your astra-mental eyes. Now look deeper and perceive the current of thoughts and ideas that underlie this direct perception of emotional significance. Now look still deeper and perceive the essential meaning that these thoughts and emotional significance give shape to.

Now once again, take a moment to sense your astra-mental skin and reaffirm your separateness and independence from your physical shell.

Now take note, with your astra-mental eyes, of the silver cord that connects your astra-mental body and your physical shell. This is the life sustaining umbilicus that keeps the autonomic functions of your physical shell continuing uninterrupted in the absence of your astra-mental body. Observe the subtle energy that flows along this cord and keeps your heart pumping and your lungs respiring. Directly perceive its emotional significance. Now look deeper and perceive the current of thoughts and ideas that underlie this direct perception of emotional significance. Now look still deeper and perceive the essential meaning that these thoughts and emotional significance give shape to.

Now once again, take a moment to sense your astra-mental skin and reaffirm your separateness and independence from your physical shell.

Now take note, with your astra-mental eyes, of the rested state of your physical shell. Observe the slow, relaxed pace of its breathing and the flaccid muscles in the face. Directly perceive the emotional significance expressed by this state of physical relaxation. Take note also of the thoughts, ideas and essential meaning that underlie your perception of emotional significance.

Now once again, sense your astra-mental skin and reaffirm your separateness and independence from your physical shell. Sense your entire astra-mental body. Sense the solid Earth region of your astral body. Add to this the fluid Water region, the light Air region and the radiant Fire region of your astral body. Sense your astral body as a unified whole and add to this awareness of the Water region of your mental body, the awareness of the Air region of your mental body. Sense your mental body's conjoined Water and Air regions and add to this the awareness of your mental body's Fire region. Sense the unification of these three regions. Sense your astra-mental body as a unified whole.

Now turn again to your right until you are once again facing away from your physical shell. Now slowly back into your physical shell and once again occupy the same space as your physical shell.

Sense your astra-mental skin, independent of your physical skin. Now close your astra-mental eyes and relax into your physical shell. Let your astra-mental body fill your entire physical frame and gently turn your awareness back to the Earth region of your mental body and the direct perception of physical sensation. Become aware of your physical skin, muscle and bone and integrate the vibrant energy of your astra-mental skin into every cell of your physical body.

Shift your attention to the Earth region of your physical body and integrate the solid energy of the Earth region of your astral body into it. Spread this energy throughout your leg region.

Move your awareness upward to the Water region of your physical body and likewise, integrate the fluid energy of your astral body's Water region into that of your physical body. Spread this energy throughout your abdominal region.

Move your awareness upward to the Air region of your physical body and integrate the light energy of your astral body's Air region. Spread this energy throughout your chest region.

Now move your awareness upward to the Fire region of your physical body and integrate the radiant energy of your astral body's Fire region. Spread this energy throughout your head region.

Hold your awareness of the conjoined astra and physical Fire regions and add to it the awareness of your conjoined astral and physical Air region. Sense these two Elemental regions as a unified whole.

Hold the awareness of these conjoined astral and physical Fire and Air regions and add to it the awareness of the conjoined astral and physical Water region. Sense these three Elemental regions as a unified whole.

Now hold the awareness of these conjoined astral and physical Fire, Air and Water regions and add to it the awareness of the conjoined astral and physical Earth region. Sense these Four Elemental regions as a unified whole.

Sense your entire physio-astra-mental body as a single unified whole.

Now send your roots deep down into the soil below and release any excess of energy that you may feel.

Turn your attention away from your roots and back to the sensing of your physical body.

Now begin your return to normal awareness. Before opening your eyes or moving your body, take a moment to listen to the noises around you, to smell the air, etc.

Now take a deep breath and exhale it gently.

Now move your hands up along your thighs and up your abdomen and chest, up to your face and back down again, awakening your body to normal sensation.

Now gently open your eyes and slowly begin to physically move about.

When this technique becomes easy for you to perform, you may move on to lesson five and the passive separation of the solitary mental body.

# ~ Lesson Five ~
# The Passive Separation and Resting
# of the Solitary Mental Body

## Introduction:

Like the previous lesson, this one is suitable only for those who have completed Step Two of IIH.

Our subject in this lesson is the passive separation of the *solitary* mental body. In Lesson Four, we separated our astra-mental body from our physical shell and now with this lesson we will enact a further separation as we vacate our astral shell. This means a constriction of our focus to just the Air and Fire regions of our mental body. I call this the solitary mental body because in this state, the mental body is bereft of its astral and physical clothing. This is the most versatile and flexible of our three temporal bodies.

The solitary mental body, composed of just the Air and Fire regions, is two-fold in nature and equates with the Individual Self or, in kabbalistic terms, the Tiphareth Self. This particular level of Self is capable of direct perception of the lower personal self *and* direct perception of the higher Self. As you know, the Air region of the mental body represents the direct perception of thoughts and ideas. This is the downward-focused aspect of the Individual Self. That part of the Individual Self which is concerned with, and involved in, the personal and physical aspects of existence. The Fire region on the other hand, represents the direct perception of essential meaning which occurs without the solid form of thoughts and ideas. This region of the solitary mental body is the upward-focused aspect of the Individual Self. That part of the Individual Self which is continuously receiving an influx from the Greater Self.

In this lesson, we will be using the same techniques presented in Lesson Four. First, we will constrict our mental body to just its Water, Air and Fire regions and thereby separate our astra-mental body from its physical shell. As before, this reveals a silver cord corresponding to what remains of the Earth region of the mental body. Then we will constrict our mental body still further to just its Air and Fire regions and separate our solitary mental body from its astral shell. This reveals a second cord of a lavender color rooted in the astral shell, corresponding to what remains of the Water region of the mental body.

The reason we are doing this specific form of separation is because in this way we completely separate and rest our three bodies. As each of our bodies rest, they naturally revert to a more pristine and healthful state. The act of letting them rest separately, significantly decreases the input from one level to the next, thus increasing the *depth* of their rest.

Without the active impress of the astral energy, the physical body rests more calmly and completely than in sleep. Likewise, the astral body, separated from both physical **and** mental input, rests as it rarely does in the course of a normal human life. And the mental body, freed in this way from both astral and physical restraints, can be led to a very deep state of restful calm.

Ordinarily, when the solitary mental body is separated, the astral body is left within the physical shell instead of being separated from it. This means that the connection between the astral and physical levels of awareness is not diminished and therefore both bodies remain relatively integrated. Ordinary separation reveals only a *single* **purple** cord instead of the two cords that the triple separation reveals. The reason such a cord is darker in color is because it is what remains of the Water **and** Earth regions of the mental body, both of which remain rooted in the astra-physical shell. In the triple separation however, the purple cord becomes two cords -- the silver cord corresponding to the Earth region and the lavender cord corresponding to the Water region. The lavender cord, since it is *just* the Water region is immediately fluid and can easily stretch to infinity.

The shade, width and degree of translucence that the lavender cord displays, will vary in direct ratio to the degree of one's focus. For example, when awareness is focused exclusively within just the Fire region of the solitary mental body, the lavender cord will be as thin as a hair and as clear as water and there will be no perception other than the direct perception of essential meaning. In such a state there is no processing of perception into words, thoughts, emotional significance or sensation of any kind. In such a state, you would not be able to hear my voice, nor would you feel it if I were to touch your physical body.

On the other hand, when awareness is focused exclusively with the Fire **and** Air regions, thoughts and words do accompany perception. In such a state the lavender cord has the width of a string and the opacity of lavender Jell-O.

With lesson five however, even though you will be primarily focused within the Air and Fire regions of your mental body, a part of your awareness will still be receiving input from your physical ears in the form of my guiding voice, and processing your perceptions via your astral body, giving them form as shape and color. Since there is this much information passing along your lavender cord, it will be the width of a finger, have the opacity of milk and shine with a distinctly bright lavender color.

In order to achieve deeper states of separation of the solitary mental body, in which there is no perception below the density of thoughts, you will have to perform this lesson without depending upon the recording to guide you. Nonetheless, this recording will sufficiently introduce you to the technique and even with its limitations, it will enable you to attain a significant degree of separation, rest and healing benefit.

So, let's turn now to the practice itself.

**Practice:**

Before we begin, make sure that you will not be disturbed. If you haven't done so already, take a moment to lock the door, turn off the phone and turn out the lights.

Situate yourself comfortably, either sitting upright, with your hands resting gently on your thighs, or lying down on your back, and clear your mind of all unwanted, mundane concerns and thoughts.

Now focus your awareness in the Earth region of your physical body and quickly relax all of the muscles in this region. Release every bit of tension.

Now move your awareness upwards to your Water region and relax all of the muscles in this region. Release every bit of tension.

Now move your awareness upwards to your Air region and relax all of the muscles in this region. Release every bit of tension.

Now move your awareness upwards to your Fire region and relax all of the muscles in this region. Release every bit of tension.

Now sense your entire head region as a whole.

Add to this your chest region and sense both together.

Add to this your abdominal region and sense all three together.

And finally, add your leg region and sense your entire physical body as a whole.

Project your roots down into the soil below you and release every bit of negativity you might be holding.

Now return your focus to sensing your entire physical body as a whole.

Now push your awareness outward slightly until you feel the vibrant energy of your astral body. Focus just upon your astral body and the direct perception of emotional significance. Willfully turn your attention away from the Earth region of your mental body and focus exclusively upon the Water region of your mental body.

Focus upon the emotional significance of the solid energy you perceive within the Earth region of your astral body.

Now move your awareness upward to the Water region of your astral body and sense the significance of the fluid energy you perceive there.

Now move your awareness upward to the Air region of your astral body and sense the significance of the light energy you perceive there.

Now move your awareness upward to the Fire region of your astral body and sense the significance of the radiant energy you perceive there.

Hold this awareness of your astral body's Fire region and add to it the awareness of the Air region. Sense these two regions of your astral body as a unified whole.

Hold this awareness of your astral body's conjoined Fire and Air regions and add to it the awareness of the Water region. Sense these three regions of your astral body as a unified whole.

Hold this awareness of your astral body's conjoined Fire, Air and Water regions and add to it the awareness of the Earth region. Sense these four regions of your astral body as a unified whole.

Focus all of your awareness upon the sensations of your entire astral body.

Hold this awareness of the Water region of your mental body and add to it the awareness of the Air region of your mental body. Incorporate the direct perception of thoughts and ideas into your direct perception of emotional significance and sense these two regions of your mental body as a unified whole.

Hold this awareness of your mental body's conjoined Water and Air regions and add to it the awareness of the Fire region of your mental body. Incorporate the direct perception of essential meaning into your direct perceptions of thoughts, ideas and emotional significance and sense these three regions of your mental body as a unified whole.

Now sense the parameters of your astra-mental body and feel your astra-mental skin.

Now, without moving your physical body at all, slowly stand upright with your astra-mental body.

Stand perfectly still within your astra-mental body and focus your awareness upon the sensations you perceive. Sense the fluid energy of its Water region, the light energy of its Air region and the radiant energy of its Fire region. Sense all three regions of your astra-mental body as a unified whole, standing upright, independent of your physical shell.

Now turn to your right until you are facing your physical shell and observe its state of rest.

Now sit down at the foot of your physical shell. Observe the silver cord that connects you with your physical shell.

Now close your astral eyes and turn your focus inward. Willfully turn your attention away from the Water region of your mental body and focus exclusively upon the Air and Fire regions. Sense the light energy of the Air region's thoughts and ideas and the radiant energy of the Fire region's essential meaning. Sense how these two regions are a unified whole.

Sense how the form provided by thoughts and ideas create a sort of mental skin that contains and expresses the radiant energy of essential meaning. Feel your mental skin. Sense how free and independent it is from your astral and physical skins.

Fill the Air and Fire regions of your mental body with the thought that you are now free of your astral shell.

Now, without moving your astral shell at all, gently float upwards until you are just a few inches above your astral shell. Focus your awareness exclusively within the unified Air and Fire regions of your solitary mental body.

Feel your mental skin and focus upon your independence from your astral shell.

Now open your mental eyes and look down upon your empty astral and physical shells. Focus upon your separateness and independence from them.

Observe the lavender cord that connects you to your astral shell. Observe also the silver cord that connects your astral shell to your physical shell.

Observe the relaxed state of both shells.

Now close your mental eyes and turn your focus inward. Focus upon the thoughts and ideas that you directly perceive in this moment.

Now turn your focus away from the Air region and towards the Fire region. Immerse yourself in the direct perception of essential meaning.

**Silence . . .**

Now gently return to the awareness of thoughts and ideas. Let your direct perceptions of essential meaning permeate the Air region of your mental body and take form.

Feel your mental skin and sense the unification of the Air and Fire regions of your solitary mental body.

Now open your mental eyes and observe the well rested state of your astral and physical shells. Willfully descend into your astral shell and gently turn your awareness back to the Water region of your mental body and the direct perception of emotional significance.

Spread your solitary mental body throughout your entire astra-mental body and sense your astra-mental skin. Sense your entire astra-mental body as a unified whole.

Shift your attention to the Earth region of your astral body and integrate the energy of your solitary mental body into it.

Shift your attention to the Water region of your astral body and integrate the energy of your solitary mental body into it.

Shift your attention to the Air region of your astral body and integrate the energy of your solitary mental body into it.

Shift your attention to the Fire region of your astral body and integrate the energy of your solitary mental body into it.

Sense all four regions of your astral body as a unified whole. Add to this the awareness of the Air region of your mental body and sense the

Water and Air regions of your mental body as a unified whole.

Now add to this the awareness of the Fire region of your mental body and sense all three regions of your astra-mental body as a unified whole.

Now open your astra-mental eyes and observe the deeply rested state of your physical shell. Sense your astra-mental skin, independent of your physical skin.

Now close your astra-mental eyes and relax into your physical shell. Let your astra-mental body fill your entire physical frame and gently turn your awareness back to the Earth region of your mental body and the direct perception of physical sensation. Become aware of your physical skin, muscle and bone and integrate the vibrant energy of your astra-mental skin into every cell of your physical body.

Shift your attention to the Earth region of your physical body and integrate the solid energy of the Earth region of your astral body into it.

Move your awareness upward to the Water region of your physical body and likewise, integrate the fluid energy of your astral body's Water region into that of your physical body.

Move your awareness upward to the Air region of your physical body and integrate the light energy of your astral body's Air region.

Now move your awareness upward to the Fire region of your physical body and integrate the radiant energy of your astral body's Fire region.

Hold your awareness of the conjoined astral and physical Fire regions and add to it the awareness of your conjoined astral and physical Air region. Sense these two Elemental regions as a unified whole.

Hold the awareness of these conjoined astral and physical Fire and Air regions and add to it the awareness of the conjoined astral and physical Water region. Sense these three Elemental regions as a unified whole.

Now hold the awareness of these conjoined astral and physical Fire, Air and Water regions and add to it the awareness of the conjoined astral and physical Earth region. Sense these Four Elemental regions as a unified whole.

Sense your entire physio-astra-mental body as a single unified whole.

Now send your roots deep down into the soil below and release any excess of energy that you may feel.

Turn your attention away from your roots and back to the sensing of your physical body.

Now begin your return to normal awareness. Before opening your eyes or moving your body, take a moment to listen to the noises around you, to smell the air, etc.

Now take a deep breath and exhale it gently.

Now move your hands up along your thighs and up your abdomen and chest, up to your face and back down again, awakening your body to normal sensation.

Now gently open your eyes and slowly begin to physically move about.

When this technique becomes easy for you to perform, you may move on to lesson six and healing through the Elemental balancing of your three bodies.

# ~ Lesson Six ~
## Elemental Balancing and Re-integration of the Three Bodies.

This Lesson is suitable only for those who have made good headway with the work of Step Four of IIH and are already proficient with accumulating the Elements.

Our subject in this lesson is the Elemental balancing of each of our three bodies. Mastery of Lesson Five is an absolute prerequisite for the pursuit of this Lesson since the Elemental balancing work requires a separation of the three bodies.

This Lesson of the Archaeous is an extension of an exercise found at the end of the astral training of Step Four in "Initiation Into Hermetics". In Bardon's version, the student accumulates the Elements into their respective regions of the physical body in order to attain an Elemental harmony. In the Archaeous however, we will be accumulating the Elements into all three of our bodies and will thereby attain a deeper degree of Elemental harmony.

We will begin with the mental body, then the astral body and end with the physical body. Great care is taken with the process of re-integrating the mental and astral bodies, and with re-integrating the astra-mental and physical bodies. In this way, the mental body's Elemental harmony is brought from the mental, into the astral and then reaffirmed by accumulating the Elements into the astral body. Then the astra-mental harmony is brought from the astral, into the physical and again reaffirmed by accumulating the Elements into the physical body.

Since the work of Lesson Six requires a very deep level of concentration and separation of the three bodies, I will not be guiding you through the process as I did in the previous Lessons. Instead, I will be describing the process and it will be up to you to then put it into practice.

So, let's move on to a description of the practice.

You begin as usual and work your way through the Archaeous up until the point at which your three bodies are separated and your focus of awareness is solely within your solitary mental body. This is the point at which Lesson Six begins.

Turn your solitary mental body until you are gazing at your resting astral and physical bodies. Take note of the cord connecting your solitary mental body to your resting astral body and the cord connecting your astral body with your resting physical body.

Focus upon the cord connecting your astral and physical bodies. As you know, this is the Earth region of your mental body. Your first task is to fill the Earth region of your mental body with the Earth Element. Do not accumulate a great amount of the Element -- only enough to fill the cord. You don't want to condense the Element, so this is to be just a gentle filling of the Earth region with the Earth Element.

Now focus your attention upon the cord connecting your resting astral body and your solitary mental body. As you know, this is the Water region of your mental body. Your next task then, is to fill the Water region of your mental body with an equal amount of the Water Element. As before, do not accumulate too much of the Element -- only fill the cord without condensing the Element.

When the Earth and Water regions of your mental body have been filled with their respective Elements, turn your focus upon the Air region of your solitary mental body. Your next task is to fill the Air region with an equal amount of the Air Element in the same manner as before. Again, just fill the Air region with the Air Element; don't condense the Element.

Then turn your focus to the Fire region of your solitary mental body and fill it with an equal amount of the Fire Element, exactly as before.

When all four regions of your mental body are thus filled with an equal amount of their respective Elements, spread your awareness throughout your entire mental body (all four regions simultaneously). Spend several moments of meditation in this state of integrated balance.

When your meditation feels complete, release the accumulated Elements in reverse order, starting with the Fire and ending with the Earth. When you are done, spend a few moments sensing the Elemental harmony and balance within your mental body.

Now turn your attention to your reclining and fully rested astral body. Gently sink down into it and regain full awareness of it. Consciously permeate it as usual, linking your astral and mental bodies intimately together. When you are ready, stand up with your astral-mental body, paying close attention to reconnecting with all of the astral sensations.

Stand still and closely integrate your astral and mental bodies. Consciously vitalize your astral body with the Elemental Equilibrium of your mental body. Bring the balancing influence of your re-vivified mental body firmly into all aspects of your rested astral energy. Special attention must be given to this re-integration. Take your time and be as thorough as possible.

Once you have fully reclaimed your astral body, turn your focus upon the Earth region of your astral body and fill it with the Earth Element. As with the filling of the mental body, you do not want to condense the Element, just fill the region.

Then turn your attention to the Water region of your astral body and fill it with an equal amount of the Water Element. Follow this by filling the Air region of your astral body with the Air Element and then the Fire region with the Fire Element.

When all four regions of your astral body are thus filled with an equal amount of their respective Elements, spread your awareness throughout your entire astral body (all four regions simultaneously). Spend several moments of meditation in this state of integrated balance.

When your meditation feels complete, release the accumulated Elements in reverse order, starting with the Fire and ending with the Earth. When you are done, spend a few moments sensing the Elemental harmony and balance within your astral body.

Now turn your focus to your resting physical body and re-integrate your astra-mental body and resting physical body. Spend several moments upon this process of re-integrating your physio-astra-mental body. Consciously integrate the Elemental harmony of your astra-mental body into every aspect of your physical body. Special attention must be given to this re-integration. Take your time and be as thorough as possible.

Once you have fully reclaimed your physical body, turn your focus upon the leg region of your physical body and fill it with the Earth Element. As before, you do not want to condense the Element, just fill the region.

Then turn your attention to the abdominal region of your physical body and fill it with an equal amount of the Water Element. Follow this by filling the chest region of your physical body with the Air Element and then the head region with the Fire Element.

When all four regions of your physical body are thus filled with an equal amount of their respective Elements, spread your awareness throughout your entire physical body (all four regions simultaneously). Spend several moments of meditation in this state of integrated balance.

When your meditation feels complete, release the accumulated Elements in reverse order, starting with the Fire and ending with the Earth. When you are done, spend a few moments sensing the Elemental harmony and balance within your physio-astra-mental body. Concentrate upon the sensations caused by this re-vivifying Equilibrium of your three bodies united. Integrate every bit of astral-mental energy you can into your physical structure, consciously guiding it into every cell of your physical body. And then release whatever excess energy remains.

Visualize your mental body as actively brightening, and willfully giving direction to, the astral. Also visualize the physical conforming its structure into agreement with this renewed astral template. This final integration and balancing should be pursued with the utmost care and concentration.

End your meditation in the usual manner, being absolutely sure to make a full return to normal, waking consciousness.

So, to summarize the process:

First you follow the Archaeous up to the point at which all three bodies are separated and your awareness is firmly rooted in your solitary mental body.

Then you load each of the four Elemental regions of your mental body with their respective Elements, starting with Earth and ending with Fire. After a few minutes in this state, you release the Elements in reverse order, from Fire to Earth. Upon completion, you re-integrate your solitary mental body with your resting astral body.

You then repeat the same exercise with your astral body by filling each region with its respective Element. After a few minutes the Elements are released in reverse order and you re-integrate your astra-mental and physical bodies.

The same work is repeated with your physical body. Again, fill each region with its respective Element and then, after a few minutes, release the Elements in reverse order.

Achieving the fully integrated and Elementally balanced physio-astra-mental body is the most healing level of the Archaeous. To quote Bardon, "If the magician should ever get into disharmony through any particular circumstances, all he has to do is practice these exercises and he will immediately redress the harmony. He will experience the comforting influence of the entire universal harmony, which is creating and keeping in him the feeling of peace and happiness, not only for a few hours, but for days."

This concludes Lesson Six of the Self-Healing Archaeous, concerning the Elemental balancing and re-integration of the three bodies. I wish you much peace, happiness and Elemental harmony!

# ~ Lesson Seven ~
## Astra-Mental Wandering

This Lesson is suitable only for those who have mastered Step Four of IIH and are making good headway with the Step Five work.

Our subject in this lesson is Astra-Mental Wandering. Mastery of Archaeous Lesson Six is an *absolute* prerequisite for the pursuit of this Lesson since the Elemental balance is what releases the astra-mental body from its bonds and enables true wandering.

One of my motivations for creating this series of audio Lessons in the first place was the many requests I received from students of IIH for a safe and sane method of astral projection that could be employed prior to reaching Step nine. The desirability of astral projection has become a very strong part of the current magical culture and many are willing to take great risks to achieve it. In fact, during my years serving as a Companion to countless students of IIH, I have been faced with many instances where the student has done considerable damage to their astral and mental bodies through their attempts to master astral projection employing today's popular techniques. So I see that meeting this need in a safer manner than is presently available and in a quicker manner than Bardon suggested, has become important to the welfare of many students of IIH.

At first, I felt a great amount of resistance to illuminating the following technique since I firmly believe that Bardon's system is THE best, most beneficial way to proceed. I had planned to merely introduce those aspects of the Archaeous which are most healing for the three bodies in the hope that this would ameliorate the damage being done through the pursuit of today's latest fad. In fact, Lesson Seven was to originally have been about the benefits of integrated self-expression through the consciously unified and Elementally balanced physio-astra-mental body, instead of being about Astra-Mental Wandering. What deterred me from this plan was the receipt of several notes indicating that folks had realized the possibilities of projection inherent to Lessons Four and Five which deal with the passive separation of the three bodies. Therefore it became imperative that I explain the *proper* way of using the Archaeous to achieve astra-mental wandering.

In order to safely astra-mental wander, there must be a state of Elemental balance within the three bodies. For example, spontaneous or unintentional astra-mental body separation occurs at times when there is a *natural* Elemental balance among all three bodies. When everything is just so and all the right factors come into temporal accord, the astra-mental body spontaneously exits the physical body. Primary among those conditions is a state wherein the three bodies achieve a temporary state of Elemental balance. There are also additional conditions that must be met at the same time, such as a behest from higher levels of Self, karmic need, etc. The bond which binds the astra-mental body to the physical body is not loosened *naturally* unless these conditions are met. Nonetheless, many popular techniques seek to override these natural conditions through an intensive accumulation and projection of raw energy. And therein lies the greatest danger of these techniques, since they abuse and ignore the safeguards that Nature has deemed necessary.

As Bardon illustrated in IIH however, when an Elemental *Equilibrium* of *all three* bodies is achieved, separation of the Astra-mental body becomes a matter of conscious intention, instead of meeting certain conditions. This is one reason why Bardon placed Mental Wandering at Step Eight and Astral Wandering at Step Nine -- by Step Eight, all three bodies have been brought into a state of Elemental Equilibrium.

From the very beginning, the Archaeous seeks to incubate this Equilibrium. First with the physical body and a process that leads toward an understanding of how the Universal Qualities of the Elements manifest within the physical body. Then with the astral body through a similar process with the same end. And finally with the mental body in the same manner. Once the Qualities are recognized and to a certain degree this realization has been integrated into the three bodies, *separation* -- NOT wandering or travel -- becomes possible. This coincides with the work of Step Three at which point one has achieved what I call the "rudimentary Astral Elemental balance", wherein the most outstanding negative personality traits have been transformed.

Then, once one has made good progress with Step Four, there is Lesson Six of the Archaeous, in which I turn to balancing the Elements, through accumulation, within each of the three bodies, followed by thorough re-integration. At this point in the IIH training, the Astral Elemental Equilibrium is close at hand, if not already in place, so Lesson Six reinforces the nascent Astral Equilibrium and speeds the practitioner toward its maturity.

Compared to Bardon's pacing, the only ingredient actually lacking in order for there to ensue safe astra-mental wandering, is the matter of the *Mental* Elemental Equilibrium. In IIH, Bardon doesn't begin directly addressing the Mental Equilibrium until Step Seven (which is another reason why mental wandering doesn't come until Step Eight), but here in Lesson Six of the Archaeous, is an exercise which directly addresses the Mental Equilibrium by the end of Step Four.

By the end of Step Four / beginning of Step Five, there is already a Mental *balance* in place, so the Lesson Six exercise will strengthen this balance and speed its evolution toward a true Equilibrium. What makes this speeding up safe, is the careful integration of the Elemental harmony into each of the three bodies in succession. This "grounds" the harmony which is what transforms transitory 'harmony' into less transient 'balance' and ultimately, into Equilibrium.

As I said, in order to safely astra-mental wander, there must be a state of Elemental balance within the three bodies. This degree of balance can be induced by the Archaeous process and in this present Lesson Seven, I will be elucidating a method by which this is achieved.

As with the previous Lesson Six, this Lesson requires such a deep level of concentration and separation of the three bodies that it would be impractical for me to lead you through the practice as I did in the early Lessons. Instead, I will once again be simply describing the process and it will be up to you to then put it into practice.

So, let's move on to a description of the practice.

Lesson Seven begins with a complete replication of Lesson Six. This is the foundation which establishes the Elemental balance of all three bodies.

So first, you will separate your three bodies and then create an Elemental harmony within your solitary mental body. You then integrate this mental harmony into your astral body and create an Elemental harmony within your astra-mental body. Next, you integrate this astra-mental harmony into your physical body and create an Elemental harmony within your physio-astra-mental body.

This whole procedure must be enacted very carefully and thoroughly, with special attention being given to the successive integrations.

At this point, you must spend a few minutes deeply focused upon the unity of your three bodies and upon their mutual Elemental balance.

When this meditation feels complete, focus upon your intention to astra-mental wander. You must build a very strong force of will into this intention.

Now constrict your awareness to your astra-mental body in the usual manner and separate your Elementally balanced astra-mental body from your Elementally balanced physical body. At first you must stand very still, right next to your empty physical shell. Focus again upon the balanced state of your bodies and upon the usual sensations of your astra-mental body. Focus your attention exclusively within your astra-mental body.

Observe the silver cord that connects your astra-mental body to your physical shell. See how thin and elastic it is. Note how much more elastic it is than when you separated your astra-mental body previously, prior to achieving the Elemental balancing of all three bodies.

Now turn your attention away from your physical body and from the silver cord. Focus exclusively within your astra-mental body and re-affirm its Elemental balance by gently accumulating the four Elements into their respective regions and then releasing them.

Now turn your attention outward to your physical surroundings. It is likely that you will feel a great sense of freedom, compounded by an eagerness to immediately fly off, but this *must* be kept in check. *You* must be in control of it, instead of it controlling you. Stand perfectly still until you feel that you are in command and able to resist any urges to fly off.

Your ability to be self-directing in the face of this strong urge is dependant upon the maturity of your mental discipline and your Elemental Equilibrium.

Once you are certain that you have command of yourself, take a few steps around the room in which your physical body rests. Examine the details of your physical surroundings with the faculties inherent to your astra-mental body.

After a few minutes of this, stop and stand very still once again. Focus inwardly and once again re-affirm the Elemental balance of your astra-mental body. If necessary, briefly accumulate and release the Elements.

When this feels complete, turn your attention to the silver cord and to your resting physical body. Observe the changes in the silver cord regarding its thinness and elasticity. Again, turn your attention back to your physical surroundings and explore them once again. This time, look for a few small details of the room and commit them to memory. Later, you will compare these memories with a physical viewing of the same details.

After a few minutes of this, turn your attention back upon your physical body. Re-affirm the Elemental Balance of your astra-mental body and then re-enter your physical body.

*Thoroughly* integrate your astra-mental body with your physical body in the manner of Lesson Six, including the accumulation of the four Elements into their respective regions. Release the Elements and then return to normal waking consciousness in the usual manner.

Immediately after you have regained your normal physical awareness and senses, you must examine your physical surroundings and discern how closely your astra-mental perceptions correspond with your physical perceptions. Look for the specific details that you memorized during your astra-mental journey and compare those memories to what you see now.

Repeat this practice of examining your immediate surroundings while inhabiting your astra-mental body and then comparing them to your physical perceptions, over and over, until such time as your astra-mental perceptions align with the physical reality. From this practice you will learn how to discern between subconscious projections and factual reality.

When you have reached the point where your astra-mental perceptions of your immediate surroundings are reliably accurate, you may then begin to venture further afield. When possible, view the places you travel astra-mentally, with your physical body later on, in order to be certain that, at a distance, your astra-mental perceptions are accurate.

Venture further and further away from your physical body as time goes by, but stay within the temporal present moment. Proceed in this way until you have become adept at visiting any place within the present moment of time-space you choose.

The method by which you get from the location of your physical body, to any other point in space, is fairly simple. It's merely a matter of forming a strong intention to visit such and such a place. This creates a mental resonance which, because of the mental plane law of 'like attracts like', immediately draws you to your location of choice. For example, if you wish to astra-mentally wander to a relative's home, you would need to create the strong mental intention to do so and this would carry your astra-mental body to their physical presence.

The practice of mastering astra-mental wandering within the physical present moment, prepares the astra-mental body for entry into the more ephemeral layers of the astral realm. Navigation within these layers of the astral is somewhat different and involves, in addition to a strongly formulated intention, the accumulation of the single Elements for exploring the Elemental realms, and the accumulation of specific frequencies of colored Light for exploring the Zone Girdling the Earth. In other words, these explorations require an alteration of your astra-mental body from its natural state.

This concludes Lesson Seven of the Self-Healing Archaeous, concerning Astra-Mental Wandering. I hope, for your sake, that you choose to use this knowledge wisely and apply it to the forwarding of your magical evolution.

# ~ Lesson Eight ~
## Techniques of Mental Wandering

This Lesson is suitable only for those who have mastered the previous Lesson Six.

There are three degrees or types of mental wandering. The first is when the solitary mental body is separated from the astra-physical shell. The second is when the astra-mental body is first separated from the physical shell and then the solitary mental body is separated from the astral shell. The third and final degree is when, having performed the separation of astra-mental from physical and then solitary mental from astral, the Fire region of the mental body is separated from the Air region of the solitary mental body.

The first degree of wandering is what Franz Bardon described in Step 8 of IIH. By this method of separating the solitary mental body directly from the astra-physical shell, one reveals a purple cord that represents what's left of the conjoined Earth and Water regions of the mental body. With this degree, one's perceptions can range from purely mental to astral and the integration of perceptions by the solitary mental body, into the emotional context is very easy. This degree is most suitable for mental wandering of the present moment, one's physical environs, other places on earth, etc. This is the precursor state for the Astral Wandering technique that Bardon taught in Step Nine of IIH.

In the second degree of wandering, one first separates the astra-mental body from the physical shell, revealing the silver cord which is just the deflated Earth region of the mental body. Then one separates the solitary mental body from the astral shell, revealing the violet cord (instead of the denser purple cord), which is just the deflated Water region of the mental body. This provides for a deeper separation of the solitary mental body and is more suitable for purely mental perceptions that involve the integration of direct perception of essential meaning with thought. It is possible to quickly integrate the mental perceptions into the emotional level but this is not automatic and therefore requires intention. It is also an easy matter to draw the astral shell to the solitary mental body and revert to astral wandering from this state.

This second degree is the most suitable for a finer mental examination of the present moment and one's physical environs, etc., but more importantly, it's the best for exploring the higher Planes or Planetary Zones. However, the conjoined Air and Fire regions of the solitary mental body cannot travel much beyond the Zone of Jupiter and can only penetrate to the "edge" of the Abyss. In other words, the solitary mental body is a creature of the sequential realm and as such, cannot enter into the non-sequential realm of eternity. Only the Fire region of the mental body can navigate the Abyss between the sequential and eternal realms.

Which brings me to the third and final degree of mental wandering -- separation of the Fire region from the solitary mental body. One starts from the second level and then separates the Fire region of the mental body from its integration with the Air region. This reveals a crystal clear cord which is all that remains of the Air region when one's awareness is totally focused within just the Fire region. With this degree there is only the direct perception of essential meaning and BEing. These perceptions can be periodically integrated into the Air region of thought, but this re-quires an act of will which removes one from a totality of focus within just the Fire region. The Fire region is like a flame, always reaching up-ward and outward. Thus the integration of the direct perceptions of the Fire region, into the Air region, requires a turning-away-from what one is directly perceiving. Consequently this interrupts the continuity of one's perceptions and one must then return to an exclusive focus upon, and separation of, the Fire region.

Only the Fire region of the mental body is capable of directly perceiv-ing, and merging awareness with, the eternal mental body

This is the highest degree of Bardon's emptiness or vacancy of mind exercise from Step One of IIH. At the level of Step One, the student is focusing their awareness within the Fire region of their mental body. This is the region of direct perception of essential meaning and a state best described as BEing. Here there is no thinking -- only perceiving and BEing. However, with the Step One exercises, this all takes place while the three bodies are still fairly integrated. In effect, the Fire region is connected by a very fat, dense cord that represents the combined Earth, Water and Air regions of the mental body. This generates a lot of back-ground noise, so to speak, that one doesn't realize is there until one has experienced the deeper quiet and greater control that comes from first separating the mental body.

As the student deepens their emptiness of mind state through contin-ued practice, the cord connecting the Fire region becomes thinner and clearer, thus revealing the various levels of mind in succession. First the layers of the brain-bound mind, then the emotion-bound mind, then the thinking-bound mind and finally revealing the perceiving-mind. It is possible, given a lot of persistent practice and perhaps an exceptional gift of native talent, to reach a state in which the cord connecting the Fire re-gion to the combined Earth, Water and Air regions, attains a crystal clar-ity. For most folks however, that takes a *long* time.

By separating the three bodies first and then separating the Fire region from the Air region, one can reach the deepest state of emptiness of mind possible. However, a lesser degree of emptiness, but one that is still su-perior to the Step One exercise, can be achieved by first separating the astra-mental body from the physical shell and then separating the Fire region from the astra-mental body, leaving behind a conjoined Water and Air astra-mental shell. This results in a translucent golden yellow cord through which the Fire region can quickly integrate its direct perceptions into the Water and Air aspects of the mental body. Although, this still means a periodic interruption of the emptiness state and of direct perception, it does take considerably less time to clarify the translucent yellow gold cord to a crystal clear state.

Since it would obviously be impossible for me to lead you through these practices, I will now simply outline the method for each degree of mental wandering. Surely you will be ably to apply this outline to your personal practice.

**Degree One:** Begin with the Elemental balancing and integration of all three bodies as instructed in Lesson Six. Once your three bodies are fully re-integrated, separate your solitary mental body from the astra-physical shell. Perceive the purple cord and then investigate your surroundings. Just as with my instructions vis-a-vis astra-mental wandering in Lesson Seven, you must verify the accuracy of your perceptions after each session. Begin by wandering very close to your astra-physical shell and then, over time, venture further and further afield. Practice integrating the perceptions of your solitary mental body into your astra-physical body during your wandering. Upon completion of your mental journey, carefully and thoroughly re-integrate into your astra-physical shell.

Travel from one place to another is caused by formulating a clear intention to travel to your chosen destination. For example, if you wish to visit with a friend in another country, you would formulate the strong intention to do so. Travel to other planes or zones is caused by intention and by consciously harmonizing the solitary mental body with the vibration of the chosen zone. For example, if you wish to visit an Elemental kingdom, you would formulate the intention and then fill your solitary mental body with the relevant Element.

**Degree Two:** Begin with the Elemental balancing and integration of all three bodies as instructed in Lesson Six. Once your three bodies are fully re-integrated, separate your astra-mental body from the physical shell. Perceive the silver cord and then separate your solitary mental body from the astral shell. Perceive the violet cord and then investigate your surroundings. As always, you must later verify the accuracy of your perceptions after each session. Begin by wandering very close to your astral and physical shells and then, over time, venture further and further afield. Practice integrating the perceptions of your solitary mental body into your astral body during your wandering. Upon completion of your mental journey, carefully and thoroughly re-integrate into your astral and physical shells. The same methods of travel apply as in degree one.

**Degree Three:** Begin exactly as in degree two. Once your three bodies are separate, focus your awareness exclusively within the Fire region of your solitary mental body. *Perceive* the essential meaning of your separation from the Air region and *perceive* the essential meaning of the crystal clear cord that connects you with it. Isolate your awareness to just the Fire Region -- to just perception and BEing.

Travel with the Fire region of the mental body is also a matter of intention and of playing with the mental realm law of "like attracts like". However, one must introduce this intention *prior* to separating the Fire region from the Air region. The intention of where one wishes to travel is very strongly formulated within the solitary mental body just prior to focusing the awareness exclusively within the Fire region. At this point an Element, Fluid or colored Light may be condensed within the solitary mental body. All of these actions create a strongly focused crystallization of the mental materia which serves as the anchor point to which your target is attracted; and visa versa, which is equally attracted *to* and *by* your target. As you and your target converge on the mental plane, you focus exclusively within the Fire region and separate from the Air region. This places your Fire region at, or in, your mental target. In other words, you *aim* your Fire region and then release it.

If you are exploring the mental plane level of your immediate physical surroundings with the solo Fire region, then it will take a fair amount of experience to "verify" them later with your physical eyesight, but by this point you should be very sure of the reliability of your mental senses.

During your experiments with the solo Fire region, you should periodically integrate your perceptions into the Air region. If necessary, completely re-unite with the Air region and then integrate your thoughts into the Water region from there as this gives a greater assurance that you will remember them clearly at a later time. Ultimately the transition between being in the solo Fire region and then integrating with the Air region and then separating the solo Fire region again, should become very fluid and rapid.

With practice, one also learns how to propel the solo Fire region *after* its separation from the Air region. This is accomplished through a process of opening oneself to what is *perceived*, as opposed to intending what one *conceives*. For example, one has aimed for and arrived at the lunar zone but now wishes to ascend from there to the mercury zone. What is required is an *opening of the self to* the direct perception of the essential meaning of the mercury zone vibration.

Ultimately, one can *open to* realms that the sequentialized solitary mental body is incapable of aiming at, simply because it cannot fully conceive of them. The solo Fire region however, is capable of *perceiving* what the sequentialized consciousness cannot conceive of. For example, when the solitary mental body is filled with the Akasha prior to separation of the Fire region and the intention of merging with one's own Greater Self is very strongly formulated, this will aim the Fire region *towards* the eternal mental body. Once separated, the Fire region *perceives* the Greater Self and then must *open itself to* the Greater Self and fully expend its Fire as a radiance that fills and becomes at-one-with the Greater Self. This same method can also be used to merge with a chosen Deity-form, to explore specific facets of the Primal Causality, etc.

When any wandering is done with the solo Fire region, very great care should be taken in the subsequent process of re-integrating the four regions and three bodies. Spend several moments, or minutes if necessary, integrating the Fire and Air regions very thoroughly. Take your time with this integration of your perceptions into your thinking mind. Likewise, thoroughly integrate the solitary mental body with the astral shell and let all those thoughts settle into the level of your emotional perceptions. And just as thoroughly, re-integrate your astra-mental and physical bodies. Affix the memory of the perceptions, thoughts and feelings from your mental journey into your mundane awareness.

This ends Lesson Eight of the Self-Healing Archaeous. I hope that these techniques help you to unveil the Eternal Splendor of the Limitless Light by serving to facilitate and encourage your own explorations of our infinite universe, with all its many wonders.

# ~ Lesson Nine ~
# The Fine Art of Integration

**Introduction:**

This final Lesson in the series is suitable only for those who have already mastered Lesson Six.

As I stated at the very beginning, the Self-Healing Archaeous follows the basic Alchemical tenet of "solve et coagula", of separation and re-unification. The separation into parts purifies those parts and the re-unification of the purified parts results in an overall improvement of the materia. This is evolution in action, the primordial process of Force taking on Form and then Form releasing its Force so that it may take on a new Form.

In Lesson One, the purification process began with the complete relaxation of every part of the physical body, which naturally required the focusing of awareness upon each body part in succession. Then there was the focusing of awareness upon each Elemental region, in succession. This focusing of the awareness upon an individual part is an important first aspect of purification. By bringing our conscious awareness fully into the part, we strengthen the astra-mental template upon which the part or region is founded. In other words, we increase the purity of the Force which has manifested as that particular Form.

Having thus purified each part, the next step in the Archaeous is to consciously re-unite each of the parts and re-assemble them into an awareness of the whole. The awareness of one Elemental region is added to that of another and the awareness of the two conjoined, is added to a third and so on, until all four regions are united in a single awareness. This is the rudimentary process of integration wherein each purified part is re-joined with all the other purified parts and awareness of each separate part is held simultaneously as a new, holistic awareness.

In Lesson Two, this same process was applied to the astra-mental body. It began with the focusing of awareness upon the astra-mental body, distinguishing it from the physical body, and then focusing upon each of its Elemental regions, in succession. Once this purification of parts had been accomplished, all the parts of the astra-mental body were re-assembled into a holistic astra-mental awareness. Then, the holistic awareness of the astra-mental body was integrated with the holistic awareness of the physical body, resulting in an even more comprehensive holistic awareness.

With Lesson Three, this same process was again repeated but this time, upon the mental body. The result was a holistic physio-astra-mental awareness.

The separation of parts in the first three Lessons occurred *in situ*, so to speak, and was solely a matter of shifting and contracting one's focus of awareness. In Lessons Four and Five however, this separation of parts was taken a step further and became a spatial separation as well, although still rooted in the focusing and contraction of one's awareness. As a consequence, the resulting purification was much more profound than that produced *in situ*. The actual passive separation of the three bodies allowed for a deeper, more exclusive focus within each body and for a deep, deep relaxation at the astral and mental levels that was not available *in situ*.

The next step in furthering the depth of purification of each part or body, came with the Lesson Six work of balancing the Elements in each of the three separated bodies. The development of the Elemental harmony exponentially increased the purification of each part and, due to the harmonizing effect upon each part, the subsequent integration of those parts was exponentially more complete.

The first six Lessons prepared one for Lessons Seven and Eight, and the next step in purification -- wandering. Astra-mental and mental wandering are educational pursuits. They expand the Self through direct experience. And while still rooted in the focusing of one's awareness, they require Self-expression as much as they do passive perception. In other words, they exercise that focused awareness in new ways which cause it to rapidly evolve.

As always, the newly purified parts must be re-integrated into a holistic physio-astra-mental awareness. But when it comes to integrating the purifications wrought through astra-mental and mental wandering, one confronts a greater labor than encountered in the earlier Lessons. One must develop new skills of integration to truly benefit from the subtle experiences one will encounter in mental and astra-mental wandering. Primarily, these new skills have to do with integrating those experiences into the mundane awareness and memory. And secondarily, they have to do with consciously integrating the lessons one learns from those experiences into each of the three bodies to such a degree that each body is further purified and transformed by those lessons learned.

Thus I have titled this final Lesson in the Self-Healing Archaeous series, "The Fine Art of Integration", for truly, this is one of the more important magical Arts.

Every bit of one's ascent *must* be integrated into the mundane levels of Self or it is for nothing. Separation without re-integration becomes destruction, and likewise, integration without periodic separation becomes stagnation. Hermetic initiation is rooted in building a solid foundation and then erecting one's ascension upon that footing, always making sure to securely bind the ascension to that solid foundation lest the whole structure topple over. Integration is what assures a sound and continuous ascent, thus it is an Art well worth mastering. And it is best to begin as early as possible because the further along the path of initiation you trod, your skills of integration will face greater and greater challenges.

The practical part of this final Lesson is divided into three sections: Integration of Astra-mental Wandering, Integration of Mental Wandering, and Integrated Self-Expression. This latter is what Bardon described as "magic action" in Step Six of IIH. I like to think of it as Physio-Astra-Mental Wandering. :)

So, on to the practical parts . . .

**Integration of Astra-Mental Wandering:**

The integration of higher perceptions and states of awareness into lower levels of consciousness is a fine art. Just like the master painter wields color and shape to express many deep layers of meaning simultaneously, so too the fine artist of integration molds the colors of thought and the shapes of emotion to capture their most sublime experiences in symbols that the lower levels of consciousness can retain and comprehend. This takes time and practice to master.

The first step of any integration into the mundane awareness is to affix the higher perceptions and thoughts into one's memory. The second step is to then actively employ the realizations that arise from those memories by making them the foundation for one's actions.

It is said that the physical brain captures everything that the eyes see and that the ears hear, but becoming consciously aware of that stored information takes something more than mere organic brain function. The ingredient that makes specific bits of that inconceivable amount of stored data consciously memorable is the emotional significance we attribute to it. If it is data that's totally innocuous, like how many cars passed by your window between noon and 3pm on Saturday, then it remains unreachable by the conscious awareness. But if it's emotionally significant, like what type of car plowed through your window at 3:15 pm Saturday, then we're certain to remember.

With astra-mental wandering, remembering is not much of an issue since these experiences are perceived through the filter of the astral body or Water region of the mental body *while* they are occurring. In other words, the experiences of astra-mental wandering occur within the milieu of emotional significance and all of the astra-mental perceptions are colored by the same. Perception occurs in symbolic forms -- shapes, colors, sounds, sensations, and so on, all of which express an emotional content. Within that emotional content lies essential meaning which is directly perceived with one's mental senses at the same instant of its astral perception. Thus the symbolic forms of the astral materia clearly communicate their essential meaning to the astra-mental wanderer.

Nonetheless, the astra-mental wanderer's primary focus is at the astral level of perception. Astral perception itself does not immediately reveal the entirety of the mental level, *direct* perception of essential meaning -- it merely *symbolizes* the direct perception. Therefore, the astra-mental wanderer should spend some time at the end of their journey reviewing their experience to ensure that later, when the astral symbol is *remembered*, the entirety of the mental level direct perception is still accessible *through* the astral symbol.

When the business of your astra-mental wandering is complete, return to the location of your physical shell and stand next to it. Spend the next few moments -- however long it takes -- reviewing your experience. Start at the beginning and go through the whole experience chronologically, trying to recall every detail. As you remember, take note of how different segments of your experience resonate with specific regions of your astral body.

When you are through with your review, re-enter your physical shell and thoroughly re-integrate your three bodies. Immediately thereafter, once again review your experience and write down sufficient notes about your experience so that you will later be able to regain your memories of events.

In the days and weeks that follow your wandering session, meditate upon your experience. Refer to your notes to refresh your memory, if necessary, and take further notes of key points that you discover during your meditations.

The purpose of these meditations is to discover and then thoroughly understand, the lessons contained in your wandering experience. Once the lessons are understood, you must then apply them to your life in whatever way seems most appropriate. You must integrate them into your experience of your Self at whatever level the lessons demand.

**Integration of Mental Wandering:**

Mental wandering is, of course, the most versatile form of wandering, yet it can present many challenges in terms of remembering one's experiences and perceptions, let alone integrating and applying their lessons. But since the mental body itself is so versatile, one is also presented with the perfect tool for adapting to every challenge. All one needs is a bit of creativity and imagination.

In Lesson Eight, I defined three degrees of mental wandering, so to shape my discussion here, I will use that same structure and describe some of the options open to each degree.

## 1. Separation of the solitary mental body directly from the physical body

Since this sort of mental wandering involves the conjoined Air and Fire regions, perception occurs in the form of thoughts and direct perception, simultaneously. However, these perceptions lack emotional significance at the time they are occurring. With a deep degree of separation, the only density of symbolic form these perceptions have is that of thoughts. There is no astral shape, color, sound, etc., so in order to gain emotional significance and astral form, these perceptions must be processed by the astral body or Water region of the mental body.

Since this degree of mental wandering reveals the denser purple cord, which is the compressed Water and Earth regions conjoined, it is very easy to create a flow of input between the solitary mental body and the Water region.

The rate of flow between the two can be regulated at will. At first, I suggest that you experiment with opening and closing it. For example, spend a few moments in deep separation of the solitary mental body from the astra-physical shell, and then expand your awareness along the purple cord ever so slightly, a degree at a time, until you feel the intrusion of emotional significance and astral form, into your thoughts. Let your thoughts settle into this level of your awareness and then return your focus to a deep separation of the solitary mental body from the astra-physical shell.

Once you get the hang of it, it becomes very easy to rapidly shift between these states and quickly integrate your solitary mental wanderings into your astral awareness. With much practice, it is possible to continuously feed your solitary mental perception into your astral awareness, without any interruption of focus within the solitary mental body. This involves a slight splitting of awareness so that an insignificant part of your focus is concentrated upon the astral level. This creates a subtle bridge through the purple cord specifically to the Water region of the mental body.

When you are finished with your solitary mental wandering, return to your astra-physical shell and hover next to it. Before re-entering it, review your wandering. Then expand your awareness down along the purple cord until you again touch the Water region. Once again review your wandering but this time in its astral form. Then fully re-integrate into your astra-physical body. Immediately write down sufficient notes so that you will be able to recapture your memories later.

As with my comments on astra-mental wandering, you must follow your solitary mental wandering with meditations and the implementation of the lessons learned. This, and this alone, is what completes the integration process.

## 2. Separation of the solitary mental body from the astra-mental body

Because the complete separation of all three bodies results in a significantly deeper and more exclusive focus within the solitary mental body, it takes a greater quantity of one's awareness to integrate the solitary mental perceptions into the Water region. As before, I suggest that you experiment with opening and closing the flow of input along the violet cord between the solitary mental body and the astral shell. Since the Water region is not conjoined with the Earth region, you will need to spend a little more effort in solidifying the astral processing of your solitary mental perceptions. With great practice, it is possible to set up so rapid a sequential exchange between the two as to be almost continuous, but this does require the splitting off of more of your awareness than before.

The main issue at first is continuity. If you interrupt your solitary wandering too often to integrate the experience into your astral awareness, then you risk loosing any sense of continuity. And if you interrupt too infrequently, you risk losing your ability to remember your experience later on. But with practice, you will learn how often is appropriate and you will also become more and more proficient.

At the end of your solitary mental wandering review your experience and then re-integrate with your astral shell. Within the astra-mental context, again review your experience and firmly affix its astral form. Then re-integrate your astra-mental body with your physical shell. Immediately review and take notes. And as always, meditate upon your experiences, learn from them and apply them.

## 3. Separation of the solo-Fire region from the solitary mental body

The perceptions from this degree of mental wandering are perhaps the most challenging to completely integrate since they are, by their nature, direct perceptions of infinity. It is also impossible to actually control the frequency with which the integration of them into the Air and Water regions will occur since there is no *thinking* will existent within the solo Fire region of the mental body. In other words, once one has separated the solo Fire region from the Air region shell, there is no *thought* of needing to return. There is only *intention* which, as I stated in Lesson Eight, is how one aims the Fire region. So it is possible to enter into the separation carrying the intention of returning to the Air region periodically in order to integrate the Fire region perceptions.

However it comes about, when you do find your perceptions beginning to take form as thoughts, spend several moments in that state of transition and very carefully let the fullness of your solo Fire perceptions settle into your thinking awareness. Let them condense to a fine Airy mist.

It is wise at this point to descend still further with these thoughts and integrate them into the Water region of your awareness, giving them some degree of astral form. Then return to the solitary mental body, again separate the solo Fire region and continue with your solo Fire wandering.

Descending all the way into the Water region with your thoughts is very disruptive to the continuity of a solo Fire wandering. In some cases it is, in fact, extremely unwise to program the intention of periodic return to thinking awareness, let alone to an astral awareness. Some solo Fire journeys must be left to find their own duration and scope; and the subsequent quality of integration into memory, left to the Divine Wisdom.

Nonetheless, it is important that you experiment with this periodic integration, followed by a return to the solo Fire region. With practice, it is possible to periodically integrate just the Air region of thoughts and store up a few segments of experience until making a larger descent into the Water region. While descending into just the Air region is somewhat less disruptive to the continuity of a solo Fire wandering, the real trick is storing segments of the solo Fire perceptions in the Air region. To accomplish this storage, one must rely upon the Water that is inherent to Air.

When your solo Fire wandering is complete, you must carefully re-integrate your awareness with the Air region shell. In the solitary mental body context, review all the thoughts that coalesce in regard to your solo Fire wandering. Be *very* thorough and patient with this step as it may take far longer than the wandering itself.

Then re-integrate with the astral shell and solidify all your thoughts with astral form. Let the Airy thoughts condense still further until they become one fluid mass, all connected, one with the other. Note the differences and similarities between which of those ideas settle into which regions of your astral body.

When the astral integration is complete, re-integrate with your physical shell. Immediately write your notes and ground these very ephemeral experiences into your waking awareness.

The experiences of the solo Fire wandering are the most important of all the wandering experiences. Their lessons are the most relevant to your advancement and therefore, they require the most thorough integration into every aspect of your being. It can takes years to fully integrate some of the lessons brought through solo Fire wanderings, perhaps even lifetimes of effort.

This is especially true of solo Fire wanderings which entail merging with one's Greater Self or Eternal Mental Body. These experiences are infinitely profound and cathartic, and produce reverberations throughout one's entire existence. Integration of the Eternal experience into the sequential layers of consciousness requires prolonged and repeated meditation. And then integrating those aspects of the Eternal experience that one has become conscious of, into the layers of personality and physicality, requires great creativity and inventiveness. One must never relent.

While these experiences are eternal and non-sequential in nature, it takes time for them to be integrated into the sequential layers of Self. Or rather, it takes time for *you* to integrate them into your mundane awareness which exists within a single moment of time-space. It is literally like trying to cram as much of infinity as you can into something the size of an atom. Ultimately, it's a matter of completely giving over to the eternal aspects of Self so that they may freely express themselves through your every thought, word and deed. Only then is the infinity that exists within an atom revealed and made manifest . . .

## Integrated Self-Expression:

In the mental exercises of Step Six of IIH, Bardon described a three-part magical action in which one is conscious of all three bodies simultaneously. I like to call this physio-astra-mental wandering, for in reality this is what it is. In this state, one is conscious of existing in all three bodies, simultaneously: one perceives with their physical, astral and mental senses, simultaneously, and each physical motion is simultaneously and consciously, performed with the astral and mental bodies in unison

This is presented as a mental exercise because it is completely dependant upon the ability to differentiate between the four regions of the mental body and to be consciously aware within all four regions simultaneously. The directorship is transferred wholly to the solitary mental body. As I've stated before, this is essentially the Individual or Tiphareth Self -- the depth *point*. With its directorship firmly in hand, the Individual Self then expresses itself *through* the Water region or astral body and *through* the Earth region or physical body.

In other words, it is an integrated Self-expression in which the astral and physical bodies serve as the vehicles through which the Individual Self expresses and manifests itself within the physical realm. When the physical arm is moved through the air, the astral and mental air is disturbed as well. Bardon called it magical action because in ceremonial ritual, all of one's movements must occur on the physical, astral and mental planes, simultaneously.

For anyone who has made it to Lesson Six in the Archaeous, the exercise I propose now, will present no difficulties. Difficulty however, may arise in the sustaining and prolonging of the state this exercise leads to.

This is a slight alteration of Lesson Six and the Elemental balancing of all three bodies.

Separate all three bodies as usual. Balance the Elements in the mental body and then re-integrate the solitary mental body with the astral shell, conjoining the Fire, Air and Water regions of the mental body. Balance the Elements in the astral body. As you do so, remain consciously aware of both your astral *and* mental bodies, simultaneously. You must sense *both* bodies at the same time and to the same degree yet still be able to differentiate between the two. This is like seeing a thing from two different perspectives at the same time. As Bardon described it, let the mental hand slip into the astral glove.

Retaining this dual, astral and mental awareness, re-integrate with your physical shell and the Earth region of the mental body. Balance the Elements in the physical body while simultaneously remaining aware of your astral and mental bodies. Sense all three bodies at the same time and to the same degree. Let the astra-mental hand slip into the physical glove.

Sustain this triple awareness of your three bodies simultaneously for as long as you are able. Just stand, sit or lie down and without moving, focus upon perceiving your physical, astral and mental surroundings simultaneously. As you look through your physical eyes, it is really your mental eyes, looking through both astral and physical eyes. As you feel your physical breathing it is really your mental will to breathe manifesting through your astral and physical respiration.

When you are able to prolong this state for 5 minutes or so, introduce physical movement. Move around your meditation space and focus upon unifying the mental, astral and physical components of each movement.

When this feels comfortable for at least 5 minutes, wander further afield. Keep working at the prolongation of the triple awareness and the retention of it in a variety of circumstances. After some time, the separation and Elemental balancing of the three bodies beforehand will become unnecessary. All one will need to do is become consciously aware of each body and then consciously unite these awarenesses into the triple awareness.

When one has succeeded in projecting the solo Fire region into the Akasha and has merged with the Eternal Mental Body of their Greater Self, then one can pursue a four-part action. This involves integrating the simultaneous awareness of the Greater Self into the triple awareness. All four perspectives -- eternal mental, temporal mental, astral and physical -- are held simultaneously in one's conscious awareness, within a single present moment of time-space. It is then the Greater Self, consciously expressing and manifesting ItSelf through the Individual, astral and physical vehicles.

When this is mastered one then has the opportunity to manifest the five-part action -- the true merging with the Divine. Here, awareness *as* The Unity is added to the four-part awareness and one exists within the physical temporal moment fully aware of The Unity, their Greater Self and Individual, astral and physical selves, simultaneously. It is then the Divine manifesting ItSelf directly into the temporal moment through the vehicles of the Greater, Individual, astral and physical levels of Self. This, of course, is the ultimate form of integration afforded by the Archaeous process.

This ends Lesson Nine and completes the Self-Healing Archaeous audio series. I pray that these Lessons, which have been my pleasure to present, serve you well along your path to perfection.

# ATTENDING THE UNITY

## THE MAGIC OF IHVH-ADNI

## THE ORIGINAL ARTICLE

1998

# The magic of IHVH ADNI --

This is the magic of combining IHVH with ADNI as I know it and practice it. I learned this magic from one whose name will forever be unspoken. After 10 years of practice, I have been granted the words to tell you of this sacred magic. But instead of telling it as I learned it, I will tell it as I have come to understand it  -- I will tell it with my own words and in my own way.

אני יהוה אדני רבונו של עולם אמן

ANI - IHVH ADNI - RBVNV ShL OVLM - AMN
(Ani - Yod Heh Vav Heh  Adonai - Ribbono Shel Olam - Amen)

Begin by situating yourself comfortably in a space where you are certain you will not be disturbed. Completely relax your body and develop a steady, deep breathing rhythm. Raise your thoughts to your Kether, inhale a breath, and with the exhale, speak the word ANI ("I am"). Prolong the Yod till your entire breath is spent. As you speak, visualize your Kether coming to life as a brilliant white sphere hovering just above the crown of your head.

With your next inhale, gather the Kethric Light. As you exhale, speak the words "Yod Heh Vav Heh" and project the Kethric Light downward. Use one quarter of your breath for each letter name, so that the final "Heh" spends the last of your air. As you speak the "Yod", project the Kethric Light down to your left temple and form there a sphere of luminous gray. Let this be your Chokmah and let it penetrate into the left side of your skull.

As you speak the first "Heh", project the Kethric Light from Chokmah, over to your right temple and form there a sphere of obsidian blackness. Let this be your Binah and let it penetrate into the right side of your skull.

As you speak the "Vav", project the Kethric Light down from Binah, to your solar plexus and form there a radiant sphere of golden-yellow. Let this be your Tiphareth and let it fill your chest.

As you speak the final "Heh", project the Kethric Light down from Tiphareth, to a point just below the arches of your feet (or if seated, to just below the tip of your spine) and form there an opaque sphere of olive-green. Let this be your Malkuth and let it encompass both your feet (or if seated, the coccyx and anus without including the sexual organs).

With your next inhale, return to your Kether and gather the Kethric Light, and as you exhale, speak the word ADNI ("ahh-don-eye"). Use your entire breath in the forceful utterance of this single word, prolonging the final Yod as necessary.

As you speak the first syllable ("ahh"), project the Kethric Light down from Kether, to Chokmah, then over to Binah, then down to Tiphareth, and ending in Malkuth. Prolong the aleph as necessary.

The second syllable ("don") is said quickly. The Kethric Light, having struck Malkuth, now erupts upward in a swirling cloud of rainbow-hued light.

The final syllable ("eye") is prolonged until the end of the available breath. During this time, the swirling Rainbow Light of Adonai becomes radiant and the channel between it and Kether flows powerfully with the Kethric Light.

Take at least one entire breath (inhale and exhale) without speaking and spend it strengthening your visualization.

With your next inhale, gather the Kethric Light-infused Rainbow Light of Adonai, and as you exhale, speak the words RBVNV ShL OVLM ("master of the universe"). Use your entire breath in speaking this phrase, prolonging the final Mem as necessary. As you speak, visualize the Rainbow Light spreading outward in all directions from you. As it radiates out into the universe, feel it permeating each and every thing it encounters.

Spend at least one breath (inhale and exhale), silently absorbed in this visualization. To finish, inhale and then with your exhale, speak the word AMN ("truth; faith"). Use your entire breath, prolonging the final nun as necessary. As you speak, feel the completeness of the Kethric Light's permeation of all things. Let the flow from Kether to Adonai and out to the universe be steady, strong and concrete.

Inhale and with your exhale release your visualization. Resume your normal breathing and normal bodily awareness.


Each word you speak should carry a specific tone and manifest a certain rhythm. The notes are dependant upon your natural vocal range, and the rhythm is dependant upon the natural pace of your breathing. The notes for the five *speaking* breaths are--

**Breath #1:** As you speak the first Aleph, you start at your lowest note and climb smoothly upward along your range till you reach a comfortable high note. The Nun and the Yod are pronounced at this high pitch.

**Breath #2:** The words "Yod Heh Vav Heh" which follow are also spoken at this high pitch.

**Breath #3:** With the first Aleph of "Adonai", you start again at your lowest note and slide upward to your highest. The second and third syllables are pronounced at this high note.

**Breath #4:** The word "ribono" is said at the high tone; "shel" is said at the lowest note; and, "olam" is said at a middle note between the two.

**Breath #5:** The closing "amen", starts from the lowest note and climbs with the Aleph to the highest. The second syllable is said at this high note.

Thus:

Aaaa ‿ neee  Yod  Heh  Vav  Heh    Aaaa ‿ don -eyeee    Ribonno  Shel Olammm    Aaaa ‿ mennn

I recommend that the non-speaking breaths number either 5 or 8, bringing the grand total to either 10 or 13 breaths.

Practice this exercise daily until you are completely comfortable with it and can perform it with facility. This discipline will eventually bring your mental and astral bodies into conformity with the visualized IHVH-ADNI structure. Each sphere and the passage of the Kethric Light between each, will become actual aspects of your finer bodies.

## The path of IHVH ADNI --

This is the natural way of things: The Ayin Soph Aur constricts and becomes the ANI; the ANI creates the Yod; the Yod creates the first Heh; the IH creates the Vav; the IHV creates the final Heh; the IHVH creates the ADNI; the IHVH-ADNI (IAHDVNHI) creates, permeates, sustains, *is* all things in our sequential universe.

This way of things is constant, never-failing, eternal. There has not ever been, nor will there ever be, a time when this is not the way of things. The root cause of this way lies in a realm which encompasses and causes the whole of time. This archetype exists beyond the influence of time, yet permeates all of time's infinite span.

This natural way of things is so integral a part of our experience, so much a part of our mechanisms of perception and of the objects we perceive, that we have naturally become blind to it. We are, so to speak, so enchanted with the infinite variety of trees that we do not notice the underlying ecosystem sustaining our forest. Nonetheless, we and the trees and all the great variety of things, exist only because of this underlying way of things -- we are, each and all, manifestations of this way. Not only are we each created by it, we are each creating it. We and the way are inseparable.

Our manifestation of the natural way of things occurs with or without our conscious, intentional participation. Yet when we do turn our individual awareness to this natural way and learn to consciously participate in its manifestation, there occurs a powerful mending of the disparity between our daily self-awareness and the Unity of all being. This act of conscious participation, clears the eternal channels of the Kethric Light coming into the present moment of our sequential, time-space universe.

When the channels are cleared through the diligent application of focused awareness, and the Kethric Light flows strongly from the eternal to the present moment, a gate opens within the human heart upon a path which leads upward along the flow of Light.

Leaving behind your physical and astral bodies, this path will lead to Tiphareth. Here you must look down upon your bodies and sense the entire flow of your present incarnation. This is the Vav which exists throughout time but does not encompass it. Throughout its span of time, it projects itself over and over into material existence. Each incarnation is experienced as a sequence of present moments. In Tiphareth, you must strive to see all the incarnations that have transpired (including your present one) since the birth of your Individual-Vav self.

When you have seen all your lives and know your Individual self, you must, as the ancients put it, "choose life", and actively return to your astral and physical bodies. You must then consciously manifest your knowledge of your Individual self in the present moment of your current incarnation. This further clears the channel of Light between the Vav and the Heh, effectively uniting them. When the VH is realized, a gate opens in the heart of the Individual self, upon a path which leads upward along the flow of Light.

As your VH, return to your Tiphareth (awareness of which is by now constant) and look upwards along the flow of Light toward Binah. There appears a veil between you and Binah which obscures your vision. You can rise along the Light only a limited distance before the veil stops your progress.

There is only one way to penetrate this veil. You must rise along the Light as far as you can and then return with it to your physical incarnation. You must thoroughly integrate this Light into the Individual, Personal and Physical aspects of your being. For each amount of Light you manifest, an equal measure more will be granted to your next rise. At first this is a slow and difficult process, but with persistence, the veil is penetrated.

The rise along the Light is not a constant progression of small increments. There are several quantum leaps toward understanding that will be encountered as you journey this path. Each leap will radically clarify your understanding and vision.

The first leap will show you the differences between Tiphareth and Binah, and will lift a primary layer off the veil. While the VH exists *within* the realm of sequence and time, Binah *causes* and *encompasses* the whole infinity of sequence/time. Binah is a non-sequentialized realm which gives birth to sequence  It causes and is the sequential realm, but experiences this sequentiality, non-sequentially.

The understanding of these essential differences opens a gate of light along the path, illuminating your way to the second leap. This leap will show you the similarities between the first Heh of Binah and the VH. This is consummated by a vision of the tapestry of commonality which weaves together the whole infinite number of Individual selves. [This is only a vision, and only of a symbolic representation of the Unity's manifestation, but it serves to show you the essential connections. This should not, despite its intensity and power, be confused with the actual experience of the Unitary consciousness.]

The vision of the commonality lifts a second layer of the veil and brings you to a sturdy, closed gate, blocking the path. The key which unlocks this similarity-gate is your understanding of the essential differences.

The path beyond this gate leads to your third and final leap. To trod this path requires that you let go of both similarities and differences. You must rise above even your own self-awareness as an Individual and merge with all the infinite number of other Individuals. Together, we are Binah. This third leap is from a sequential self-awareness to a non-sequential awareness which perceives the whole of sequence within itself.

This brings you to the dark shore of Binah and further clears the channel of Light between the first Heh and the VH, effectively uniting them.

The unification of HVH brings your awareness to an eternal perspective. Your Individual work is placed in a infinitely larger context. The work itself is no longer sequential -- only the manifestation of it is.

As you manifest this eternal Light within the layers of time and space, the dark shores of Binah brighten with the Light of the Yod. Truly, the connection to the Yod and the ANI occur -- in time/space terms -- simultaneous with the realization of Binah. It is only the transition from the eternal level of awareness to the sequential level which makes it seem, from the sequential perspective, as if the journey from the HVH to the Yod and on to the ANI, takes a span of time. It truly takes no time to occur, but at the same time, its manifestation is sequential and therefore requires a span of time to fulfill itself.

From our sequential perspective, this shift from HVH to the Yod is best illustrated by the differences and similarities between the two words understanding and wisdom. Understanding is a process -- a gateway through which we seek out threads of commonality and differentiation. In Binah we connect with the ability to understand any thing we focus our attention upon. The instant at which the nascent Binah understanding realizes that it secretly understands all things simultaneously, the innate quality of wisdom emerges. Wisdom is an inherent power, a formless force which manifests as understanding. But wisdom is not itself a process in the way that understanding is. Wisdom encompasses understanding and experience, manifesting itself spontaneously, practically, and completely.

Wisdom comes when, through experience, understanding encompasses itself. This happens, as I have said, beyond the ken of time and manifests as a further clearing of the channel of Light between the Yod and the HVH, effectively uniting them. The IHVH shares simultaneously in the Unitary consciousness of ANI and the downward focused HVH-Binah consciousness. It consciously integrates the Unity into the manifest ADNI. This is symbolized by IAHDVNHI, the true RBVNV ShL OVLM.

# The labor of IHVH ADNI --

Consciously manifesting this visualized passage of Kethric Light through mundane actions, is an essential step toward truly conforming your astral body to the mental impress. Permanent change manifests in the astral body only when that change reaches down into the substantive level of one's physical life. If the Kethric Light is not brought down solidly into Malkuth (the mundane realm of your day-to-day life), little real change in the astral body will result -- your harvest will be ungraspable, insubstantial things of air.

Working with the downward flow of Light and tending to its completion, is just as important as pursuing the upward path toward ultimate Unity. The one supports the other and either alone leads to instability. The work with the downward flow into manifestation must therefore be engaged simultaneous with the journey upward.

This work bears the fruit of the upward journey and constitutes the lesser magic of IHVH-ADNI:

### The First Work

When you have reached the stage of facility with the IHVH-ADNI visualization in which the visualization comes easily to you (i.e., the initial conformation of your mental body), turn your attention to the pause between "Adonai" and "ribono shel olam". Lengthen the time of this pause and meditate deeply upon the Rainbow Light of Adonai.

This is the covenant between Force (sunlight) and Form (water vapor), showing itself (rainbow). It represents the immanent, creative manifestation of the Kethric Light.

As you meditate, strive to become at one with the Rainbow Light. Strive to feel its creative power and radiance as your own. Each repetition of this meditation will bring you closer into alignment with the Rainbow Light, but it will likely take quite a span of dedicated effort to achieve a complete union.

At the end of each meditation, regardless of your level of unification with the Rainbow Light, speak the words "ribono shel olam" with your conjoined self-ADNI awareness. Strive to feel the resultant radiation of Light into the universe as your own self moving outward into your own self. Permeate your universe-self with your IHVH-ADNI-self.

Practice this meditation over and over until you reach a genuine state of union with the Rainbow Light and IHVH-ADNI. It took me nearly three years of persistent effort with this meditation, to pass from the conformation of my mental body, to conformation of my astral body and the initial union with the Rainbow Light. It will take you a span of time commensurate with your effort and abilities -- perhaps shorter than my span, perhaps longer. Each person is unique in this.

### The Second Work

As you progress toward union with the Rainbow Light, you will experience the profound IHVH-ADNI energy. At first it will be just a miniscule contact with its immensity. When you sense this energy, focus your attention upon it. Feel the quality and the quantity of it.

Working again within the breaths between "Adonai" and "ribono shel olam", pause to meditate upon this energy. Define, as I said, the quality and quantity of the energy you sense at that moment. Now repeat the words and visualization from "Ani" through "Adonai", and double the quantity of the energy you sense. As you reaffirm the visualization from within the visualization, strive to consciously double your contact with this energy.

Work with this doubling of your tolerance and contact, until you are comfortable with both levels and the process as a whole. Next, work by the same means at tripling the amount of energy. To do this, you will perform the words and visualizations from "Ani" through "Adonai", three times in total. Each repetition is to add an equal quantity of energy to the mix.

Each time you speak the subsequent words, "ribono" through "Amen", consciously radiate the energy you've accumulated with as complete a unification with the self-ADNI awareness as you can in that moment manifest.

When you reach comfort and facility with this triple invocation of energy, strive to accumulate the triple quantity of energy within a single speaking of "Ani" through "Adonai". When you master this, work at doubling and then tripling this new quantity, and so on.

As you increase both your tolerance and your depth of contact with this energy you will be supporting the process of achieving a true union with the Rainbow Light. However, the IHVH-ADNI energy and self-awareness is infinite and cannot therefore, be reached incrementally --

there is simply not enough time to complete an infinite number of sequential increments.  One begins incrementally and eventually reaches a point where there is a quantum leap in consciousness -- from the sequential orientation, to the non-sequential wholeness of true union.

### The Third Work

Another support to the process of unification is to formulate a prayer at the end of your pause between "Adonai" and "ribono".  As you speak the rest of the phrase, radiate your prayer along with the Kethric Light.  Tinge the Light with your prayer and let it be a manifestation of the IHVH-ADNI self-awareness.  See how the universe conforms itself to this prayer.

Note whether or not and to what degree your will actually manifests as the days, months and years  proceed.  Learn from this constant self examination, the ways in which your will is an extension of the IHVH-ADNI will.  You will find that you are effective only when your personal willings participate with the divine will.  This will lead you along the path toward conforming your will to the divine will.

As you progress toward unity, your will will slowly come into harmony with that of IHVH-ADNI.  The moment of first union itself, will be marked by your personal will coinciding perfectly with the will of IHVH-ADNI.  At that moment you are IHVH-ADNI, but infinitely more importantly, IHVH-ADNI is you.  At that moment, personal will is transcended and the personal suddenly encompasses the infinity of all being.  Your lips become the lips of IHVH-ADNI and you speak with One voice.  This is so sublime a state of awareness that there is no room for the petty concerns of personal will.  Or rather, One's sense of personal will encompasses the simultaneous experience of all personal willings -- there is still self-awareness, but that Aware Self encompasses all of Its infinite manifestations equally, completely and non-sequentially.

# THE MAGIC OF IHVH-ADNI

# THE AUDIO LESSONS

In 2002 I recorded a series of nine guided audio "Lessons" in The Magic of IHVH-ADNI (TMO). What follows are the scripts of those recordings.

# LESSON ONE
## PRONUNCIATION, TONALITY AND RHYTHM

I learned the Magic of IHVH-ADNI several years ago. I find it to be a very potent discipline, one that has greatly forwarded my own evolution. And so, I make it my gift to you in hope that it will forward *your* personal evolution as well.

One problem with the printed version is that many readers are in the dark as to the proper pronunciation. But with this recording, that problem is now overcome.

Since the question of how to pronounce the canticle properly is the most frequent question, that is where I will begin.

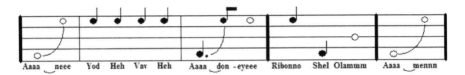

Aaaa___neee  Yod  Heh  Vav  Heh  Aaaa__don-eyeee  Ribonno  Shel Olammm  Aaaa__mennn

*Ani, IHVH-ADNI, Ribonno Shel Olam, Amen.*

That is the proper pronunciation, tonality and rhythm.

Let's break it down into the five component breaths.

The first breath is *Ani*. This Hebrew word, spelled Aleph-Nun-Yod, means "I am".

The speaking begins with your lowest natural note and rises smoothly to end with your highest natural note. *Ani*. You should hold the final "Yod" until your breath is fully spent.

The second breath is *IHVH*. This is the so-called, unspeakable Name of G-d in the Jewish Tradition. Thus we speak it as four separate letters, subsumed by a single breath. Each letter should take up about one quarter of your exhale and each is spoken at your highest natural note. In other words, the same note you ended your first breath with. Thus: *Ani, IHVH*.

The third breath is *ADNI*. This Hebrew word, spelled Aleph-Daleth-Nun-Yod, translates into English as "Lord". and is the spoken substitute for the unspeakable Name, IHVH. However, in Kabbala, ADNI is a specific title and is not just a substitute for IHVH. Often, it modifies the IHVH and we arrive at IHVH-ADNI, or even see the two combined into IAHDVNHI.

ADNI is given the same tonality as the Ani. *Ani*. *ADNI*. Both begin at your lowest natural tone and rise to your highest. ADNI however, has three syllables instead of Ani's two, so the "don" of ADNI is spoken very briefly and the Yod is extended. The Aleph is what rises upward along the scale and both the "don" and the Yod are spoken at the highest note. Thus: *ADNI*.

The fourth breath is the phrase ***Ribonno Shel Olam***. This Hebrew phrase translates into English as "Master Unto the Ages" or alternately, "Master of the Universe". The "universe" in this case is the entire temporal realm, so I prefer "unto the ages" over "of the universe".

The first word of this phrase, "Ribonno", means master, but not in the slave-driver sense. You will note that it shares the same Hebrew root as the word "Rabbi" and this is the sort of mastery implied here. "Ribonno" is said at your highest note, which is where you left off in the third breath at the end of ***ADNI***. ***Ribonno***. Speaking "Ribonno" should expend one quarter of your fourth breath.

The second word in this phrase is ***Shel***. It also expends one quarter of your breath. "Shel" means "unto" or "of the" and is spoken at your lowest natural tone. Thus: ***ADNI, Ribonno Shel***.

The third and final word in this phrase is ***Olam***. It consumes the final half of your fourth breath and is spoken at a middle-range tone. It is the only word in the entire canticle spoken at this tone. Thus: ***Ribonno Shel Olam***.

The fifth and final spoken breath is the word ***Amen***. This is a common ending for prayer in the Judeo-Christian traditions. It's meaning and the philosophy behind it however, are very complex. Its simplest translation into English is "Truth", but it also means "Faith". It's composed of the letters Aleph-Mem-Nun and has two syllables. Therefore, it is spoken exactly the same as the opening ***Ani***, with each syllable receiving equal breath. Thus: ***Amen***.

So, let's put it all back together:

*Ani* -- inhale -- ***IHVH*** -- inhale -- ***ADNI*** -- inhale -- ***Ribonno Shel Olam*** -- inhale -- ***Amen***.

Let's try it together. Speak with me:

***Ani, IHVH, ADNI, Ribonno Shel Olam, Amen.***

And again:

*Ani, IHVH, ADNI, Ribonno Shel Olam, Amen.*

And one final time:

*Ani, IHVH, ADNI, Ribonno Shel Olam, Amen.*

Very well!

This ends Lesson One. I suggest that you practice pronouncing until it comes easily -- until you achieve the proper pronunciation, tone and rhythm *automatically*. Only then should you move on to Lesson Two and begin learning the three-part magical speaking of the canticle.

# LESSON TWO
## THREE-PART MAGICAL SPEECH

Lesson One concerned the proper pronunciation, tonality and rhythm. Now we will focus upon how to *speak* the canticle. This is a different matter than how to *pronounce* it.

The Magic of IHVH-ADNI employs a form of magical utterance. There are three levels to this manner of speaking. First is mental speech, second is astral speech and third is physical speech.

Mental speech is inaudible or silent. Here you "speak" it only with your mind -- no breath and no vocalization. When you speak the canticle mentally, you must also hold the canticle's meaning in your mind. This is not just about hearing the words in your mind, it's also meant to be a matter of simultaneously *thinking* its meaning. In other words, it's important that you bring your understanding of the canticle's words into your mental utterance.

Let's try this now. As I speak the canticle aloud, you should do so only in your mind, but make what's in your mind sound mentally like my utterance.

*Ani, IHVH, ADNI, Ribonno Shel Olam, Amen.*

And again:

*Ani, IHVH, ADNI, Ribonno Shel Olam, Amen.*

And a final time:

*Ani, IHVH, ADNI, Ribonno Shel Olam, Amen.*

Very well.

The second form of magical speech is the astral. Astral speech involves combining the silent mental speech with breath. In fact, it's *astra-mental* speech, not mere whispering as some maintain. With the astra-mental speech there is to be absolutely no vibration of the vocal chords.

Here is what it sounds like with breath and mind alone:

*Ani, IHVH, ADNI, Ribonno Shel Olam, Amen.* [Whisper]

Now try saying astra-mentally along with me:

*Ani, IHVH, ADNI, Ribonno Shel Olam, Amen.* [Whisper]

Let's do that one more time, but this time be sure you're saying it *mentally* as well as with your breath:

*Ani, IHVH, ADNI, Ribonno Shel Olam, Amen.* [Whisper]

Now, let me add a new factor into the mix with the astra-mental speech. "Breath", in Kabbala, has a special meaning beyond just atmosphere that you inhale and exhale. Its deeper meaning is "the breath of life", the "Ruach". In magical speech, "breath" refers to emotion -- the astral substance that binds mind and physical matter together. So, when using your breath for magical speech, you are combining your emotional sense of the canticle with your mental understanding of it. You are combining your inner passion with your rational understanding and expressing them in unison.

So, let's try it one more time in astra-mental mode, this time focusing on your mental understanding of the canticle, adding in your emotional passion and expressing both with your physical breath.

*Ani, IHVH, ADNI, Ribonno Shel Olam, Amen.* [Whisper]

This brings us to the third form of magical speech, the physical. Here is where the canticle is made *physically* manifest through simultaneous vibration of the vocal chords. But here again, it's not just a matter of mundane speech. This is physio-astra-mental speech -- the combining of mental understanding, emotional passion and physical vibration. All three must occur simultaneously. Your understanding and your emotional passion must manifest and be audible as your breath passes over your vocal chords and sets them vibrating.

The theory here is that all things vibrate and when one vibrating thing intersects another vibrating thing, they each change their vibration accordingly. When you say the canticle with the physio-astra-mental speech, you are projecting the specific astra-mental vibration of the canticle outward (or inward) and physically impregnating the universe with it. This is what causes the universe to change in response to your speech.

To be truly effective, you must totally commit yourself to speaking the canticle. Put every bit of yourself into it. Let it flow through you of its own accord. In other words, don't be shy.

So, let's try the physio-astra-mental speech, but let's build up to it.

We will begin with the silent mental speech. I will speak the canticle aloud but you should speak it only with your mind and understanding along with me.

*Ani, IHVH, ADNI, Ribonno Shel Olam, Amen.*

Now let's add the factor of emotional passion and express it astra-mentally.

*Ani, IHVH, ADNI, Ribonno Shel Olam, Amen.* [Whisper]

And now, let's give our vocal chords a good flexing and say it with our whole being, including every cell of our physical bodies.

*Ani, IHVH, ADNI, Ribonno Shel Olam, Amen.*

And again.

*Ani, IHVH, ADNI, Ribonno Shel Olam, Amen.*

And again.

*Ani, IHVH, ADNI, Ribonno Shel Olam, Amen.*

Very well!

This ends Lesson Two. I suggest that you practice these three modes of magical speech until they become second nature. Only then should you move on to Lesson Three and begin learning the energetics that accompany the canticle.

# LESSON THREE
## ENERGETICS

Lesson One concerned the proper pronunciation, tonality and rhythm of the canticle; Lesson Two, the three modes of magical speech; and now, with Lesson Three, we will focus upon the energetic work that empowers the canticle and makes it truly magical.

This involves integrating your creative imagination with the spoken canticle. Thus creating a magical ritual very similar to the "Middle Pillar" exercise and the "Rose Cross", popularized by the Golden Dawn.

Again, for ease of explanation, I will be dividing the canticle into five parts corresponding to the five speaking breaths.

The first step occurs simultaneous to the speaking of *Ani*. Here your consciousness must rise up, along with your vocalization. Let the "Ani" resonate at your crown and visualize there a sublimely radiant sphere of white brilliance. Let this be your Kether, your crown, your highest ideal of Self and of Divinity. Make it a thing of intense, undeniable power.

Let's try it now. As we speak the "Ani", create your Kethric sphere just above the top of your head and let it shine there for a moment or two.

*Ani.*

Now hold your Kethric sphere exactly where it is with your mental will. Stabilize it. Feel it. Let it be your own personal doorway to the Kethric Light. Now speak the "Ani" again and make it grow still stronger.

*Ani.*

Very well. Now let it dissipate completely.

The second step, composed of four sub-steps, occurs simultaneous to the speaking of the "IHVH". While it *is* four energetic steps, it's really *one* operation, and must be accomplished smoothly and in one motion. However, to explain it, we must go one semi-step at a time and then tie them all together.

With the "Yod" you are to pull a beam of Kethric Light down, out of your "Ani" sphere, and create a luminous gray sphere at your left temple. This is your Chokmah, your innate Wisdom.

With the first "Heh", you pull Light from your luminous gray sphere, over to your right temple and form there an obsidian black sphere. This is your Binah, your deepest Understanding.

With the "Vav", you pull Light from your obsidian black sphere, down to your solar plexus and form there a radiant sphere of golden yellow. This is your Tiphareth, your own radiant Beauty.

With the final "Heh", you complete this phase by pulling down Light from your golden yellow sphere and forming an opaque sphere of olive green just below the arches of your feet. This is your Malkuth, your own sphere of influence.

Throughout this drawing down, you must remain cognizant of the fact that this is Kethric Light and that the channels between Kether and each sphere are to remain open at all times. In other words, you are not pulling down just a single quanta of Light which you then deposit at your feet. Instead, you are opening up the channels to the Light and letting it rush through them continuously.

So, let's give this a few tries, slowly at first. We'll spend one breath for each letter.

First, establish your Kether with "Ani".

*Ani.*

Now, when we say the "Yod", bring a channel of Light down to your left temple and make it luminous gray.

*Yod.*

And when we say the first "Heh", bring the Light over to your right temple and make an obsidian black sphere.

*Heh.*

And with the "Vav", bring the Light down to the center of your chest and make it a radiant golden yellow sphere.

*Vav.*

Now finish with the final "Heh" and bring the Light all the way down so that you're standing on an opaque olive green sphere.

*Heh.*

Hold this visualization. Let the Kethric Light pour continuously into you.

Now, holding this visualization, let's repeat again and thus stabilize the structure. Don't worry about how fast you go just yet. Spend one entire breath on each letter.

*Ani, I, H, V, H.*

Once again.

*Ani, I, H, V, H.*

Very well. Now, still holding your visualization, let's go a bit faster. Spend one breath on the "Ani", firming up your Kether, and then do all four letters of IHVH within a single breath.

*Ani, IHVH.*

Once again.

*Ani, IHVH.*

Very well. Now let your visualization dissipate completely.

The third energetic step comes in three parts and occurs simultaneous with the speaking of *ADNI*.

The first part occurs during the speaking of the first syllable, "Aleph". With your inhale, raise your awareness to your Kether. With the exhale and speaking of the "Aleph", actively *push* the Light down, all the way to your Malkuth in a single lightning flash.

With the speaking of the second syllable, "don", the Kethric Light, having struck your Malkuth with some force, now erupts upward in a swirling cloud of Rainbow-hued Light.

And with the speaking of the final, extended "Yod", you are to increase the density and clockwise rotation of this cloud of Rainbow Light.

Now let's try this new step. First we will speak the "Ani, IHVH" in two breaths as before. Remember to bring the Kethric Light downward -- first to your left temple, then your right temple, your solar plexus and ending at your feet.

*Ani, IHVH.*

Now, holding your Light structure as it is, let's try adding in the "ADNI". Remember to rise to your Kether with the inhale, push the Light downward to your Malkuth with the "Aleph", and then let it erupt in a swirling Rainbow-hued cloud of Light.

*ADNI.*

Spend a silent moment now and stabilize the swirling cloud of Rainbow Light. Make certain that it is fed constantly by the descending Kethric Light.

Now, leaving your visualization in place, let's do the entire sequence again, overlaying it upon what we have already established.

*Ani, IHVH, ADNI.*

And again.

*Ani, IHVH, ADNI.*

Very well. Now let your visualization dissipate completely.

With the fourth step of the energetics, we will cast the accumulation of Rainbow Light outward. The idea here is that as you release it from your body and cast it into the universe, it will affect the materia of the universe and transform it to your will. Therefore, you must formulate in your mind what sort of change you wish to affect. For now, our intention will be a simple blessing of good will to all.

The fourth step is singular and occurs simultaneous to the speaking of the phrase, ***Ribonno Shel Olam***. With the inhale of breath after the "ADNI", you are to gather up the entire body of Light, and then with the exhaled speech, you forcefully eject it outward. Let it veritably explode into the external universe. Carefully visualize the Rainbow Light spreading ever outwards until it reaches the very edge of the Infinite Universe.

Now let's try this fourth step. First we must re-establish our Light structure with the "Ani, IHVH, ADNI".

*Ani, IHVH, ADNI.*

Now hold this structure and stabilize it. Let's repeat two more times.

*Ani, IHVH, ADNI.*
*Ani, IHVH, ADNI.*

Very well. Hold this structure.

Now as you inhale, gather up the Light and then release it with the "Ribonno Shel Olam".

[Inhale]

***Ribonno Shel Olam.***

Let it go completely in one gigantic explosion. See it and feel it penetrating to the very edges of the Infinite Universe.

Very well. Now let's do the entire thing twice more.

*Ani, IHVH, ADNI, Ribonno Shel Olam.*
*Ani, IHVH, ADNI, Ribonno Shel Olam.*

Very well. Now let your visualization dissipate completely.

The final, fifth step occurs simultaneous to the speaking of *Amen*. This is a more passive step in that you merely observe and confirm the return of the Light you've just emitted.

During the inhale which follows the explosive release of the "Ribonno Shel Olam", you are to visualize that the Light, having indeed reached the edge of the Infinite Universe, now rebounds inward. Draw it back into yourself and when your inhale is complete, speak the word "Amen". As you speak "Amen", visualize the returned Light solidifying, calming and stabilizing. The "Amen" ends the operation by concretizing what you have emitted, embedding its influence within the entire materia of the universe.

Now, let's try the canticle from "Ani" through "Amen".

*Ani, IHVH, ADNI, Ribonno Shel Olam, Amen.*

And again. Be very aware of what you are doing at an energetic level throughout.

*Ani, IHVH, ADNI, Ribonno Shel Olam, Amen.*

And now one final time. This time be aware of your energetics and also remember that you are speaking it magically, with the combined physical-astra-mental speech.

*Ani, IHVH, ADNI, Ribonno Shel Olam, Amen.*

Very well!

This ends Lesson Three. I suggest that you practice the canticle, combining the three modes of magical speech with the energetics you've just learned, over and over again, until it also becomes second nature. Only then should you move on to Lesson Four and begin learning some of the applications of the Magic of IHVH-ADNI.

# LESSON FOUR
## APPLICATIONS

Having successfully pursued Lessons One, Two and Three, you should now be capable of performing the canticle with ease. You should be able to speak the canticle at the proper tonality and rhythm, using the three-fold magical speech while empowering it with your energetic visualizations. All of this should be an easy matter for you to accomplish by now.

Therefore, we will now focus upon the ways that you can use the Magic of IHVH-ADNI.

There are two points in the canticle where a pause is appropriate. The first point is between "ADNI" and "Ribonno Shel Olam". This is a crucial juncture in the structure of the canticle. It's the point between the accumulation of Light and the expulsion of Light.

When you speak the segment from "Ani" through "ADNI", you are accumulating a certain quantity of Light energy and you are holding it to yourself. This is a very dynamic energy which should be sensed as a physically energizing pressure.

To begin with, I suggest three repetitions of the first segment. Let's do this together to demonstrate. There will be a brief pause of one or two breaths between each repetition.

*Ani, IHVH, ADNI.*

Okay, now hold the energy and during this pause, stabilize the Light structure.

Now a second time. Layer the Light energy you accumulate over what is already present. Let this repetition double your accumulation.

*Ani, IHVH, ADNI.*

Take a moment to sense the increased energy and stabilize the Light structure.

Now a third time. Layer this over what is already present and let it triple the original accumulation.

*Ani, IHVH, ADNI.*

Very well. Now release this accumulated energy by performing the canticle all the way through to "Amen".

*Ani, IHVH, ADNI, Ribonno Shel Olam, Amen.*

In future, as you say the "Ani, IHVH, ADNI" part of this final repetition, you should not actually accumulate a fourth charge of the Light energy. Instead, merely set what has already been accumulated, into motion. Stir it up and dynamize it, and get it prepared for your expulsion.

Now let's go through the entire process of triple accumulation and expulsion straight through. Remember, we start with three repetitions of the segment "Ani" through "ADNI" for our accumulation, and then close with a single repetition of the entire canticle for our expulsion.

*Ani, IHVH, ADNI.*
*Ani, IHVH, ADNI.*
*Ani, IHVH, ADNI.*
*Ani, IHVH, ADNI, Ribonno Shel Olam, Amen.*

Let's do that once more.

*Ani, IHVH, ADNI.*
*Ani, IHVH, ADNI.*
*Ani, IHVH, ADNI.*
*Ani, IHVH, ADNI, Ribonno Shel Olam, Amen.*

Very well. At the end of such an accumulation, you should be certain that you have rid yourself of the entire accumulation of Light energy. You will of course, still feel energized by the experience, but you must not feel overly so. If you feel that you have not completely expelled your accumulation, then simply visualize any excess flowing out through your feet and into the receptive earth.

Now, the next phase of our work involves impregnating this accumulated Light energy with our intention, desire or will. We must give it a specific purpose. Our purpose will be to create a blessing of well-being for everything that our energy encounters on its journey to the edges of the infinite universe.

This operation occurs during the pause between "ADNI" and "Ribonno Shel Olam". Once we have accumulated our triple charge of Light energy, we will spend a few "empty" breaths where all we do is focus our intention and impress it upon the accumulated energy.

Let's begin our triple accumulation.

*Ani, IHVH, ADNI.*
*Ani, IHVH, ADNI.*
*Ani, IHVH, ADNI.*

Now, focus upon our intention of blessing and make the accumulated charge of energy conform to it with your mind. With your mind and with your emotional passion, cause the Light energy to assume the correct vibratory rate for manifesting a sense of well-being in all that it encounters. Just let yourself do this, don't try to figure out how to do it, or what "well-being" looks like, or anything of the sort. Just do it. Let it flow of its own accord. Your subconscious instinct knows what to do without even thinking about it.

Very well. Now let's repeat the canticle all the way through and send our blessing energy outward to the edges of the infinite universe.

*Ani, IHVH, ADNI, Ribonno Shel Olam, Amen.*

Wonderful!

Let's add one final ingredient and then we will practice the entire triple accumulation, impregnation of blessing and then expulsion, three times through.

This last factor is what I call "shepherding". By this I mean that we add our own conscious intent into the mix while the Light energy we've just sent outward, rebounds back toward us.

The Light energy we send out, should reach the philosophical edges of the infinite universe in that moment when the last of our breath is spent on "Ribonno Shel Olam". With the inhale that follows, the Light energy begins to rebound. It echoes back toward us, just like the ripples in a pond reverberate back upon their source.

This is another critical juncture since this is when the changes caused by the first, outward wave of Light energy, are concretized. This echo, having been touched by the Divine through its brushing against the philosophical edges of the infinite universe, is a special substance. It is a universal fixative. It's what "sets in stone", so to speak, the changes we have wrought through our blessing.

When we add our conscious intent to this particular phase of our creation, we can multiply its effect exponentially.

So, this final factor in our canticle is where we get to add extra oomph to the effectiveness of our intended blessing. This process is similar to what I said about making the accumulated Light energy reflect and manifest our intention. This is also something that you need to just *do*, without rationalizing it. You will know instinctually what to do.

As you perceive the returning wave of blessing, make the ripples reflect your intention. See your intention crystallizing within the essence of everything the wave passes through. Use your mind's power to aid the universal fixative.

And then, with the closing "Amen", make it a completely concrete reality. At that moment, the echoing ripples return to you.

So, with this final ingredient included, let's perform the entire extended canticle. We will begin with our triple accumulation and then pause for three complete breaths while we impregnate our accumulation with our blessing of well-being to all. Then we will expel our blessing with the "Ribonno Shel Olam" and pause for another three breaths while we shepherd its return. And then we will close with the "Amen".

*Ani, IHVH, ADNI.*
*Ani, IHVH, ADNI.*
*Ani, IHVH, ADNI.*

Now impregnate the accumulation.

Now expel it.

*Ani, IHVH, ADNI, Ribonno Shel Olam.*

Now shepherd its return.

Now concretize it.

*Amen.*

Wonderful!

Now let's do that again, but before we do, I want to remind you about the three-fold magical speech. Remember that you are not just speaking normally, but physical-astra-mentally. You are speaking with your mind, your heart *and* your body.

Very well, let's proceed but this time I will not speak during our two three-breath pauses.

*Ani, IHVH, ADNI.*
*Ani, IHVH, ADNI.*
*Ani, IHVH, ADNI.*
+
+
+
*Ani, IHVH, ADNI, Ribonno Shel Olam.*
+
+
+
*Amen.*

Wonderful!

Now let's do the entire operation one last time.

*Ani, IHVH, ADNI.*
*Ani, IHVH, ADNI.*
*Ani, IHVH, ADNI.*
+
+
+
*Ani, IHVH, ADNI, Ribonno Shel Olam.*
+
+
+
*Amen.*

Perfect!

Now we must turn our attention away from what we have just accomplished. This is an important step in any magical operation. At the end, you must create a true end and sever the link between your mind and what has just transpired. The more abruptly and firmly you do this, the better.

The canticle that forms the exterior of the Magic of IHVH-ADNI can be used in many different ways. What you have just learned is the complete working of the canticle, or what I call the "full form". I realize that there is a lot to keep track of during the full form, but don't worry, it will become automatic with practice. What now takes intense concentration, slow thinking and lots of empty breaths, will eventually occur within the span of mere seconds.

Likewise, your perception of the Light energy will increase and mature with practice, as will the quantity you are capable of accumulating.

The simplest form of the Magic of IHVH-ADNI mimics the breath cycle itself. With the simple form, there is no accumulation, impregnation or shepherding. The Kethric Light is merely drawn down and expelled, drawn down and expelled, over and over for as many repetitions as seems appropriate. This practice has a tonic effect upon the astra-mental body and helps establish the kabbalistic light structure within. It clears the channels of Light within your whole being.

The full form has many ritual uses. Primarily it makes for quick and powerful accumulation of energy. The segment from "Ani" through "ADNI" can be repeated as many times as desired and you can thus accumulate as large or as dense a charge of Light energy as you desire.

The full form's Light energy can be directed outward toward all others, or be more specifically aimed at a single person or group. Or it can be turned directly inward upon your own self. With the blessing we just performed, we have spread our Light energy outward to all others. If you wish to focus it upon a specific target, then the times for targeting are during the impregnation of your intention upon the accumulated Light energy, and then again during the shepherding phase. In any event, you must still send it out to the edges of the infinite universe, but when you wish to focus on a target, you must make your target the exact center point of the returning wave. In other words, your target must be the point at which the echoing ring of waves shrinks back to nothing. If *you* are the target, then the wave of Light energy returns finally to you and no where else.

One thing that you should be aware of is that this canticle does not work if the desire you impress upon the accumulated Light energy would result in a harmful or negative effect. There are two reasons for this. Number one is the Kethric source of the Light employed. And number two is because we are sending this Light out to the philosophical edges of the infinite universe. In other words, we are touching the Divine. The Divine touch is transformative and when we send a negative or harmful energy unto it, it is returned to us in a new form. When what we send to the Divine is overly negative, it returns *only to us*. But when we send blessing, it returns multiplied a thousand-fold and not only to us alone.

This ends Lesson Four. I suggest that you experiment with these new additions to your practice and become familiar with their inclusion. When you feel ready, you may move on to Lesson Five and learn how to create and maintain your own personal shield, using the Magic of IHVH-ADNI.

# LESSON FIVE
## CREATING A TRIPLE SHIELD

With this Lesson we will explore another specific use of the Magic of IHVH-ADNI -- the creation of your own triple shield.

By "triple shield" I mean a three-part shield that encases your physical, astral and mental bodies, independently and simultaneously. The triple shield is constructed in three steps. First, the physical body is shielded, then the astral body and finally, the mental body.

For each part of the triple shield, we will accumulate three quanta of the ADNI Rainbow-hued Light and wrap it around ourselves. Then, during the pause between "ADNI" and "Ribonno Shel Olam", we will impregnate this accumulated Light with our instructions for our shielding and bind it to the universal storehouse of Light so that it may exist continuously without our needing to replenish it.

Then, with the "Ribonno Shel Olam", we will release this accumulated Light in the usual manner and cast it out to the philosophical edges of the infinite universe. In this way, we bless our shield and connect it to the universal storehouse of Light -- the Divine. As we shepherd the return of this Light, we direct it to surround our bodies and shield us as we have willed. And then, with the "Amen", it becomes concrete fact.

In this Lesson, I will lead you through the construction of all three parts of the triple shield, starting with the physical shield and ending with the mental shield. However, you may want to create only one part of the shield at a time. If so, then follow along until the physical shield is complete and return to the Lesson another time. With your second working, redo your physical shield and then create your astral shield on top of that. Finally, on your third working, redo your physical and astral shields and add on your mental shield as a final layer.

The philosophy or quality that underpins a shield is vitally important. Personally, I prefer a shield that alerts me to any incoming or ambient negative influences and then gives me the option to either let them in or reject them entirely, as I see fit. We can learn many important lessons from our encounters with negative forces and unpleasant circumstances, so avoiding them entirely misses the point.

This is the type of shield I will be directing you to create. However, should you desire to create a different sort of shield, based upon a different philosophy, then you should feel free to modify my instructions as *you* see fit.

So, let's move on to the practice itself.

It is best if you stand upright for the creation of your shield, but if this is impossible or uncomfortable, then sitting erect will suffice.

We will begin with a cleansing by employing the canticle's short form, three times in succession. This rids our three bodies of all negativity that we may be holing at this moment. Let's cant together now.

*Ani, IHVH, ADNI, Ribonno Shel Olam, Amen.*
*Ani, IHVH, ADNI, Ribonno Shel Olam, Amen.*
*Ani, IHVH, ADNI, Ribonno Shel Olam, Amen.*

Very well.

Now feel the dimensions of your physical body. Try to feel your *whole* body, all at once.

Now let's accumulate our three quanta of Rainbow Light by canting the "Ani" through "ADNI" three times in succession. As you accumulate the light, wrap it around the exterior of your physical body and circulate it clockwise (left to right in front of you and right to left in back of you). Let the density and vibrancy of the Light increase with each repetition.

*Ani, IHVH, ADNI.*
*Ani, IHVH, ADNI.*
*Ani, IHVH, ADNI.*

Very well. Now hold this Light, keep it circulating and increase its density.

Now we will impregnate this accumulated Light with our instructions. First we must impress upon it the nature of its purpose.

Whether it be with words or thought alone, is up to you, but you must instruct this Light to act as a permanent barrier to all incoming or ambient negative energies.

Instruct it to alert you when negative energies are present.

Instruct it to always remain active, even when your mind is on other things, until such time as you consciously decide to release it.

Instruct it to constantly replenish itself from the universal storehouse of Light.

Spend a few moments now, focused upon this Light shield and see to it that it conforms to your desire.

And now we will send our accumulated Light out along its journey to the Divine. As you speak the "Ani" through "ADNI", instead of accumulating another quanta of Light, use the descending Light to enhance the structure of what you have created. With the "Ribonno Shel Olam", release the Light and let it touch the edges of the infinite universe. As it rebounds upon you, shepherd its course and make sure that it connects with the universal storehouse of energy, drawing its energy from the entire universe. And finally, with the "Amen", see that it forms a solid shield of Light surrounding your physical body.

Let's cant together now.

*Ani, IHVH, ADNI, Ribonno Shel Olam, Amen.*

Wonderful! Now spend a few moments visualizing and stabilizing your physical shield.

Now we will create our astral shield. As with the physical shield, we will begin by sensing the dimensions of our astral body. Try to sense your *whole* astral body, all at once.

Now let's accumulate our three quanta of Rainbow Light by canting the "Ani" through "ADNI" three times in succession. As you accumulate the Light, wrap it around the exterior of your astral body and circulate it clockwise in concert with your physical shield. Let the density and vibrancy of the Light increase with each repetition.

*Ani, IHVH, ADNI.*
*Ani, IHVH, ADNI.*
*Ani, IHVH, ADNI.*

Very well. Now hold this Light, keep it circulating and increase its density.

Now we will impregnate this accumulated Light with our instructions.

That this Light is to act as a permanent barrier to all incoming or ambient negative energies.

That it is to alert you when negative energies are present.

That it is to always remain active, even when your mind is on other things, until such time as you consciously decide to release it.

That it is to constantly replenish itself from the universal storehouse of Light.

Spend a few moments now, focused upon this Light shield and see to it that it conforms to your desire.

And now we will send our accumulated Light out along its journey to the Divine. Let's cant together now.

*Ani, IHVH, ADNI, Ribonno Shel Olam, Amen.*

Wonderful! Now spend a few moments visualizing and stabilizing your astral shield. Unite your astral shield with your physical shield so that they function as a single entity.

Now we will create our mental shield. As before, we will sense the dimensions of our mental body. Begin by sensing your entire astra-physical body. This effectively spreads your mental body out over your entire corpus. Now try to sense your *whole* mental body, all at once.

Now let's accumulate our three quanta of Rainbow Light by canting the "Ani" through "ADNI" three times in succession. As you accumulate the Light, wrap it around the exterior of your mental body and circulate it clockwise in concert with your astra-physical shield. Let the density and vibrancy of the Light increase with each repetition.

*Ani, IHVH, ADNI.*
*Ani, IHVH, ADNI.*
*Ani, IHVH, ADNI.*

Very well. Now hold this Light, keep it circulating and increase its density.

Now we will impregnate this accumulated Light with our instructions.

That this Light is to act as a permanent barrier to all incoming or ambient negative energies.

That it is to alert you when negative energies are present.

That it is to always remain active, even when your mind is on other things, until such time as you consciously decide to release it.

That it is to constantly replenish itself from the universal storehouse of Light.

Spend a few moments now, focused upon this Light shield and see to it that it conforms to your desire.

And now we will send our accumulated Light out along its journey to the Divine. Let's cant together now.

*Ani, IHVH, ADNI, Ribonno Shel Olam, Amen.*

Wonderful! Now spend a few moments visualizing and stabilizing your mental shield. Unite your mental shield with your astra-physical shield so that they function as a single entity.

We will close as we began, with three repetitions of the canticle's short form. This will fuse our three-part shield into a true triple shield that functions as a single entity.

*Ani, IHVH, ADNI, Ribonno Shel Olam, Amen.*
*Ani, IHVH, ADNI, Ribonno Shel Olam, Amen.*
*Ani, IHVH, ADNI, Ribonno Shel Olam, Amen.*

Wonderful!

Now let's turn our attention away from our shield and let it begin functioning on its own.

It is wise to revisit this creation of your shield at least once a week for the first month. Until you get the hang of connecting your shield to the universal storehouse of Light, it may need periodic recharging. This can be accomplished by simply accumulating the Light and binding it to the shield you have already created. As you do this, be sure to reiterate your instructions, especially your instruction that it replenish itself from the universal storehouse of Light.

You can at any time make changes to your shield simply by modifying your instructions and impressing them upon the Light itself. You can also terminate your shield or turn it off temporarily. Your shield is your own creation so you get to set its parameters.

Ordinarily, your shield will recede to the background of your awareness, but you can easily call it up by merely thinking about it. This will ignite your shield to full force, so to speak, and it will become a consciously protective ally.

Using this same technique, combined with the transference of consciousness that Franz Bardon described in his "Initiation Into Hermetics", you can generate shields around other objects or people. Alternately, you can create a shield and then project it around an external object; or you can cause one to coalesce around an external object without it first passing through your own body. You can even extend your own triple shield to encompass another person or object. The options are as limitless as your creative imagination.

I wish you many happy, fruitful years of experimentation and shield-crafting!

This ends Lesson Five. You may continue on to Lesson Six whenever you want now that you have created your triple shield.

# LESSON SIX
## CONSCIOUSNESS RAISING

In this sixth Lesson, we will diverge from the thread we have followed till now and examine an entirely different use of the canticle. This time we will not be using it to create anything. Instead, we will use the canticle as a tool for the raising of our own conscious awareness.

The canticle expresses five distinct levels of consciousness which can be correlated to the four Hermetic Elements, plus the fifth, Aethyr or Akasha. In the ascending order which we shall be using, these levels are as follows:

The first level corresponds to the final Heh of IHVH and the Element Earth. This is Malkuth and your personal life circumstances. This is your conscious awareness as it normally exists within your physical body. From the Malkuth perspective of the final Heh, you reach upwards to Kether (Ani) and pull the light all the way downward into your body, *and* you perform this operation from within your physical body. This is the perspective from which you've learned to practice the Magic of IHVH-ADNI through the preceding Lessons.

The second level corresponds to the Vav of IHVH and the Element Air. This is Tiphareth and your Individual Self. The experience of the Individual Self is best described as one of detachment from direct involvement in the personal chaos of normal life. From the Tiphareth perspective of the Vav, the Individual Self looks down upon the mundane life circumstances and perceives them in a broader context.

When the Individual Self draws down the light from Kether, it is not as far an upward reach and when the light descends into the Vav, there is a sense of completion and empowerment similar to that experienced from the Malkuth perspective when the light descends into the final Heh. After the light reaches and fills the Vav, the Individual Self willfully pushes it further downward into the final Heh of Malkuth. In this way, it is the Individual Self that directly empowers the mundane personal self.

The third level corresponds to the first Heh of IHVH and the Element Water. This is Binah and your Greater Self. From the Binah perspective of the first Heh, the Greater Self looks down upon the countless number of Individual Selves that it projects into the stream of space-time, along with the mundane life circumstances of each Individual Self's incarnations and perceives them in the broadest of contexts. The Greater Self is the eternal mental body or core spirit that fills our particular being.

The Greater Self can focus its attention on any single Individual Self and its incarnation, or focus itself throughout all of its Individuals simultaneously. The Greater Self is a vastly inclusive and fluid level of awareness.

When the Greater Self draws down the light from Kether, it is right at hand, hardly a reach at all except in the symbolic sense. And when the light descends into the first Heh, there is the same sense of completion and empowerment that is experienced from the Tiphareth perspective when the light descends into the Vav and from the Malkuth perspective when the light descends into the final Heh.

After the light reaches and fills the Heh, the Greater Self willfully pushes it further downward into one or all of its projected Vav's or Individual Selves. And from there, each Individual Self pushes it downward still further into their mundane incarnations. In this way, it is the Greater Self who causes the Individual Self to empower the mundane personal self.

The fourth level corresponds to the Yod of IHVH and the Element Fire. This is Chokmah, highest level of Greater Self.

It is difficult to describe what differentiates between Chokmah and Kether or Unity. In fact, the ancient kabbalists described their closeness with the symbol of the Yod, saying that the uppermost point of the Yod was actually Kether and only the downward stroke was Chokmah. This symbolism provides an important clue in that it attributes the downward movement and direct action of a pen stroke to Chokmah, while reserving the passive point of origin for Kether.

In essence, Chokmah is the unity of all the Greater Selves. Chokmah is the unity-of-parts, whereas Kether itself is a singular, completely integral whole.

From the Chokmah perspective of the Yod, the Chokmah Self looks down upon the infinite number of Greater Selves that fill eternity, along with all of the Individual Selves that they project into the stream of space-time and the mundane life circumstances of each Individual Self's incarnations. The Chokmah Self perceives all of these parts as parts of its own self.

The Chokmah Self can focus its attention on any single Greater Self, or focus itself throughout all of its Greaters simultaneously, just as we can focus on our little finger alone or all of our fingers at once.

The Chokmah Self doesn't draw down the light from Kether, per se. Instead, the Chokmah Self ignites the Kether and the light is immediately at hand. Chokmah *is* the downward movement of the light of all-potential, into actualization.

And when the light fills the Yod, the sense of completion and fulfillment is overwhelming and beyond words. The Chokmah Self then pushes the light downward into the realm of the Greaters and on down, eventually reaching the material incarnations. In this way, it is the Chokmah Self who causes the Greater Self to empower the Individual Self, who in turn empowers the mundane personal self.

The fifth and ultimate level corresponds to the Ani or "I am" and to the Akasha. This is Kether, The Unity, The One Self.

In Kether itself, there is no experience of light for it becomes clear that what is perceived from below as light, is in truth consciousness. From the perspective of Unity, everything is composed of this consciousness, of the essence of the Unity itself. Thus Kether is a whole thing, not a mere unity of parts. It is potential *and* actualization, simultaneously.

From the Kethric perspective of the Ani, the Unitary consciousness emanates into Chokmah and from there into the entire realm of *BE*ing. When it reaches Chokmah, it is then directed – *as light* -- by the Chokmah Self into whatever direction is desired.

So, these are the five levels of awareness symbolized within the Magic of IHVH-ADNI canticle.

When the light strikes Malkuth with force and the ADNI rainbow-hued light erupts, it rises all the way back up to Kether. When the canticle is performed from the Malkuth perspective that you've already learned, then the sensation of empowerment elicited by the ADNI eruption is felt primarily at the Malkuth level. But when the canticle is performed from the Tiphareth perspective, as the Individual Vav Self, then the sensation of empowerment is felt at that level more so than at the Malkuth level. And when it's performed from the Binah perspective of the Greater Self, the empowerment is felt at that level primarily, and so on.

At each level, the rainbow-hued cloud of ADNI light is sent outward with the recitation of Ribonno Shel Olam *from the perspective of that level,* and is returned to that same level. In other words, when you perform the operation from the Tiphareth perspective, it is with your Tiphareth body that you expel the accumulated light and your Tiphareth body is where the light returns to once it has touched the edges of the infinite universe.

So, on to the practice itself. I will explain the process of ascent using the canticle and also describe a few alternate exercises to experiment with.

We will start with three repetitions of Ani. As you say the Ani or "I Am", sense your entire physical body and make this your center of self awareness. Only when it comes to speaking the canticle itself should the Ani raise your awareness to your Kether. So, our first three Ani's will focus our awareness into our Malkuth and the fourth Ani which begins our recitation of the canticle itself, raises our awareness to our Kether. The point here is that it must be *from* Malkuth that we raise our awareness *to* our Kether. It is from our Malkuth that we must perform the entire operation.

Very well. Let's begin now with our three Ani's and then move directly into performing the canticle from the Malkuth perspective.

*Ani*
*Ani*
*Ani*
*Ani, IHVH, ADNI, Ribonno Shel Olam, Amen*

Wonderful!

Now we will move up one level and perform the same sequence but from the Vav or Tiphareth perspective of the Individual Self. While you are saying the initial three Ani's, you must focus your awareness upon your Individual Self. The simplest way to do this is to visualize yourself standing atop a cloud, looking down in a fairly detached manner upon your every day life. The main distinguishing feature of this perspective is that of detachment from immediate involvement in all the emotions and events of your mundane life.

With the three Ani's, you must make this body the central focus of your awareness. It must be your "I Am". When it comes time to begin the canticle itself, you must raise your awareness from your *Tiphareth* to your Kether.

As you bring the light down from Kether, pay close attention to the sensations elicited as it strikes and fills your Vav. Also notice how it feels when the ADNI light arises to the Vav; how it feels to radiate this light from the Tiphareth perspective when you recite the Ribonno Shel Olam; and finally, how it feels when this light, having rebounded off the edges of the infinite universe, returns to your Tiphareth Self.

Very well. Let's begin now with our three Ani's and then move directly into performing the canticle from the Tiphareth perspective.

*Ani*
*Ani*
*Ani*
*Ani, IHVH, ADNI, Ribonno Shel Olam, Amen*

Wonderful!

When you practice this apart from this recording, you should feel free to increase the number of initial Ani's as it suits you. Keep repeating the Ani until you are firmly rooted in the Tiphareth perspective.

Now we will move up another level and perform the same sequence but from the first Heh or Binah perspective of the Greater Self. While you are saying the initial three Ani's, you must focus your awareness upon your Greater Self. The simplest way to do this is to visualize yourself standing atop a small planetoid in deep space. You stand as a giant upon a very, very small asteroid and all around, you see countless stars, each with its own planetary system. Each of these stars is a part of you and each is given sustenance from your own Self. These are your Individual Selves, your Vav's.

Once you have achieved this perspective, you must identify the Individual star that projects your corporeal self, your own Malkuth, for that is where you will be sending the descending light during the canticle itself. With the initial Ani's, you must focus your awareness in your Greater Self and make this your "I Am", but you must also be sure that you are still connected to your own Tiphareth and Malkuth. It is from here that you reach up to Kether as you begin speaking the canticle itself.

As the light descends into and fills your first Heh, pay close attention to the sensations this elicits. Once it does fill your Greater Self, you must then direct it downward, into your own Individual Self. On its return upward as the ADNI, again pay close attention to the sensations this elicits in your Greater Self. Notice also how it feels to radiate this swirling cloud of ADNI light as you speak the Ribonno Shel Olam, from the Binah perspective, and how it feels when, having touched the Divine, it returns to your Binah Self.

Very well. Let's begin now with our three Ani's and then move directly into performing the canticle from the Binah perspective.

*Ani*
*Ani*
*Ani*
*Ani, IHVH, ADNI, Ribonno Shel Olam, Amen*

Excellent!

Now we will move up another level and perform the same sequence but from the Yod or Chokmah perspective. While you are saying the initial three Ani's, you must focus your awareness upon your Chokmah Self. The simplest way to do this is to visualize yourself standing amid a universe filled with nothing but particles of light. Each of the infinite number of light particles is a Greater Self. You will know automatically which exact particle of light is the Greater Self that connects to your particular incarnated body.

The procedure is exactly the same as before so I will not go into the usual minute detail.

Let's begin now.

*Ani*
*Ani*
*Ani*
*Ani, IHVH, ADNI, Ribonno Shel Olam, Amen*

Excellent!

Now we will move up to the ultimate level and perform the same sequence but from the Ani or Kethric perspective of the Unity. While you are saying the initial three Ani's, you must focus your awareness upon your Kethric Self. The simplest way to do this is to create the feeling that you are the Kethric light itself. That you are all consciousness, all being, all of existence. This is you body, your "I Am".

The procedure here is not exactly the same as before since you are now the source of light and you draw nothing down. Instead, the canticle, when performed from the Kethric perspective, is an operation entirely devoted to the emanation of light. Taken to its fullness, performing the canticle from the Kethric perspective mimics the cyclic breath of the universe itself as it emanates into existence and then returns to its source only to emanate again, and so on.

Let's begin now.

*Ani*
*Ani*
*Ani*
*Ani, IHVH, ADNI, Ribonno Shel Olam, Amen*

Excellent!

Now we will perform one final recitation of the canticle from the normal Malkuth perspective in order to firmly ground us back into our normal mundane awareness.

*Ani.*
*Ani*
*Ani*
*Ani, IHVH, ADNI, Ribonno Shel Olam, Amen*

Very well. This ends the instructional portion of Lesson Six.

Now I will discuss a few alternate approaches for you to experiment with and explore.

In the preceding instructions, I indicated that you should guide the descending light down into your own Malkuth. This however, is not your only option. From Tiphareth, you can also guide the light down into any or all of your past incarnations. From Binah, you can guide the light down into any or all of your Greater's manifest Individuals. From Chokmah, you can guide the light pretty much anywhere you like, and from the Unity you can emanate the light into the entire universe if you so choose.

Another alternative is that you can truly follow the light down with your conscious awareness. For example, from Binah, you can descend *with* the light into Tiphareth, sense your Tiphareth body and then descend *with* the light into your Malkuth and sense your Malkuth body. And as the ADNI light erupts and rises upwards, you can re-ascend with your conscious awareness until you reach the level from which you started. This has the effect of greatly integrating your various levels of Self, unlike the method you've just performed which merely opens the channels of light between these levels.

A final alternative that I will mention is what I call "Breathing the Unity". Here, you begin by working your way up to your Kether by following the steps you've just learned. Then you spend some time emanating your Kethric light into the whole universe, then inhaling it back into yourself and then emanating it anew, over and over with each repetition of the canticle from the Kethric perspective. Then you follow your emanation of light with your conscious awareness, outward into the entire universe and back to your Kether, over and over. Given enough practice and facility with the Magic of IHVH-ADNI, this can be a sublimely powerful meditation.

This ends Lesson Six, the final Lesson in the Magic of IHVH-ADNI. I pray that you use this magic well and create much beauty in the world.

**[Note: Although presented in the audio Lesson as a single work, this need not be so and may be practiced one level at a time instead of attempting all five levels in succession.]**

# LESSON SEVEN
## SETTING THE TONE OF THE TEMPORAL MOMENT

I wish to introduce you to an advanced usage of The Magic of IHVH-ADNI that I call "Setting the tone of the temporal moment". By this technique one creates conditions within the material realm that are in harmony with the realization of a specific desire.

For example, once a week I drive 35 miles each direction, along both freeway and narrow back roads, to volunteer a few hours at a food bank. Each week before departing, I use this Setting the Tone technique to assure that I will have a safe journey to and fro, that my time at the food bank will be pleasant, and that I will succeed in putting smiles on several faces whilst there. As a consequence, I have never had an accident on either the freeway or on the narrow back roads, my time at the food bank is always pleasant, and I invariably succeed at making folks smile.

Another example was one day, I was having difficulties with my computer's CD burner and I had a fair sized order for CD's that needed burning. So I used this technique to set the tone of smooth operating. It was like making a groove into a blank record, after which it was no problem to deposit myself and my CD burner into that groove. As a consequence, I was able to finish the needed CD burning without further difficulty.

As a final example, I used this technique right before sitting down to write this new Lesson. With it, I set the tone for a successful completion of my task, for clarity of mind and for a lack of importune interruptions.

These, of course, are just three, rather mundane examples of what is possible to accomplish with this technique. Nonetheless, it is best to begin with something simple and practical when learning this technique, so I will be using my final example as a template for my explanation of the technique.

First, I will give a detailed description of the technique within the context of my template and then I will guide you through the technique, step by step, as you apply it to a matter of your own choosing.

It took me a matter of just a few seconds to set the tone for this writing session but, I dare say, it will take me far longer to describe in detail what occurred during those few seconds. This is just as well since when you're first learning this technique, it's essential that you take your time and move very slowly through the visualizations I will be describing.

But before I go any further, I must say something about visualization. For the trained magician, there's but a hair's breadth of different between visualizing something and perceiving it as an accomplished fact. The reason for this is the strength of the trained mental will. When a thing is visualized with a strong mental will, a strong presence is created within the mental realm itself. Within the mental realm the Law of "like attracts like", holds sway, so when you insert a strong visualization into the mental realm, the realization of that visualization is immediately drawn to it and the visualization becomes a fact of reality instead of just an imagination. Of course, it takes time for this mental template to sink through the layers of density and become a physical reality, but on the mental plane, the transition from imagination to factual reality is instantaneous.

This mental plane Law of 'like attracts like' is important. It's the key to how one travels around the infinite mental plane, it's the root of many forms of magic, and it's the basis upon which several of the exercises of IIH were constructed. For example, the Step Three work with the Elements is based upon this Law. The student begins by creating a multi-sense imagination that the Element surrounds them and stretches infinitely in every direction. This creates a very strong presence within the mental realm to which is attracted the mental reality of the imagined Element. In this way, the student connects with the real Element through the application of their own imagination. And because this is a multi-sense imagination it will sink immediately into an astral density and the student will connect with the astral Element as well. But it is only because of the mental formation, and consequent mental connection, that the astral connection results. In other words, without the mental connection, no astral connection would ensue.

In Lesson Seven, I will instruct you to visualize certain things, but really these need to become more than mere imagination and grow into actual perceptions of factual reality. However, your imaginations will become stronger and stronger through repeated practice and you **_will_** achieve that transition from imagination to perception of factual reality.

So, on to my description --

I begin by uttering the Ani. Simultaneously, I am placing my awareness in Kether. In Kether, I look down upon the whole of reality, the eternal and the temporal. My perspective is as if from above and implies a certain detachment, yet I am completely connected with all that I see. It and I are one, yet I have focused my awareness above it so that I can look down upon it.

The primary thing that catches my Kethric eye is a thin white thread that stretches from my Kethric Self all the way down to my little Rawn-self who just uttered the word Ani. This thread passes through Chokmah and thereby highlights Chokmah to my vision. It passes also through the Greater Self, Sowantha, of which the small Rawn-self is an aspect, and thereby highlights Binah to my vision. Furthermore, it passes through the Individual-Rawn Self and thereby highlights Tiphareth to my vision. And at its end, the thread lies rooted in the small Rawn-self who first uttered the Ani.

I focus my Kethric consciousness upon this single white thread and as I speak the Yod through my small Rawn-self, I follow that descending thread and lower my Kethric Self into Chokmah, the place of choice. I fill Chokmah with my Kethric awareness and choose to follow the thread further.

As I utter the first Heh through my small Rawn-self, I follow the thread and lower my Kether-Chokmah Self into Binah and the Sowantha Greater Self. I fill Sowantha with my Kether-Chokmah awareness and sense my eternal surroundings. Then with my Kether-Chokmah-Binah awareness, I look down upon my Individual-Rawn Self within the temporal realm.

As I utter the Vav through my small Rawn-self, I follow the thread and lower my Kether-Chokmah-Binah Self into Tiphareth and the Individual-Rawn Self. I fill the Individual-Rawn with my Kether-Chokmah-Binah awareness and sense my temporal surroundings. Then with my Kether-Chokmah-Binah-Tiphareth awareness, I look down upon my small Rawn-self within the finite temporal moment.

As I utter the final Heh through my small Rawn-self, I follow the thread and lower my Kether-Chokmah-Binah-Tiphareth Self into Malkuth and the small Rawn-self. I fill Rawn with my Kether-Chokmah-Binah-Tiphareth awareness and sense my time-space surroundings.

Then with my unified Kether-Chokmah-Binah-Tiphareth-Malkuth awareness, I speak the Adonai as the Rainbow-hued cloud of light erupts around me. This light exists as a consequence of the unification of these five layers of my awareness within this temporal moment.

Then I inhale this cloud of light into the material body of my small Rawn-self by pulling it inward with a clockwise spiral motion, like water going down the drain of a sink.

If you have trouble visualizing this clockwise spiral motion then I suggest that you plug a sink and fill it with water. Then un-plug the sink and as the water drains, move your hand clockwise through the water and create a strong clockwise current. This is how the in-draw feels -- it pulls in from the edges toward center in a right-to-left arc. The expulsion of the light outward uses this same clockwise motion, in which case, the light fans out from center.

Through my exhale I speak the Ribonno Shel Olam with my Kether-Chokmah-Binah-Tiphareth-Malkuth awareness and send this light outward unto eternity. I see the Rainbow-hued light spread immediately throughout the temporal universe and I follow its passage inward and feel it as it strikes in succession my Tiphareth, Binah, Chokmah and Kethric Selves.

This raises my Kether-Chokmah-Binah-Tiphareth-Malkuth awareness up to Kether and I am united in Kether in the same way I am united in Malkuth.

With the inhalation of my material body within the finite temporal moment, my Kether-Chokmah-Binah-Tiphareth-Malkuth awareness is drawn back down into Malkuth and as I speak the Amen with my unified consciousness and will, the cloud of light re-solidifies around my material body.

As I inhale, I draw the cloud of light again into my material body with a clockwise spiral motion. As I exhale, I speak the Amen again with my fully unified awareness and send the light outwards into the fabric of time, again with a clockwise spiral motion.

I should explain that sending the light into the fabric of time is different than sending the light out to the edges of the infinite universe. Here I am sending it outward from the present finite moment of rigid time-space, into the ocean of possible futures that surround this finite present moment. This feels very different than sending the light out into just the present moment alone. When sending it into the fabric of time, there is a sense of boundlessness; whereas, when sending it into the present moment alone, there is a contrasting sense of rigidity and physicality, as if you're passing through matter itself. Here however, you're not passing through matter; instead, you're passing through the, as yet unwoven, fabric of time.

Since the desire I bring to the use of this magic today is that I might find the right words in writing this Lesson, I send that mental desire out with the light on its journey into the fabric of time. My mental impress acts as a magnet that draws what I seek to me and draws me to what I seek. The cloud expands until its edges reach the possible future temporal moment in which there is a realization of my desire. At that point, the spreading lights ceases to expand. I have made contact with the potential future I sought and there is no reason to probe further.

With an inhale of breath I draw the light back into my material body, again using a clockwise spiral motion. As the light returns to me, I feel that it has bound my goal and I together. It has connected us and forms a bridge between us. That bridge is built out of my desire to be successful in the creation of Lesson Seven.

What I have done here is to anchor the light upon a specific possible future. This enables me to locate that specific moment again with the next sending and provides me with the target I need to harmonize my present moment with. In other words, I will now begin the process of truly setting the proper tone for the moments that ensue between the present one and the possible future that I've anchored the light to. By using the Adonai-light to fill the temporal gap between my present moment and that specific possible future moment, I have created a vibrational continuum between the energetic frequencies of these two different moments in time-space. I am at one place in that spectrum of Rainbow-hued light and the future moment is at another point in the spectrum, and before me lies an unbroken continuum of color which blends my point in the spectrum with that of the future moment.

So, having drawn the light back into my material body and into the present moment, I exhale and speak the Amen again with my fully unified awareness, sending the light outwards into the fabric of time once more. It expands with a clockwise spiral motion until it reaches my target moment once again. As it expands, the continuum between moments becomes clearer and more solid and these two moments are brought into closer harmony. This also strengthens my grasp upon that future moment which increases its likelihood a thousand-fold.

With the inhale, I draw the light back again into my material form and into the present moment. This alters the present moment and brings it into closer harmony with the likely future moment.

For a third and final time, I again speak the Amen with my fully unified awareness and send the light out on its final journey to my target moment. As the light expands, the continuum between moments is enlivened and brought still closer to the realm of probability and ultimate actualization. When it touches the target moment, the target is moved firmly into the realm of probability. So much so, in fact, that it is now unlikely that it would **_not_** occur.

With the final inhalation, I draw the light back into my material body and draw the vibration of my target moment back with me and into the present moment. As the light returns, the continuum becomes absolutely solid and there is no doubt that this target moment containing success will manifest.

I close with a moment of thankfulness and return to my relatively mundane awareness.

When I sat down to write several minutes later, I completely surrounded myself and my target moment, with white light and thereby set myself on the path which invariably leads to that future moment.

This final step of encircling oneself and one's target with white light is what sets you upon the path to your goal. No matter how long a time has lapsed between your work of setting the tone and your actually setting foot on the path, circling both ends of the continuum with white light will bring you immediately into harmony with the path. The work of setting the tone carves the metaphorical groove and circling yourself and your target with white light puts you in that groove which leads to only one place -- your target.

For example, I will not finish writing Lesson Seven in one sitting. I will have to go water my garden soon which means that I will have to later reclaim my position in this groove. It will take several days possibly to complete this task of writing, recording and then posting it on my website, so I will need to jump in and out of that groove, so to speak, several times before I've met face to face with my target moment. All I have to do to get back into the groove is to surround myself and my target with white light.

As I hinted at the beginning, this setting the tone technique has countless applications and an equal number of possible variations. One internal variation that I'd like to mention has to do with the initial phase of anchoring. Aside from your target moment, you can also anchor the light to interim moments that exist within the continuum of separation between your present moment and your ultimate target. This is especially beneficial for longer range goals.

For example, with the working I just described, I could have also anchored onto the moment that I finish writing Lesson Seven and the moment I finish the recording, in addition to my target moment of total completion. Having these three anchors instead of just the one, makes the journey to a final destination somehow easier to manage. It's like when taking a long road trip. If one sees a few familiar landmarks along the way, the long journey then splits itself into shorter parts. This provides clear markers that help define one's progress. Multiple anchors are, as I said most practical for longer term goals, so I have not felt the need for them here in this instance.

Anchoring is also an important factor when you wish to adapt this technique for healing another person or for bestowing the Blessing of IHVH-ADNI upon another person. Both of these adaptations will be covered in future Lessons.

Well, I think I've completely exhausted my ability to describe the technique to you so let's move on to the practice.

**Practice:**

Before we begin, you must decide upon the desire you wish to apply this technique to. For this first practice it should be something fairly simple and short term. If you haven't already settled upon a choice, then put this recording on pause and decide now.

Since we will be going so slowly through the utterance of the canticle, please feel free to take any empty breaths that you might need. Do not hold your breath in or out in any event.

Begin by stilling your mind and body and focusing your awareness within the present moment of time and space. When you speak the Ani which begins the canticle, you want to raise your awareness up to your Kether in synchrony with the rising tone of the word, so that by the time you are uttering the final Yod of Ani, you are firmly rooted in your Kethric awareness.

So, let's begin.

> Inhale <

*Ani*

Your awareness is now focused in Kether. The entire creation is spread out below your center of awareness. You see below you, the layers of eternity and temporality. Weaving its way up to you, you see a thin white thread. It is rooted in your material form and leads all the way up to your Kethric awareness. It exists because you have spoken the Ani.

You see that it passes through Tiphareth and illumines your own Individual Self. It passes through Binah and illuminates the Greater Self of which you are a part. And it passes through Chokmah, illuminating that sphere as well.

When these images are clear to your perception, you are ready to speak the IHVH and follow that thread down to your material form. As you speak the Yod, begin your descent and, with your Kethric awareness, follow the white thread into Chokmah.

> Inhale <

*Yod*

Your Kethric awareness is now centered in Chokmah. This region appears in a soft grey light with the bright white thread passing through the center of it. Fill your Chokmah with your Kethric awareness and then, with your combined Kethric and Chokmah awareness, gaze over at Binah and see the bright white thread which spans this distance.

When these images are clear to your perception, you are ready to speak the first Heh and follow that thread over to your Greater Self. As you speak the Heh, begin your descent and, with your combined Kether-Chokmah awareness, follow the white thread into Binah.

> Inhale <

*Heh*

Your Kether-Chokmah awareness is now centered in Binah. Fill your Greater Self with your Kether-Chokmah awareness and then, with your combined Kether, Chokmah and Binah awareness, look around you.

Above, you see the White Brilliance of Kether and below you, you see the relative darkness of the temporal realm. Surrounding you within the eternal realm, you perceive an infinite number of other Greater Selves.

Now take note of the bright white thread that leads from the heart of your Greater Self, down into the temporal realm, highlighting your Individual Self residing in Tiphareth.

When these images are clear to your perception, you are ready to speak the Vav and follow that thread down to your Individual Self. As you speak the Vav, begin your descent and, with your combined Kether-Chokmah-Binah awareness, follow the white thread into Tiphareth.

ᴠ Inhale ᴗ

### Vav

Your Kether-Chokmah-Binah awareness is now centered in Tiphareth. Fill your Individual Self with your Kether-Chokmah-Binah awareness and then, with your combined Kether, Chokmah, Binah and Tiphareth awareness, look around you. Above, you see the Violet Blackness of Binah and below you, you see the relative darkness of the material realm. Surrounding you is the entire temporal realm and you perceive an infinite number of other Individual Selves.

Now take note of the bright white thread that leads from the heart of your Individual Self, down into the material realm and the finite moment, highlighting your material self residing in Malkuth.

When these images are clear to your perception, you are ready to speak the final Heh and follow that thread down to your material self. As you speak the Heh, begin your descent and, with your combined Kether-Chokmah-Binah-Tiphareth awareness, follow the white thread into Malkuth.

> Inhale <

### Heh

Your Kether-Chokmah-Binah-Tiphareth awareness is now centered in Malkuth. Fill your material self with your Kether-Chokmah-Binah-Tiphareth awareness by becoming of each of these levels of your awareness simultaneously. Sense your Kether, Chokmah, Binah, Tiphareth and Malkuth all at once, as a single, cohesive, multi-layered consciousness.

When this unified state of awareness which combines the eternal and temporal realms, occurs within the finite moment of time-space, the Rainbow-Hued Light of Adonai spontaneously erupts.

With your united consciousness, you speak the Adonai in celebration and affirmation of this eruption of Light.

> Inhale <

### *Adonai*

The Rainbow-Hued cloud of Adonai Light now spins clockwise around your material body which houses your unified consciousness.

As you inhale in preparation to speak the Ribonno Shel Olam with your unified consciousness, draw this cloud of Adonai Light into the center of your material body. As you then speak the Ribonno Shel Olam, send the Light you have brought into your core, outward to the edges of the infinite Universe as usual, and also send it inward to Tiphareth, Binah, Chokmah and Kether.

> Inhale <

### *Ribonno Shel Olam*

Follow the Light with your unified consciousness all the way out to the metaphorical edges of the universe and all the way in to Kether, brushing upon everything that exists in between.

With an inhale, draw this transfigured Adonai Light back to your material body and into the finite moment of time-space, wherein is housed your unified consciousness. Again, spread your awareness to all the layers of your multi-layers consciousness simultaneously.

And as you speak the Amen, see that the transfigured Adonai Light surrounds your material body, spinning clockwise.

> Inhale <

### *Amen*

With the Adonai Light spinning around you, spend a few moments focused upon your single desired outcome.

With your inhale in preparation to speak the next Amen, you must draw the Adonai Light back into the core of your material body. At the same time, transfer your strongly formed desire into the Adonai Light. Impress it very strongly upon the Light as you draw it into your body. And then, as you speak the Amen itself, you must send this Light which carries the impress of your desire, outward and into the, as yet, unwoven fabric of time.

> Inhale <

*Amen*

With your unified consciousness, ride the expanding wave of out flowing Light as it penetrates the darkness of infinite possibilities. You are looking for the one possible future moment in which your desire is realized. Just flow outward with the wave of light, keeping your mind focused upon your desired outcome, and this moment in future-time will find you. You will know when you have encountered it by the fact that it stops the expansion of Light outward.

For a brief moment, let your unified consciousness rest in that future moment.

And now with an inhale, draw the Light back to your material body and into the finite present moment, as usual giving it a clockwise spiral motion.

Spend a few moments focusing upon the connection that now exists between this present moment and that future moment. You've snared it in your web of Adonai Light and have plucked it from the realm of infinite, undifferentiated possibilities and transformed it into a specific possibility.

With your inhale in preparation to speak the next Amen, you must again draw the Adonai Light into your core and re-affirm its impregnation with your desired outcome. With the subsequent speaking of the Amen, you again send the Light out into the fabric of time, but this time around you are aiming for a known goal -- your future moment.

> Inhale <

*Amen*

As before, with your unified consciousness, ride the expanding wave of light as it very quickly makes its way to the now familiar future moment that holds the realization of your desire.

For a brief moment, let your unified consciousness rest in that future moment.

And now with an inhale, draw the Light back to your material body and back into the finite present moment, as usual giving it a clockwise spiral motion. This time however, you must draw that future moment back with you. Bring its definable uniqueness back into the definable uniqueness of the finite present moment.

Spend a few moments focusing upon how much stronger the connection between this present moment and that future moment has become. See how this present moment has been changed by your having made this connection. You have brought that possible future closer and it's now a likelihood, instead of a mere possibility.

With your inhale in preparation to speak the final Amen, you must again draw the Adonai Light into your core and re-affirm its impregnation with your desired outcome. With the subsequent speaking of the Amen, you again send the Light out into the fabric of time, but this time it's as if you're carving a clear pathway between you and your future moment.

> Inhale <

### Amen

As before, with your unified consciousness, ride the expanding wave of light as it very quickly makes its way to the now familiar future moment that holds the realization of your desire. As you progress outward, carve a very distinct path that connects your present moment with your future moment.

For a brief moment, let your unified consciousness rest in that future moment.

And now with an inhale, draw the Light back to your material body and back into the finite present moment, as usual giving it a clockwise spiral motion. Again, you must bring the definable uniqueness of the future moment back into the definable uniqueness of the finite present moment. As you travel back to the present moment with the Light, follow the path you laid down during the expansion and make this pathway more distinct.

Spend a few moments focusing upon how strong, clear and solid the connection between this present moment and that future moment has become. See how both this present moment, and that future moment, have been changed by your having made this strong connection. You have brought that future likelihood still closer and it's now an inevitability, instead of a likelihood.

In this present moment, you are positioned squarely on the path that leads to this inevitable moment in which your desire has been realized.

With your unified awareness, focus in this present moment and once again, spread your unified awareness throughout the multiple layers of your consciousness simultaneously. See the cloud of Rainbow-Hued Light that surrounds, say a brief prayer of thanks for this blessing, and utter a final Amen.

> Pause <

> Inhale <

*Amen*

Release your visualizations and return firmly to your mundane awareness. Open your eyes if they were closed and move your body around a bit.

> Pause <

Once you have fully returned to your normal state of awareness, mentally surround yourself with white light. And then, mentally surround your future moment with the same white light.

This ends the practice of Setting the Tone of the Temporal Moment and concludes Lesson Seven in The Magic of IHVH-ADNI. I wish you many wonderful returns as you explore the infinite possibilities of this technique.

# LESSON EIGHT
## HEALING FROM AFAR

In Lesson Seven, "Setting the tone of the Temporal Moment", I introduced two new factors that this present Lesson builds upon. These are: sending the Adonai Light out into the, as yet unwoven, fabric of time and, what I called, anchoring the Light.

In Lesson Eight, "Healing From Afar", we begin as we did in the previous Lesson, with two main differences. One, we will be sending the Adonai Light out into the **woven** fabric of the **present** moment of time-space. And two, instead of searching for a possible future moment, we will seek out a known person -- the person we have chosen to be the recipient of our healing efforts. We will anchor the Adonai Light upon this person and steadily draw our own mental awareness to that person's location in the present moment of time-space.

Once our mental awareness is standing next to the physical body of this person we will focus our healing efforts upon them. To simplify matters for this Lesson, the only healing technique we will employ is to surround this person with the Adonai Light, but any other healing technique of your choosing can be substituted during your own solitary practice.

When our healing work is completed, we will then return with the Adonai Light to our own physical bodies and end in the usual fashion.

As I guide you through the practice of this technique, I will be moving along more quickly than in the last Lesson, assuming that you have already become familiar with the technique of unifying the layers of awareness.

So, without further ado, let's move on to the practice of healing from afar.

**Practice:**

Before we begin, you must decide upon the person you wish to apply this technique to. For this first practice it should be someone you know very well. If you haven't already settled upon a person, then put this recording on pause and decide now.

Since we'll be going somewhat slowly through the utterance of the canticle, please feel free to take any empty breaths that you might need. Do not hold your breath in or out in any event.

Begin by stilling your mind and body and focusing your awareness within the present moment of time and space.

So, let's begin.

> Inhale <

*Ani*

Your awareness is now focused in Kether. The entire creation is spread out below your center of awareness.

> Inhale <

*Yod*

Your Kethric awareness is now centered in Chokmah.

> Inhale <

*Heh*

Your Kether-Chokmah awareness is now centered in Binah.

> Inhale <

*Vav*

Your Kether-Chokmah-Binah awareness is now centered in Tiphareth.

> Inhale <

*Heh*

Your Kether-Chokmah-Binah-Tiphareth awareness is now centered in Malkuth. Fill your material self with your Kether-Chokmah-Binah-Tiphareth awareness by becoming conscious of each of these levels of your awareness simultaneously. Sense your Kether, Chokmah, Binah, Tiphareth and Malkuth all at once, as a single, cohesive, multi-layered consciousness.

When this unified state of awareness which combines the eternal and temporal realms, occurs within the finite moment of time-space, the Rainbow-Hued Light of Adonai spontaneously erupts.

With your united consciousness, you speak the Adonai in celebration and affirmation of this eruption of Light.

> Inhale <

## *Adonai*

The Rainbow-Hued cloud of Adonai Light now spins clockwise around your material body which houses your unified consciousness.

As you inhale in preparation to speak the Ribonno Shel Olam with your unified consciousness, draw this cloud of Adonai Light into the center of your material body. As you then speak the Ribonno Shel Olam, send the Light you have brought into your core, outward to the edges of the infinite Universe as usual, and also send it inward to Tiphareth, Binah, Chokmah and Kether.

> Inhale <

## *Ribonno Shel Olam*

Follow the Light with your unified consciousness all the way out to the metaphorical edges of the universe and all the way in to Kether, brushing upon everything that exists in between.

With an inhale, draw this transfigured Adonai Light back to your material body and into the finite moment of time-space, wherein is housed your unified consciousness. Again, spread your awareness to all the layers of your multi-layered consciousness simultaneously.

And as you speak the Amen, see that the transfigured Adonai Light surrounds your material body, spinning clockwise.

> Inhale <

## *Amen*

With the Adonai Light spinning around you, spend a few moments focused upon the person you wish to heal.

With your inhale in preparation to speak the next Amen, you must draw the Adonai Light back into the core of your material body. At the same time, transfer your strongly formed image of this person and your desire to locate them into the Adonai Light. Impress it very strongly upon the Light as you draw it into your body. And then, as you speak the Amen itself, you must send this Light which carries the impress of your desire, outward and into the fabric of the present moment of time-space which surrounds your physical body.

> Inhale <

*Amen*

With your unified consciousness, ride the expanding wave of out flowing Light as it penetrates the spatial substance of the present moment. You are looking for the one person that you have chosen to focus your healing upon. Just flow outward with the wave of light, keeping your mind focused upon this person, and you will automatically be drawn to them. You will know when you have encountered them by the fact that they stop the expansion of Light outward

For a brief moment, let your unified consciousness rest in their presence.

And now with an inhale, draw the Light back to your material body, as usual giving it a clockwise spiral motion.

Spend a few moments focusing upon the connection that now exists between yourself and this person. You've snared them in your web of Adonai Light.

With your inhale in preparation to speak the next Amen, you must again draw the Adonai Light into your core and re-affirm its impregnation with your desire to heal this person. With the subsequent speaking of the Amen, you again send the Light out into the fabric of the present moment of time-space, but this time around you are aiming for a known location.

> Inhale <

*Amen*

As before, with your unified consciousness, ride the expanding wave of light as it very quickly makes its way to the now familiar location that holds the physical body of the person you seek.

For a brief moment, let your unified consciousness rest in their presence.

And now with an inhale, draw the Light back to your material body, as usual giving it a clockwise spiral motion.

Spend a few moments focusing upon how much stronger the connection between yourself and this person has become.

With your inhale in preparation to speak the final Amen, you must again draw the Adonai Light into your core and re-affirm its impregnation with your desire to heal this person. With the subsequent speaking of the Amen, you again send the Light out into the fabric of the present moment of time-space.

> Inhale <

**Amen**

As before, with your unified consciousness, ride the expanding wave of light as it shoots like an arrow to the time-space location of the person you wish to heal. As you progress outward, gather more Light from the Universal substance and add this to the wave of Adonai Light.

When you arrive, stop and stand very still next to the physical body of this person.

Now condense part of the Rainbow-hued Adonai Light until it surrounds the person standing before you. Make it spin in a clockwise direction around them.

> Pause <

While the condensed Adonai Light swirls around them, say a prayer with your unified consciousness to the effect that this person will draw from the Adonai Light whatever they need to achieve healing.

> Pause <

After you've uttered your prayer, repeat your intention, with your unified consciousness, in the form of a command.

> Pause <

*See* that it is so.

> Pause <

Now you must turn your attention away from this person and fix it back upon your own physical body. With an inhale, draw the remaining Adonai Light back to your physical body and follow along with your unified consciousness.

With your unified awareness, focus yourself within your physical body and once again, spread your unified awareness throughout the multiple layers of your consciousness simultaneously. See the cloud of Rainbow-Hued Light that surrounds you, say a brief prayer of thanks for this blessing, and utter a final Amen.

> Pause <

> Inhale <

**Amen**

Release your visualizations and return firmly to your mundane awareness. Open your eyes if they were closed and move your body around a bit.

> Pause <

This ends the practice of Healing From Afar and concludes Lesson Eight in The Magic of IHVH-ADNI. I pray that you use it well and bring much healing into the world.

# LESSON NINE
## THE BLESSING OF IHVH-ADNI

By now, you are very familiar with the blessing that the practice of this magic confers upon the practitioner. With this final Lesson in the audio series, you will learn how to confer this same blessing upon another person. In order to effectively confer the Blessing of IHVH-ADNI, you must have thoroughly mastered the previous Lessons, most especially Lessons 7 and 8.

The procedure has three parts, the first two of which are exactly like the previous Lesson, "Healing From Afar". The first part is our utterance of the canticle and the unification of the various levels of our consciousness. The second part is the sending out of the Adonai Light into the woven fabric of the present moment of time-space, anchoring it to the person we wish to confer the Blessing upon and then projecting our own mental awareness to their physical location in time-space. Once we are standing next to this person with the mental presence of our unified consciousness, we begin the third part which is the Blessing itself.

Our first action in the Blessing is to draw in the Adonai Light until it surrounds us and the person we are to Bless. Then we begin to recite the canticle from the beginning and, in effect, unify our consciousness and the other person's consciousness, simultaneously.

When we speak the Ani and focus our awareness in Kether, we see two white threads instead of just one. This is our own thread and the thread of the person we have enveloped in our Adonai Light. Since we have established such a strong mental harmony between ourselves and this other person, our utterance of the Ani has the same effect upon the both of us as it ordinarily does upon us when we utter the Ani in solitude. It draws two threads up from the material realm.

In Kether, these two threads are one. In Chokmah the one thread splits into two and each connects to a different Greater Self in Binah. That is, unless you and the person you are Blessing both stem from the same Greater Self. In such a case, the thread remains one all the way to Binah and then splits to connect with separate Individual Selves in Tiphareth. Ultimately, these threads lead to two different people who are sharing the same mental proximity within the temporal present moment -- yourself and the person you wish to Bless.

As we speak the IHVH, we descend along both threads simultaneously and draw the Kethric Light of unified consciousness down them both equally. Since we occupy such close mental proximity within the temporal realm, our two threads will be very close together at each level of our descent. When, together, we reach Malkuth wherein our mental presence is standing right next to this person's physical body, the Rainbow-hued Adonai Light erupts to surround the both of us and we speak the Adonai.

When we speak the Ribonno Shel Olam, we send the Adonai Light outward to the metaphorical edges of the infinite universe _and_ inward all the way back up to Kether. As we go inward, we ascend along _both_ threads simultaneously.

And with the inhale that precedes the closing Amen, we draw back the Adonai Light that we have sent outward and inward, inwardly following along both threads in our descent, until it once again surrounds the both of us. As we speak the Amen, it solidifies around us and Blesses us.

This completes the Blessing and all that's left is our return to our own physical bodies, a prayer of thanksgiving and the resumption of normal waking consciousness.

Assuming that you have indeed mastered the previous 8 Lessons, I will be leading you through the first two parts of the procedure fairly quickly and then slowing down for the third part, the Blessing itself.

Lesson Nine, "The Blessing of IHVH-ADNI", is the final Lesson in The Magic of IHVH-ADNI audio series. Within this Foundation of nine Lessons, are buried many treasures from which to build a Temple worthy of housing your Divine spirit. I pray that you use this sacred magic to Bless your own life and to multiply those Blessings a thousand-fold that they may rain down as a shower of Beauty upon the whole world.

So, let's move on to the practice of the final Lesson, The Blessing of IHVH-ADNI.

**Practice:**

Before we begin, you must decide upon the person you wish to apply this technique to. For this first practice it should be someone you know very well. If you haven't already settled upon a person, then put this recording on pause and decide now.

Begin by stilling your mind and body and focusing your awareness within the present moment of time and space.

> Pause <

So, let's begin.

> Inhale <

*Ani*

> Inhale <

*Yod*

> Inhale <

*Heh*

> Inhale <

*Vav*

> Inhale <

*Heh*

> Inhale <

*Adonai*

> Inhale <

*Ribonno Shel Olam*

> Inhale <

*Amen*

With the Adonai Light spinning around you, spend a few moments focused upon the person you wish to Bless.

Transfer your strongly formed image of this person and your desire to locate them into the Adonai Light and then send this Light which carries the impress of your desire, outward and into the fabric of the present moment of time-space which surrounds your physical body.

> Inhale <

*Amen*

With your unified consciousness, ride the expanding wave of out flowing Light as it penetrates the spatial substance of the present moment until you locate this person.

For a brief moment, let your unified consciousness rest in their presence.

And now with an inhale, draw the Light back to your material body.

Spend a few moments focusing upon the connection that now exists between yourself and this person. You've snared them in your web of Adonai Light.

Now again send the Light out into the fabric of the present moment of time-space, but this time around you are aiming for a known location.

> Inhale <

*Amen*

For a brief moment, let your unified consciousness rest in their presence.

And now with an inhale, draw the Light back to your material body and spend a few moments focusing upon how much stronger the connection between yourself and this person has become.

With your inhale in preparation to speak the final Amen, you must again draw the Adonai Light into your core and re-affirm its impregnation with your desire to Bless this person.

Now send the Light out into the fabric of the present moment of time-space a final time.

> Inhale <

*Amen*

As before, with your unified consciousness, ride the expanding wave of light as it shoots like an arrow to the time-space location of the person you wish to Bless.

When you arrive, stop and stand very still next to the physical body of this person.

Now condense the whole of the Rainbow-hued Adonai Light until it surrounds both yourself and the person standing before you. The two of you stand within a clockwise spinning circle of Adonai Light.

> Pause <

Take a moment to expand your awareness throughout all the levels of your consciousness simultaneously, bringing your awareness into a unified state as you stand with your mental presence next to the person you wish to Bless.

Now begin to speak the canticle from the beginning.

> Inhale <

*Ani*

Your awareness is now focused in Kether. Weaving their way up to you, you see two thin white threads. They are rooted in Malkuth and lead all the way up to your Kethric awareness. They exist because you have spoken the Ani.

When these images are clear to your perception, you are ready to speak the IHVH and follow those threads down to the material realm. As you speak the Yod, begin your descent and, with your Kethric awareness, follow the single conjoined white thread into Chokmah.

> Inhale <

*Yod*

Your Kethric awareness is now centered in Chokmah. Fill your Chokmah with your Kethric awareness and then, with your combined Kethric and Chokmah awareness, gaze over at Binah and see the two bright white threads which span this distance.

When these images are clear to your perception, you are ready to speak the first Heh and follow both threads over to Binah and into both your own Greater Self, and that of the other person simultaneously. As you speak the Heh, begin your descent and, with your combined Kether-Chokmah awareness, follow the white threads into Binah.

> Inhale <

*Heh*

Your Kether-Chokmah awareness is now centered in Binah. Fill both your Greater Self and that of the other person, with your Kether-Chokmah awareness. Take note of the bright white thread that leads from the heart of your own Greater Self and the one that leads from the heart of the other person's Greater Self. Observe how each leads down into the temporal realm, highlighting your Individual Selves residing in Tiphareth.

When these images are clear to your perception, you are ready to speak the Vav and follow both threads down into your own Individual Self and that of the other person simultaneously. As you speak the Vav, begin your descent and, with your combined Kether-Chokmah-Binah awareness, follow the two white threads into Tiphareth.

> Inhale <

*Vav*

Your Kether-Chokmah-Binah awareness is now centered in Tiphareth. Fill your own Individual Self and that of the other person with your Kether-Chokmah-Binah awareness. Take note of the bright white thread that leads from the heart of your own Individual Self and the one that leads from the heart of the other person's Individual Self. Observe how each leads down into the material realm, highlighting your mental presence and the other person's material presence, standing side by side in Malkuth.

When these images are clear to your perception, you are ready to speak the final Heh and follow the threads down into the material realm. As you speak the Heh, begin your descent and, with your combined Kether-Chokmah-Binah-Tiphareth awareness, follow the two white threads into Malkuth.

> Inhale <

*Heh*

Your Kether-Chokmah-Binah-Tiphareth awareness is now centered in Malkuth. Fill your mental awareness and the material body of the other person with your Kether-Chokmah-Binah-Tiphareth awareness by becoming conscious of each of these levels of your awareness simultaneously. Sense your Kether, Chokmah, Binah, Tiphareth and Malkuth all at once, as a single, cohesive, multi-layered consciousness.

The Rainbow-Hued Light of Adonai spontaneously erupts and, with your united consciousness, you speak the Adonai in celebration and affirmation of this eruption of Light.

> Inhale <

## Adonai

The Rainbow-Hued cloud of Adonai Light now spins clockwise around you and the other person.

As you inhale in preparation to speak the Ribonno Shel Olam with your unified consciousness, draw this cloud of Adonai Light into the center of your mental presence and into the material body of the other person simultaneously. As you then speak the Ribonno Shel Olam, send the Light you have brought into _both_ cores, outward to the edges of the infinite Universe as usual, and also send it inward to Tiphareth, Binah, Chokmah and Kether.

> Inhale <

## Ribonno Shel Olam

Follow the Light with your unified consciousness all the way out to the metaphorical edges of the universe and all the way in to Kether, brushing upon everything that exists in between. As you ascend inward, follow both threads simultaneously.

As you inhale in preparation to speak the Amen, draw this transfigured Adonai Light back to Malkuth and into the finite moment of time-space, again following both threads in your descent. And as you speak the Amen, see that the transfigured Adonai Light surrounds your mental presence and the other person's material body, spinning clockwise.

> Inhale <

## Amen

Focus your mind upon the Blessing of the Adonai Light that infuses both of you.

Now you must turn your attention away from this person and fix it back upon your own physical body. With an inhale, draw a portion of Adonai Light back to your physical body and follow along with your unified consciousness.

With your unified awareness, focus yourself within your physical body and once again, spread your unified awareness throughout the multiple layers of your consciousness simultaneously. See the cloud of Rainbow-Hued Light that surrounds you, say a brief prayer of thanks for this blessing.

> Pause <

And utter a final Amen.

> Inhale <

**Amen**

Release your visualizations and return firmly to your mundane awareness. Open your eyes if they were closed and move your body around.

> Pause <

This ends the practice of conferring the Blessing of IHVH-ADNI and concludes the final Lesson Nine in The Magic of IHVH-ADNI.

# THE MAGIC OF
# IHVH-ADNI

# FURTHER DEVELOPMENTS

Between 2003 and 2006 I wrote three additional articles which expanded upon the material presented in the audio Lessons.

# THE FINAL FORM
## 2003

In the nine Lessons of The Magic of IHVH-ADNI audio series, I taught two "forms" of TMO: the Simple Form and the Full Form. The Simple Form mimics the breath cycle itself. There is no accumulation, impregnation or shepherding involved as the Kethric Light is merely drawn down and expelled, over and over for as many repetitions as desired, creating a tonifying and cleansing effect upon the practitioner's three bodies.

The Full Form on the other hand, involves accumulation, impregnation of the accumulation with specific intent and shepherding of the Light once it's been expelled. All of the magical uses of TMO employ the Full Form and this is the more versatile of the two forms presented in the audio Lessons.

Now I would like to publicly introduce the Final Form of TMO. Although I've mentioned this Form before in passing, I will now explain it in detail.

In essence, the Final Form is an extension of Lesson Six, "Consciousness Raising". Here however, the canticle itself is not spoken, neither physically, astrally, nor mentally. Instead of speaking, the practitioner *becomes* the canticle and enacts the rising, descent, expulsion and contraction of the Light with their own consciousness. The canticle becomes an act of creating, shifting and unifying a micro-focus within an overall Macro-focus.

The first step is to establish the Macro-focus within which TMO occurs. This is accomplished by raising one's focus to Kether. In the Simple and Full Forms, the utterance of the "Ani" guides this ascent of consciousness, but in the Final Form, there is nothing other than the independent ascent of your conscious awareness to the Kethric level.

From the Kethric perspective one not only sees the entire Creation "below" the point of focus, but one also *IS* all that lies "below". The Kethric consciousness is a state of immanence in which one personally experiences *EVERY* thing simultaneously. Here there is no single micro-focus -- only Macro-focus.

In the Simple and Full Forms, the next step would be to utter the "Yod" and descend into Chokmah, but in the Final Form there is no utterance to guide this descent and focalization. Instead, one must independently form a micro-focus within Chokmah without any mental, astral or physical utterance.

In Chokmah, a micro-focus is formed and one then sees the single thread that connects to one's own Greater Self residing in Binah. Having perceived the thread and what lies below Chokmah, one then reconnects the Chokmah micro-focus to the Kethric Macro-focus and holds the two simultaneously within Chokmah. In other words, within Chokmah one experiences the Chokmah micro-focus (which perceives the thread leading to Binah) *and* one perceives/experiences the entire Creation from the Kethric perspective, simultaneously.

Once the micro- and Macro-foci have been united, one then shifts the micro-focus to Binah and the experience of one's own Greater Self. Ordinarily, this shift would be guided by the utterance of the first "Heh", but here it must again be an independent formation of the micro-focus within Binah.

Once the micro-focus is formed within the Binah Greater Self, one perceives the entire realm of sequence "below", along with the single thread that connects to one's own Individual Self in Tiphareth. Then one reconnects with the Chokmah micro-focus and the Kethric Macro-focus and holds all three perspectives *simultaneously* within the Binah micro-focus.

This same formula is continued downward as one shifts micro-focus to their own Individual Self in Tiphareth. Once the micro-focus is formed within the Individual Self, one perceives the totality of the temporal realm as it exists in the present moment, along with the single thread that leads to the mundane self "below". Then, as before, one reconnects the Tiphareth micro-focus to the Binah and Chokmah micro-foci and the Kethric Macro-focus so that all four perspectives are experienced *simultaneously* within the Tiphareth micro-focus.

And then to conclude the descent and unification of consciousness, the micro-focus is shifted to Malkuth and formed within the material self. Once the micro-focus is formed, one senses the physical body and its surroundings, all of which are confined to the immediate present moment. Then one reconnects the Malkuth micro-focus to the Tiphareth, Binah and Chokmah micro-foci and the Kethric Macro-focus so that all five perspectives are experienced *simultaneously* within the Malkuth micro-focus.

The instant that all five levels of Self exist simultaneously within one's mundane consciousness, the Rainbow-hued Adonai Light erupts. With the Final Form there is no need for uttering the "Adonai" to ignite the Adonai Light since this is accomplished by the unification of all five levels within Malkuth.

A few moments are spent uniting all five levels of Self as one stands amid the swirling Adonai Light. Then, one draws the Light inward at the Malkuth level, into the center of the physical self, and then expels it outward for the Divine Blessing. As the Light expands, one observes its expansion *outward,* throughout the entire temporal universe, and *inward,* to Tiphareth, Binah, Chokmah and ultimately, Kether. As it passes inward, one *experiences* its passage through each of the four micro-foci and its entry into the Kethric Macro-focus.

Once the expansion has reached the edges of the temporal universe and has penetrated to one's Kethric perspective, one then "pushes" it back down, through the levels of Self, and constricts it inward, through the expanses of space, till it once again surrounds the mundane self in Malkuth.

All of this movement of the Adonai Light is perceived as movement *within* the Macro-focus and it is performed *by* the five unified levels of Self.

What I have just described can be called the Final-Simple Form. There was no accumulation, no impregnation of the Adonai Light with a specific intention and no shepherding of the Light as it returned. I suggest that one practice this first, before moving on to the Final-Full Form. The Final-Full Form of course, involves an accumulation of the Adonai Light, an impregnation of the accumulated Light with a specific intention and the shepherding of its return.

Accumulations are exponentially more powerful when one performs the Final Form than when using Full Form. The Final Form also affords the opportunity of opening a continuous channel of the Adonai Light, one which will continuously increase in volume and intensity if one allows it to. This is accomplished by prolonging the period of unification of all five levels of Self within the Malkuth micro-focus. As this multi-level awareness is held in Malkuth, the Kethric Light continues to flow into Malkuth, building an ever-increasing intensity of the Adonai Light. One should, of course, be careful not to over-do and should avoid exceeding the limitations of their three temporal bodies.

Alternately, one can let the Adonai Light simply flow outward instead of confining it as when accumulating the Light. By this method, one holds the unification of the five levels of Self within Malkuth and allows the growing mass of Adonai Light to continuously expand outward within the temporal present moment. One can also set a limit to this expansion and thereby fill a room with the Adonai Light, for example.

Impregnation of a Final Form accumulation is done by the unified levels of Self, not just by the mundane level of one's awareness. In other words, the intention is formulated simultaneously within all five levels of Self and impressed upon the accumulated Light. With the Final Form, the formulation of intention can alternately be accomplished *during* the descent and unification of consciousness, thus producing an Adonai Light that already carries intention and which doesn't require subsequent impregnation. When combined with the prolongation of the unified state within Malkuth, one can very quickly fill a room with Adonai Light that *already* carries an intention, thus producing a more immediate result.

In the Final-Full Form, the shepherding of the returning Adonai Light is also accomplished by the five unified levels of Self, not just by the mundane awareness. This provides for much greater control and much greater attention to detail as the returning wave moves *through* the Self. One *experiences* its entire passage *and* its effect *as* it is occurring.

Applying the Final Form to the various "applications" of TMO that I describe in the audio Lessons will exponentially increase their effectiveness and their versatility. For example, using the Final Form in a healing ritual allows one to create a more intimate connection with the healing subject. When using the Final Form, that connection begins at the level of Binah and continues downward to Malkuth, due to the fact that *EVERY* thing (and *EVERY* one) exists within the Kethric Macro-focus. Thus, the healing subject is *experienced* as an aspect of Self. This makes it possible to enlist the aid, insight and cooperation of the healing subject's own Greater Self (as their Holy Guardian Angel) and Individual Self.

The TMO Working Group has found the Final Form most useful and at this point, most of our members are employing it during our group rituals. It has allowed us a great amount of fluidity and places us in a very efficient and effective relationship with our healing subjects. Because of the degree of intimacy we can achieve with our subjects, our perceptions of their condition are very precise and informative. The use of Final Form in our group ritual has also increased our unity as a group and has opened us *collectively* to still higher states of group functionality and awareness.

Mastery of Lesson Six of the audio series ("Consciousness Raising") is necessary before one can begin working with the Final Form, so this should not be viewed as a beginning technique. :)

# TMO AND THE ARCHAEOUS
## 2004

Many times in the past I've stated that TMO (The Magic of IHVH-ADNI) and the Self-Healing Archaeous lead to the same end, which is to say, both result in a unification of consciousness within the temporal moment. TMO achieves this through Kabbalah and the Archaeous, through Hermetics.

The greatest difficulty that practitioners new to TMO face is the issue of conceptualizing the five levels of Self-Awareness represented by the "Ani IHVH" (i.e., Kether, Chokmah, Binah, Tiphareth and Malkuth). In order to simplify this process I would like to present to you a method that relies upon the Archaeous for reaching those levels of Awareness.

The very first step in TMO is the utterance of the "Ani" and the immediate raising of one's awareness to the level of Kether or The One Self. If one has already experienced this all-inclusive level of Self-Awareness, then this rise presents no difficulty. However, if this level has not been experienced previously then the practitioner must do their best to conceptualize what it is like and creatively establish a facsimile of that experience. Given time and persistent practice, this creative conceptualizing will eventually become perception and fact, but until that occurs, the generation of the Adonai Light remains very weak and the integration of awareness, incomplete.

With the Archaeous technique however, this rise can be accomplished in a more factual manner from the outset. Instead of immediately jumping from the mundane awareness to the Kethric Awareness as TMO demands, with the application of the Archaeous technique the TMO practitioner is provided the opportunity to rise *sequentially* and gradually. This improves the quality and accuracy of the practitioner's creative conceptualization and ultimately, speeds the shift toward factual perception.

Our starting place is the mundane or Malkuth awareness. This a composite awareness which integrates all four Elemental regions of the temporal mental body, the Akashic mental body and The One Self, into the temporal present moment. In other words, it combines all the levels of Self-Awareness that TMO is concerned with, but at varying degrees. For example, while centered in the Malkuth awareness, one is generally only slightly, if at all, aware of The One Self and of the Akashic mental body, but is aware to a greater degree of the four regions of the temporal mental body, with the Earth region being foremost.

Since the Malkuth awareness is composed of all the levels of Self-Awareness, the rising or traveling up those levels involves a shedding of layers. It's very much like undressing and stepping out of one garment at a time until the naked Self is revealed. First one steps out of the Earth region of the temporal mental body and sheds awareness of physical sensation. Then one steps out of the Water region, shedding awareness of emotional significance, and then the Air region, shedding awareness of thought. This reveals the Fire region of the temporal mental body and the focused state of pure perception known as the "depth point" or Tiphareth Self. Then even this level of Self-Awareness is shed and one merges with the Akasha and becomes at one with the eternal mental body or Greater Self. And finally, this focalized consciousness is shed and one merges with The One Self or Kether.

This is then followed by a conscious and intentional descent of The One Self into each of the layers of awareness one has just shed. This intentional descent re-integrates awareness of each of these layers into the temporal present moment of the Malkuth consciousness. And since all the layers of Self-Awareness are therefore *equally* united within the temporal present moment, the Adonai Light is generated.

**Practice:**

Begin with the complete relaxation of your physical body. Become aware of all four Elemental regions of your physical body: the Earth, Water, Air and Fire regions. This is the Earth region of your temporal mental body -- your direct perception of physical sensation.

Now shift your awareness to your astral body and release your awareness of physical sensation. Focus exclusively upon the perception of emotional significance contained within the four Elemental regions of your astral body. This is the Water region of your temporal mental body -- your direct perception of emotional significance.

Now shift your awareness to your thinking mind and release your awareness of emotional significance. Focus exclusively upon the perception of thought and the four Elemental types of thoughts that fill your awareness. This is the Air region of your temporal mental body -- your direct perception of thought and idea.

Now shift your awareness to your perceiving mind and release all awareness of thought. Focus exclusively upon pure perception and an emptiness of mind. This is the Fire region of your temporal mental body -- your direct perception of essential meaning.

Take a moment now to perceive the three regions that you have shed. Below you lies your thinking awareness, your awareness of emotional significance and your awareness of physical sensation. You perceive them as separate and distant from your focalized awareness -- they lie at your feet like clothes that you no longer wear. Yet at the same time, you know that they are *your* clothes and you have only shed them temporarily.

Now turn your awareness away from what lies below you and perceive what surrounds you. You find yourself still within the realm of time and sequence but you are no longer stuck in physical space and matter. Here, your surroundings stretch infinitely in every direction and you stand at the exact center of the infinite universe.

Now, as a focalized awareness composed only of Fire, you must release your focus and expand to encompass the whole infinite universe that surrounds you. You must let go of being *a* flame and become the infinitely radiant Fire itself which merges with the Akasha. This infinite expanse of Self is your eternal or Akashic mental body, your Greater Self.

You now *are* the Akasha and below you, you now perceive your entire temporal mental body, surrounded by the entire temporal realm. You are free from space *and* time, and from thinking, feeling and sensing. Yet at the same time, you know that they are *your* clothes and that you have only shed them temporarily.

You are pure perception, awareness and will in their non-sequential state, yet still you are focalized and do not encompass The All. You do not yet experience the infinite number of other similarly focalized awareness in the same way as you experience yourSelf. You can experience many of them individually as yourSelf, but not *all* of them *simultaneously*. To do this you must expand and *become* them *all*.

Let go of your focalization and expand. You must become pure Light. You don't stand *within* The Light; instead, you *are* The Light. Nothingness surrounds you and you are focused inward upon Self.

As The One Self of Kether, you directly experience *every* one of the infinite number of focalized quantas of consciousness that exist throughout all of eternity, *simultaneously*. There is no thing that you do not experience and know as your Self.

When you reach this state or have successfully created your facsimile conception of this state of Awareness, utter the "Ani" (I am).

Now you will reverse this process of ascent and expansion and begin to descend, through a process of contraction and focalization. You will, as it were, put back on all the clothes you have shed, piece by piece until you are again fully encased within your Malkuth awareness. The difference however, is that when you reach your Malkuth, you will have *consciously* united each level of awareness so that you remain fully cognizant of them *all* within the temporal present moment.

The descent begins with a decision to focalize and constrict awareness and with a choosing of which particular focalized quanta of consciousness you wish to descend into. This decision and choice is Chokmah -- Wisdom, the ability to choose correctly. As you constrict your Kethric Awareness, you utter the "Yod" and choose to aim toward your Binah or Greater Self. In Chokmah, you perceive your own Greater Self at a distance and you feel your Self-Awareness pulled down into it.

As you constrict and descend into your Binah Greater Self, utter the first "Heh". Again, you *are* the Akasha and below you lies the entire infinite temporal realm, along with your temporal mental body. Above you, lies Kether and the All-Encompassing Awareness as The One Self. Surrounding you, within the eternal realm itself, are an infinite number of other Akashic mental bodies.

Immediately below you lie many Individual Selves all of which you project into the infinite stream of time and sequence. You must now choose the one temporal mental body that you originally arose from and descend into its Fire region. As you slip into this familiar garment of your Tiphareth Individual Self, utter the "Vav".

Again, you are a perceiving point *within* the temporal realm. You stand within the stream of time itself and immediately below you lie the Air (thinking), Water (feeling) and Earth (sensing) regions of your temporal mental body which root you firmly in space as well as a specific moment of time. Above you lie your Greater Self and The One Self. Surrounding you are an infinite number of other Individual Selves.

Now look below you and perceive the Air, Water and Earth regions of your temporal mental body. Perceive your separation from thinking, feeling and physical sensing. And now descend further and put back on the garment of thought and then that of emotion and finally that of physical sensation. When you are once again aware of your physical body, utter the final "Heh" that signifies Malkuth.

Now very rapidly reclaim your full awareness of the Water, Air and Fire regions of your temporal mental body, your awareness of your eternal Akashic Mental body and of The One Self. Consciously integrate all these levels of Self-Awareness within your Malkuth awareness and utter the "Adonai". All these levels of Self-Awareness now exist simultaneously and with your full consciousness, *within* the present moment of time-space.

When this conscious integration of Self-Awareness occurs within the temporal present moment the Adonai Light becomes manifest and will swirl around your physical body as a Rainbow-Hued cloud. This cloud is composed of all the colors of the rainbow but not in the ordered sequence of a rainbow. Instead, it is composed of random flashes of all the colors which, even though they are random, still exist in harmony and balance.

Now you will circulate this Adonai Light throughout all the unified levels of your Self-Awareness. Inhale the Adonai Light into your lungs and into the very center of your being and then push it outwards with the utterance of "Ribonno Shel Olam". Send it outward from the center of your physical body into the material realm surrounding you and also from the very center of your being to all the other levels of Self within.

With your unified Self-Awareness, perceive the Adonai Light's inward passage. With your Individual Self, perceive its passage through your Tiphareth; with your Greater Self, perceive its passage through your Binah; and with The One Self, perceive its arrival in Kether. The Adonai Light arrives inward at Kether in the same moment it arrives outward at the edges of the material universe, whereupon it begins of fold back upon itself and return to its point of origin -- *your* Malkuth Awareness.

As the Adonai Light constricts, follow its progress just as you did with its expansion. When it once again reaches your Malkuth Awareness and swirls once again around your physical body, utter the "Amen".

The TMO process can be accomplished in its entirety based solely upon Archaeous techniques. In other words, the TMO canticle and its Kabbalistic symbolism can be set aside and one can perform the whole process as an exercise in the direct manipulation of one's conscious awareness using the Archaeous' Hermetic techniques.

This, of course, is pretty much the same thing as performing the TMO "Final Form", which brings home my point that both the Archaeous and TMO lead to the same end.

# THE PATH OF BRILLIANCE
## *THE BRILLIANT WAY AND THE BRILLIANT FORM.*
### 2004

The Path of Brilliance is an outgrowth of my own work with advanced forms of The Magic of IHVH-ADNI (TMO) [1] and the Self-Healing Archaeous [2] techniques. What distinguishes it from both of these disciplines is its direct incorporation of the Kethric Brilliance. In the TMO context, the Path of Brilliance manifests as the Brilliant Form of TMO and in the Self-Healing Archaeous context, it manifests as the Brilliant Way.

Prerequisites to <u>truly</u> practicing the Path of Brilliance are:

1. The ability to clearly sense one's own physical, astral and mental bodies and to directly perceive one's Akashic or eternal mental body.

2. Mastery of the Elements sufficient to be able to load the Elemental regions of one's own physical, astral and mental bodies with their respective Elements.

3. Mastery of the Electric and Magnetic Fluids sufficient to load the Fluidic hemispheres of one's own physical, astral and mental bodies with their respective Fluids.

4. Direct personal experience of the Kethric Brilliance sufficient to be able to invoke it into the physical, astral, mental and Akashic realms and to emanate it in those same realms.

If you do not already posses these prerequisites then it is still possible to derive some small benefit from practice of the Brilliant Way and Brilliant Form through imagining, to the best of your ability, the four bodies, the loading of the Elements and Fluids and the invocation / emanation of the Kethric Brilliance. However, the benefits and effectiveness of this sort of practice would be minor in comparison to the true practice.

## The Brilliant Way

For ease of introducing you to the Path of Brilliance, I will begin with a description of the Brilliant Way, which is rooted in the purely Hermetic techniques presented in the Self-Healing Archaeous. If you have not already pursued the Self-Healing Archaeous then I suggest that you master at least the first three Lessons of the audio series before you think of attempting the Brilliant Way technique.

Like TMO, the Brilliant Way involves a process of ascent, descent, re-ascension, re-descent and finally, emanation, of conscious awareness. And like the Archaeous, the Brilliant way involves the physical, astral, mental and Akashic bodies and their Elemental regions. Where it differs from both is its incorporation of the Kethric Brilliance.

The first phase is the initial ascent of conscious awareness -- from the very limited mundane level, "upwards" and "outwards" to the infinitely inclusive level of Kether -- from the infinitely finite "_**I**_ am" to the infinitely infinite "I _**Am!**_". In a sense, this ascent is a preparation of the vessels which will serve as vehicles for the Kethric Brilliance during the subsequent descent phase. These vessels must first be Elementally and Fluidically balanced before they can truly invoke the Kethric Brilliance and then emanate it without distortion.

The very first step of the initial ascent is the expansion of our awareness from its normal mundane state to a more holistic awareness of our _whole_ physical body. Normally, the mundane awareness is focalized in head. We peer out _through_ our eyes at the world, listen to it _through_ our ears, etc. So our first task is to bring our conscious awareness down into the rest of our body. To do this, become aware of your head region and then your chest region, then your abdominal region and finally, of your leg region.

Now load the leg region |3| of your physical body with the Earth Element.. This is <u>not</u> to be a dynamic accumulation in which you experience a specific tension of the Earth Element; rather, it is a process of _abandoning_ your leg region _to_ the Earth Element and of _letting_ it _be_ the Earth Element. _Feel_ its cold dryness; its absolute cessation of motion; its thirst and its chill; its _desire_ for heat and moisture, for change and motion. _Feel_ its latent fertility, just waiting for the moisture of Water and the warmth of Fire to touch it.

Now load the abdominal region |4| of your physical body with the Water Element. As before, this is not to be a dynamic accumulation but rather, an _abandoning_ of the abdominal region to the Water Element. Let it _be_ the Water Element and _feel_ its cold wetness; its continuous fluidity and constant state of change; its _desire_ for heat and its _longing_ to quench the Earth's dryness. Let the Water seep down into the topmost layer of the dry Earth below, thus uniting your Earth and Water regions.

Now load the chest region |5| of your physical body with the Air Element. _Abandon_ your chest region to the Air Element and let it _be_ the Air. _Feel_ the Air's warmth and dampness; its lightness and weightlessness; its freedom bound only by its _desire_ for guidance and direction. Feel its _need_ to give its heat where there is cold and its moisture, where there is dryness. Let the Air feed its heat to the upper layer of the cold Water below, thus uniting your Water and Air regions.

Now load the head region |6| of your physical body with the Fire Element. _Abandon_ your entire head to the Fire Element and let it _be_ Fire! _Feel_ the Fire's intense heat and searing dryness; its burning, flame-like intensity. _Feel_ its radiant quickness and its absolute and desperate _need_ to quicken the slow cold and evaporate the putrefying dampness. Let the Fire warm the Earth and Water below, bringing the Earth to fertility and evaporating the uppermost layer of the Water, turning it into Air. Unite all four Elemental regions of your physical body and feel the dynamic interaction of all four Elements and regions.

Now load the right hemisphere [7] of your physical body with the Electric Fluid. As with the Elemental loadings, this is <u>not</u> to be a dynamic accumulation but rather, an *abandoning* of the hemisphere to the Electric Fluid. Let the hemisphere *be* the Electric Fluid. *Feel* its dynamic radiance and its undeniable *need* to affect and transform its surroundings.

Now immediately load the left hemisphere [8] of your physical body with the Magnetic Fluid. *Abandon* this entire hemisphere to the Magnetic Fluid and let it *be* the Fluid. *Feel* its dynamic power of attraction and contraction as it draws the radiance of the Electric Fluid unto itself. Feel the incredible *desire* of the Magnetic Fluid for the Electric Fluid and vise versa and in this way, unite the two Fluidic hemispheres of your physical body. Feel also the Fluidic hemispheres of each of the Elemental regions and how each Element is itself divided into two hemispheres, positive and negative which, like the Fluidic hemispheres, are bound together by an inseparable and mutual desire.

Spend a few moments focused upon this completely balanced Fluidic and Elemental composite physical body. Unify the four regions and two hemispheres of your physical body until they are a perfectly balanced whole.

Now invoke the Kethric Brilliance. *Abandon* your entire physical being to it and *be* the Kethric Brilliance. *Feel* its infinite reach; its ability to permeate *all* things equally and without discrimination. *Feel* its qualities of an infinite will-to-good and all-pervading awareness. *Feel* how it obliterates *all* barriers and *all* differences and turns all things into pure White Brilliance.

Now emanate the Kethric Brilliance outward, into the entire physical realm surrounding your physical body. *Abandon* yourself to the radiant properties of the Kethric Brilliance. *Be* that radiance and *feel* your awareness expanding <u>with</u> the Kethric emanation. *Feel* the Kethric Brilliance permeate *all* things equally and without discrimination, touching *all* things with its will-to-good and *consciously* filling *all* things with its all-pervading awareness. *Consciously* turn *all* things into pure White Brilliance.

Spend several moments focused upon this state of emanating the Kethric Brilliance <u>through</u> your perfectly balanced physical body, <u>into</u> the physical realm surrounding you.

Now expand your self-awareness until you become directly aware of your astral body. Become aware of its Fire region and descend into its Air region, then Water region and finally, into its Earth region.

Now load each Elemental region of your astral body |9| with its respective Element in the same way as you did with your physical body. Follow this by loading each hemisphere with its appropriate Fluid and spend several moments focused upon the Elemental and Fluidic balance and unity of your astral body.

Now invoke the Kethric Brilliance into your astral body and then emanate it outward, into the entire astral realm surrounding your astral body.

Spend several moments focused upon this state of emanating the Kethric Brilliance through your perfectly balanced astral body, into the astral realm surrounding you, while *simultaneously* emanating the Kethric Brilliance through your physical body, into the physical realm surrounding you. In other words, you are emanating the Kethric Brilliance *simultaneously* into the physical and astral realms surrounding you.

Now shift your awareness to your temporal mental body or Individual Self. Focus your awareness in its Fire region and descend into its Air, water and then Earth regions.

Now load the Earth region of your temporal mental body |10| with the Earth Element. Next, load the Water region |11| with its Element; then the Air region |12|; and finally, load the Fire region |13| with the Fire Element. Follow this by loading each hemisphere of your temporal mental body with the appropriate Fluid and spend several moments focused upon the Elemental and Fluidic balance and unity of your temporal mental body.

Now invoke the Kethric Brilliance into your temporal mental body and emanate it outward, into the entire mental realm surrounding your temporal mental body.

Spend several moments focused upon this state of emanating the Kethric Brilliance through your perfectly balanced temporal mental body, into the mental realm surrounding you, while *simultaneously* emanating the Kethric Brilliance through your astral body, into the astral realm surrounding you *and*, through your physical body, into the physical realm surrounding you. In other words, you are to *simultaneously* emanate the Kethric Brilliance through your temporal mental body, astral body and physical body, into the physical, astral and mental realms which surround your three temporal bodies.

Now shift your awareness to the Fire region of your temporal mental body and project your awareness into the Akashic realm of your Greater Self or eternal mental body. Invoke the Kethric Brilliance into your Greater Self and emanate it outward, into the Akashic realm surrounding your eternal mental body.

Spend some "time" focused upon this state of emanating the Kethric Brilliance through your eternal mental body, into the Akashic realm surrounding you, while *simultaneously* emanating the Kethric Brilliance through your temporal mental body, into the mental realm surrounding you *and*, through your astral body, into the astral realm surrounding you *and*, through your physical body, into the physical realm surrounding you. In other words, you are to *simultaneously* emanate the Kethric Brilliance through your eternal mental body, your temporal mental body, astral body and physical body, into the physical, astral, mental and Akashic realms which surround your awareness.

Now merge your awareness with Kether ItSelf and abandon yourself completely to the Kethric Brilliance. Within that Brilliance, recognize your Greater Self, Individual Self, astral self and physical self, all united together in actively rooting the Kethric Brilliance into the present moment of physical time-space. Emanate the Kethric Brilliance into all these levels of Self *simultaneously*.

Now, while maintaining this holistic Awareness, condense a micro-focus and cause it to descend to your Greater Self, then to your Individual Self, then into your astral body and finally, into your physical body. Become consciously aware of your physical body with this micro-focus and invoke the Macro-focus of the holistic Awareness within your physical micro-focus. Now emanate the Kethric Brilliance with your micro- and Macro-foci *simultaneously*. In other words, you are to *simultaneously* be the Kethric Brilliance and emanate it into each realm through all of your bodies.

Spend several *minutes* [14] focused in this state of unification and un-interrupted emanation.

Now raise this micro-focus through your various bodies until you once again reside with your awareness in Kether. Follow this by shifting your micro-focus back down through each body until your are again focused within your physical body. You may repeat this ascent and descent of micro-focus as many times as it pleases you to do so.

When you are satisfied and feel you have done enough, stabilize your awareness within your physical body, gently release your Macro-focus and return to your mundane physical awareness in the normal manner.

## The Brilliant Form

The Brilliant Way merges very effectively with the practice of TMO, resulting in TMO's most powerful "form" -- the Brilliant Form TMO.

To begin, follow the initial ascending phase of the Brilliant Way exactly as outlined above. Once you reach Kether and the merging with the Kethric Brilliance, utter the "Ani".

Descend with the "IHVH" by blending the normal TMO method with that of the Brilliant Way in the following manner, remembering throughout to maintain your Macro-focus simultaneously with the movement of your micro-focus: With the "Yod", bring your micro-focus into your Chokmah and emanate the Kethric Brilliance within Chokmah. With the first "Heh", shift your micro-focus to your Binah and emanate the Kethric Brilliance through your Greater Self (eternal mental body), into the Akashic realm. With the "Vav", bring your micro-focus into your Tiphareth and emanate the Kethric Brilliance through your Individual Self (temporal mental body), into the mental realm. With the final "Heh", bring your micro-focus into your Malkuth by first shifting your micro-focus into your astral body and emanating the Kethric Brilliance through your astral body into the astral realm, and then, shifting your micro-focus into your physical body and emanating the Kethric Brilliance through your physical body, into the physical realm.

With the "Adonai", unify your emanations on the various levels so that they are consciously simultaneous within your micro-focus of Malkuth and allow the Adonai Light to erupt as usual.

You will find that the eruption of Adonai Light is continuously fed by the simultaneous multi-level emanation of the Kethric Brilliance and will continue to grow until it either matches the clarity of your emanation of the Kethric Brilliance *or* you will it to halt its growth. When the density of your accumulation of the Adonai Light reaches a comfortable level or quantity, instruct it stop increasing.

At this point you may impregnate the accumulated Adonai Light as per usual. Draw it into yourself as usual with your inhalation and then send it out for the Divine Blessing as usual with the "Ribonno Shel Olam". As it spreads outward and inward, let it ride *with* the Kethric Brilliance which permeates every level of your Self-Awareness.

With the return wave of the Adonai Light, center it upon your desired focus as usual, letting it rest upon its target with the "Amen". During this process, let it flow *with* the Kethric Brilliance which permeates every level of your Self-Awareness and observe how the presence of the Kethric Brilliance increases the penetrating power and effectiveness of the Adonai Light.

If needed, you may rapidly convert the Kethric Brilliance (that you are simultaneously emanating at the level of your target) into more Adonai Light by consciously willing the Kethric Brilliance to *become* the Adonai Light at that level. This will transmute the Kethric Brilliance immediately into the Adonai Light upon the level at which you are working with your micro-focus.

When you are finished with your work, shift your micro-focus to your physical body and firmly root yourself in your physical body awareness. Gently return to normal mundane awareness in the usual manner.

## The Path of Brilliance

Similar to the Akasha, the Kethric Brilliance cannot be accumulated dynamically (i.e., condensed to a pressurized state within the temporal realm). Instead, it can only be emanated with varying degrees of clarity. The greater the degree of clarity with which it is emanated — the greater the degree of its manifestation. If it is emanated with a low degree of clarity, then its manifestation will be hardly noticeable; and if emanated with perfect clarity, then its manifestation will produce immediate effects and be quite noticeable.

But while the Kethric Brilliance ItSelf cannot be condensed or accumulated, it can be transformed into another substance which can then be condensed into an accumulation of whatever density one wishes. Since the Kethric Brilliance is the primal root of all that exists, it can be transmuted into any substance one chooses by merely willing it to be so. In other words, if you wish to transmute the Kethric Brilliance in the Electric Fluid for instance, all you would do is mentally will that the Kethric Brilliance condense itself into the Electric Fluid. In essence, you are drawing the Electric Fluid out of the Kethric Brilliance to the exclusion of everything else that is *potentially* contained within the Kethric Brilliance.

The maximum degree of density of the transmuted Kethric Brilliance will depend upon the degree of clarity of the emanated Kethric Brilliance. For example, if you emanate a low clarity of Kethric Brilliance and then transmute it into an Element, your subsequent quantity of that Element will be fairly limited and thus produce only a small accumulation of the Element. Conversely, if you are able to emanate the Kethric Brilliance with perfect clarity then any transmutation of it will produce a resulting accumulation of infinite potential.

An accumulation produced by transmutation of the Kethric Brilliance will possess a greater power of penetration than a normal accumulation of the same substance derived by normal means. The Kethric Brilliance is, to use an appropriate term of Alchemy, *the* "Universal Solvent" and possesses an *infinite* power of penetration. Thus any direct transmutation of the Kethric Brilliance inherits some degree of this same power (depending, as before, upon the original clarity of emanation).

The primary effect of the emanation of Kethric Brilliance is harmonization. In fact, when performing the Brilliant Way, one can reach a state of perfect harmony between one's inner state of awareness and one's external physical, astral, mental and Akashic environment. And by emanating the Kethric Brilliance in the presence of others, one can establish a deep harmony with them at any level one chooses. This is a very beneficial asset for any sort of healing work.

A very pleasant exercise in regard to harmonizing with one's environment is to perform the Brilliant Way while walking in a natural setting. Balance the Elements and Fluids within your physical body, invoke the Kethric Brilliance and then emanate it into your physical surroundings. Follow this with the same procedure for your astral body and astral environment; your temporal mental body and mental environment; and finally, with your eternal mental body and your Akashic environment. When all four levels are united and you're simultaneously emanating the Kethric Brilliance into your environment at all four levels, you become fully integrated with your surroundings and attain a perfect state of environmental harmonization. This state will produce a heightened degree of perceptual awareness and the ability to communicate directly with your environment. Here one finds the true value and immense Beauty of power *with*, as opposed to power *over*.

Another effect is an increased mobility of the micro-focus within the Macro-Focus [15]. In the presence of the Kethric Brilliance, translocation of the micro-focus can be instantaneous. For example, with the Brilliant Form TMO, the micro-focus can be instantly shifted to any level of self-awareness and to any location within the four realms (physical, astral, mental and Akashic), making the treatment of multiple subjects or attending to several targets, very easy and rapid.

With sufficient practice of the Brilliant Way technique it is possible to load and balance the Elements and Fluids within your three temporal bodies, *instantly*, by merely invoking the Kethric Brilliance. In other words, the Fluidic and Elemental balancing becomes a *consequence of* the presence of the Kethric Brilliance instead of its precursor. This is similar to the creation of a finger ritual [16] in which repetition builds a "volt" that can be activated by a single simple action instead of a series of complex actions.

Notes:

1. See http://www.tmo-wg.net for more info.

2. See http://www.abardoncompanion.com/Arch-info.html for more info.

3. The "leg region" is attributed to the Earth Element and encompasses the area from the tops of your hips downward, including your genitalia, to the soles of your feet and also, your hands from wrists to fingertips.

4. The "abdominal region" is attributed to the Water Element and encompasses the area from your diaphragm muscle downward to your pelvis, excluding your sexual organs; and also your forearms, from elbows to wrists.

5. The "chest region" is attributed to the Air Element and encompasses the area from the base of your neck downward to your diaphragm muscle and also, your upper arms from elbows to shoulders.

6. The "head region" is attributed to the Fire Element and encompasses the whole head and neck.

7. The "right hemisphere" is attributed to the Electric Fluid and encompasses the **_most_** dominant half of your body. In the average person, this will correspond to whichever hand you use automatically. For the average right-handed person, this will be the right-hand side of the body and for the average left-handed person, this will be the left-hand side of the body. However, the Fluidic hemispheres have more to do with one's astral character, so there will be exceptions to this "rule". Each of the two hemispheres perfectly bisect the body and all four regions into equal left-right halves.

8. The "left hemisphere" is attributed to the Magnetic Fluid and encompasses the **_least_** dominant half of your body. For the average right-handed person, this will be the left-hand side of the body and for the average left-handed person, this will be the right-hand side of the body.

9. The Elemental regions of the astral body surround the same area where the Elemental regions of the physical body are located. Thus the Earth region of the astral body is the lowest, surrounding the physical leg region, and is composed of the foundational emotions from which all the rest of your emotions spring. The Water region surrounds the physical abdominal region and is composed of those emotions which translate the foundation into action. The Air region surrounds the physical chest region and is composed of those emotions that communicate the foundation. And finally, the Fire region surrounds the physical head region and is composed of the most fleeting and passionate emotions whose expression is transformative.

10. The "Earth region" of the temporal mental body is, effectively, your physical awareness. So in this case, you are to load your entire physical body with the Earth Element.

11. I.e., load your emotional awareness or entire astral body with the Water Element.

12. I.e., load the thinking aspect of your awareness with the Air Element.

13. I.e., load the perceiving aspect of your awareness with the Fire Element.

14. Maintain this state for as long as it pleases you to do so.

15. See http://www.ABardonCompanion.com/TMO-FinalForm.html for an explanation of micro- and Macro-focus in the TMO context.

16. See Franz Bardon's "*Initiation Into Hermetics*", Step Four, Physical Training.

# KNOW THYSELF
## A GUIDE TO RECOGNIZING THE ESSENTIAL SELF

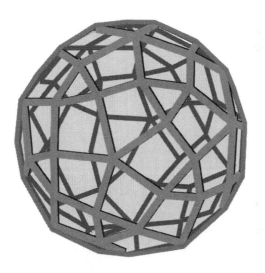

## AUDIO SERIES

In 2006 I developed an audio series consisting of an introduction followed by three meditations exploring the nature of Self.

# INTRODUCTION

In Hermetics, like any other system of philosophy, we use a variety of terms which may or may not be used commonly, without really defining the specific meaning we wish to convey with their use. Most often, we intend to communicate something more with them than their common, every day definitions would imply and it is assumed that you either already know what distinguishes their use from the ordinary meaning or will figure it out. One such term is "self" and although it is true that if you are seriously pursuing the work of Franz Bardon's *Initiation Into Hermetics*, you will eventually be led to an understanding of its Hermetic use, it is nonetheless *very* advantageous if you have prior knowledge and can recognize the essential Self from the outset. Clarifying what is truly meant to be communicated by this seemingly simple word in the *Hermetic* context, will be the subject of all that follows and, as usual, this will be an experiential journey, not just an intellectual one.

Self is a very complex, multi-layered combination of factors whose definition varies depending upon one's perspective. Nonetheless, we can define an essential, or core Self (with a capital 'S'), from which all of these layers spring and to which, all of the various factors cling. Simply put, the essential Self is the ***intentional*** aspect of our overall awareness which is capable of ***objective*** perception and expression.

The words ***intentional*** and ***objective*** are important here because the essential Self is **always** intentional and objective. It is this quality that distinguishes it from the other aspects of human consciousness which make up the overall awareness.

Our overall or mundane awareness is a mixture of ***intentional*** and ***unintentional*** factors. The intentional aspect can be equated with the "conscious mind" and the unintentional aspect, with the "subconscious mind". However, I do not particularly like these terms for Hermetic use since they do not really speak, in any practical way, to the true differences and connections between these factors, so I will abandon them and stick to "intentional" and "unintentional".

It is the intentional awareness that looks at an object and perceives its details; it is the unintentional awareness that simultaneously perceives everything else in the field of peripheral vision (outside of the intentional focus) and, normally, the unintentional awareness is what places all of these perceptions into personal, emotional context. The intentional awareness thinks things through before speaking; the unintentional awareness colors all of those thoughts by relating them to memories and emotional attitudes. The intentional awareness is spontaneous and "in the moment"; the unintentional awareness is habitual and always seeks to relate the present moment to past moments.

Of course, the intentional awareness is capable of reshaping the contents of the unintentional awareness and of thus intentionalizing those contents. This is essentially the process of character transformation described in Steps One and Two of *Initiation Into Hermetics*. Once the transformation of the unintentional awareness's subjectifying content is complete, it can then be used *objectively* by the intentional awareness in perception and expression. In other words, it becomes a *tool* of the essential Self instead of something that *obscures* the essential Self.

From here on, we will concern ourselves primarily with the intentional aspect of awareness since this is our route to understanding the essential Self.

The intentional awareness has a twin nature. It is both a perceiver and an expresser, either sequentially or simultaneously. It perceives its external environment and/or itself, and it expresses itself by transforming itself and/or its environment.

Perception is Watery and Magnetic. The perceiver is affected by the perception and in some way transformed by the experience. When we perceive something, we experience the *objective* effects that the object of perception exerts upon our senses and simultaneously, we experience the reaction to those effects generated by the *subjectifying* aspects of awareness. Perception places the perceiver into context with the universe.

Perception is physically, astrally and mentally nourishing. It exercises and stimulates our senses and thus energizes our bodies. It broadens our range of experience and causes us to grow and evolve.

Expression, on the other hand, is Fiery and Electric. Expression seeks to change the Universe so that it comes into context with us or in some way reflects our essence. In expression, we release and externalize our inner content. We then learn and grow by evaluating the success or failure of our expression and thus the contextual appropriateness of our expression evolves.

Expression itself is physically, astrally and mentally depleting. It drains us of energy as we externalize our inner content. However, we gain considerable nourishment in the process of perceiving the results of our expression and reaping the benefits when our expression has been successful -- so much so that this can far outweigh any depletion.

As I noted earlier, perception and expression can occur separately or simultaneously. It can be said that the emotional reaction we generate in response to perception is an action of the expressive awareness; and similarly, that we cannot express without simultaneously perceiving the effects of our expression. Like Fire and Water, Electric and Magnetic -- perception and expression are sides of the same coin.

Perception and expression occur either in a subjective mode or an objective mode or, most usually, as a combination of these two modes.

Subjective mode is Earthy. It is all about personal context. For example, when we smell an aroma, we immediately associate it with a memory and an emotional valuation (good/bad/indifferent) and thus *interpret* the aroma in the context of our heretofore accumulated personal experience.

Objective mode on the other hand, is Airy and is all about distancing oneself from personal contextualization. Objective mode perceives the aroma as what *it* is instead of as how we *feel* about it or what memories we may have that relate to it.

Another example is the sensation of cold. In subjective mode, we suffer and shiver and experience cold as a thing to be avoided. In objective mode, we note the perception of cold and its effects upon our body but without an emotional valuation of good or bad -- it simply *is* – and we don't suffer, even if we are shivering.

In the context of the expressive awareness, subjective mode is very emotive and personal. Conversely, objective mode is very dispassionate and impersonal expression – one which reflects a broader context than the purely personal. An angry tirade is an example of subjective mode expression and the Step Two mental exercises from *Initiation Into Hermetics* (where you are isolating each sense, even from the emotions, and using them creatively) is an example of objective mode expression.

With perception, objective mode is the most nourishing since it entails no creative subjectification and thus no expenditure of energy. Furthermore, objective perception is a much more holistic experience and more growth ensues.

With expression, subjective mode is the more nourishing since it exercises and stimulates the self-contextualizing and self-affirming aspects of the personality. Subjective mode expression is ultimately more holistic than objective expression.

By nature, the intentional awareness primarily perceives and expresses by focusing itself, either upon the object of perception or the receptacle of expression. It is also capable of rejecting focus entirely and entering a non-focal state of pure BEing, akin to Bardon's Step One emptiness of mind, but we will not dwell on that possibility just yet since it has little to do with the initial recognition of essential Self.

The intentional awareness can expand and contract its focus. It can limit its field of perception or expression to a single infinitely finite point or it can expand its field to encompass infinity itself, all by act of will or intention. It can hold just a singular focus or it can expand to engage many focal points simultaneously. In this regard, the intentional awareness is very fluid and adaptive, capable of adopting any shape or size it wishes.

The intentional awareness can also move its self-aware focus from one place to another. For example, it can focus itself within your right big toe and then relocate its focus to your left thumb. Similarly, it can project its self-aware focus form its normal anchoring in your own physical body, into an external object or person. It can focus upon the contemplation of one idea and then engage another idea in the next moment. All of these are aspects of its motive power to relocate its self-aware focus.

As I stated earlier, our normal, mundane awareness manifests as a combination of intentional and unintentional factors. However, western society is generally built around encouraging the unintentional and subjective factors of awareness and inhibiting the intentional and objective factors. A good example of this is the invasive presence of commercial advertisements which manipulate the unintentional ("subconscious"), subjectifying awareness into purchasing brand 'X' because it will make you feel good, sexy, happy, etc. Unfortunately, this sort of consumption-based manipulation is present in nearly all aspects of western culture – we see it in politics, in the educational system, in medicine, science and religion, and so on. In the face of such overwhelming and intrinsic manipulation, most become used to living in the unintentional-subjective mode and have little inkling of the immensely powerful intentional-objective awareness that slumbers within.

Once recognized though, the intentional-objective awareness of the essential Self begins to permeate the whole of one's existence and little by little, becomes the true seat of mundane awareness. This unleashing of the intentional-objective powers of the essential Self is the major portion of the early work of Hermetic initiation. In the very first exercises of Step One, the intentional-objective awareness is focused inwardly, upon the mind, the character and the body. Although it is no where stated that the student is immediately exercising their essential Self in this perceptual process of self-examination and self-discovery, it still has the effect of rending the first veil and setting in motion a self-revelatory process.

In Step Two, the veil is further rent through combining the expressive, creative power of the intentional-objective awareness with its perceptual powers. With the mental exercises, the student uses their expressive intentional-objective power as they work creatively with each of their senses in isolation, while simultaneously using their perceptual intentional-objective powers to perceive and evaluate their sensory creations. With the astral exercises, the student employs their intentional-objective creative power in the transformation of their character, while simultaneously exercising their intentional-objective perceptual powers in monitoring of the character's habitual nature. And finally, with the physical exercises, the student uses their expressive intentional-objective powers to create desired states within their physical body, while simultaneously strengthening their perceptual intentional-objective power to experience and verify those states. All in all, the work of Step Two begins to shift the seat of awareness away from the unintentional-subjective and leads it firmly toward taking root in the intentional-objective.

Step Three firmly sets the seat of awareness to intentional-objective mode by training the intentional-objective awareness how to work *with* the intentional-subjective awareness. This is seen in the finalization of the character transformation in which the unintentional content that rules the subjectifying awareness, has been objectively intentionalized. This transforms the subjectifying character into an *objectively-intentional* creature that *expresses* the essential Self. The Step Three mental, astral and physical exercises also effect the same unification of the objective and subjective powers of the intentional awareness by working with multi-sensorial creations that evoke subjective responses amidst objective expression.

If the work of Step Three has not successfully and permanently shifted the seat of normal awareness to that of the intentional-objective awareness of the essential Self, then the work of Step Four will be nearly impossible to accomplish. This is most notable when it comes to the mental "transplantation of consciousness" because *only* the intentional-objective awareness is capable of transferring its self-awareness from one place to another. Likewise with the astral exercises – *only* the intentional objective awareness is capable of truly connecting with the elements sufficient for their accumulation and *only* the intentional-objective awareness is capable of shifting its focus from one internal body part to another. And as many have discovered in working with the physical exercises of Step Four, *only* the intentional-objective awareness of the essential Self is capable of successfully and wisely wielding the expressive powers of the Elements without causing self-harm.

When Franz Bardon wrote *Initiation Into Hermetics*, the world was just at the beginning of the "commercial age" which has so drastically inhibited easy access to the intentional-objective awareness within western society. In his time, I imagine that pursuing the work of the Steps would have fairly rapidly unveiled the nature of the essential Self to the student. Today however, the situation is somewhat different and many are having difficulty with this point. It is, as I stated at the outset, my hope that the series of meditations and exercises which follow will help lead all those who are pursuing the work of IIH, very rapidly to the recognition of their essential Self and thus make their progress that much easier and secure.

# KNOW THYSELF MEDITATION ONE
## PHYSICAL PERCEPTION

In this meditation exercise, we will explore the nature of perception through our physical senses. We will identify the different aspects of awareness involved and examine the roles that each aspect plays in physical perception.

In order to effectively fulfill this task, there are certain environmental details that must be seen to first. Perform this meditation exercise in a room where you are assured privacy for the duration. Your room needs to be moderately lit – not too bright nor too dim – and contain at least one object for you to look at. The nature of this object does not matter. You must be able to sit or recline comfortably, without having to expend any energy to keep yourself upright. The ideal position for this meditation exercise is reclining, with your head slightly elevated above your chest, and your chest, slightly elevated above your abdomen. This can be achieved by lying on your back with a couple of pillows propped beneath your head and shoulders.

Since we will be working with all of the physical senses, you will also need to have readily available something to taste, something to smell and something to hear. It doesn't particularly matter what items you choose, so long as they can be sensed through taste, smell and hearing. In regard to sound, it would be best if you can work in a non-soundproofed room and thus rely on environmental sounds external to your room, but if this is not possible, I recommend a small bell or a piece of pottery or glass that you can make ring by gently tapping.

So, pause this recording and assemble everything you need.

Once everything is ready, make yourself as physically comfortable as you can and take a few moments to get settled.

(pause)

So, to begin . . .

Focus your eyes on the object you have chosen to observe visually.

(pause)

In the few moments you have been looking at your object, several things have transpired, all of which *together* have constitute your perception of this object. However, the *only* information your eyes have provided are the objective details of your object – all the rest of the information within your perception has come from other sources.

Look very intently at your object now and intentionally note each of its objective attributes. Note its size, its shape, its texture and its colors. These are the *objective* details that your eyes reveal to your intentional awareness.

(pause)

Now take notice of the emotional feelings and reactions that the objective details of your object evoke within you. How does its shape make you feel? Or each of its colors? Its size and texture?

(pause)

At first, these emotional responses involve you and you truly experience them, but now I want you to consider them *objectively*, without any direct involvement. Note them and accept them as *objective* facts. Focus your eyes on one specific aspect of your object at a time and objectively perceive your spontaneous emotional reaction to each one.

(pause)

And now, look at the object as a whole and objectively perceive your emotional reaction.

(pause)

These spontaneous emotional reactions to objective visual information arise from within the unintentional awareness and are rooted in your past experience with the same or similar objective details that are possessed by your object. This input from the unintentional awareness gives each objective detail personal *significance*.

Take a few moments now to once again observe the objective details of your object and again perceive the emotional responses that arise. Try to trace these emotional responses back to the memories that founded them.

(pause)

Throughout the past few minutes of looking at your object and of perceiving your emotional responses to its features, you may have noticed an internal voice that provides a running verbal description of what you are perceiving. It voices your thoughts as they occur and gives names to everything you are perceiving and feeling. This voice also has its origin in the unintentional awareness and it is the means by which the unintentional awareness intellectually integrates your perception of the objective details with your emotional responses. It acts like a glue that holds the objective details and their emotional significance together in a way that you can comprehend.

When your attention is focused, the inner dialogue will naturally pertain in some way to your focal object. When your mind is unfocussed however, the inner voice becomes mind chatter and it can then range over a broad spectrum of topics, ideas, feelings, etc., ultimately reflecting the contents of the unintentional awareness.

Once again, view the objective details of your object and this time, objectively note the contents of your inner dialogue.

(pause)

Now shift your attention to your emotional reactions and note the dialogue that accompanies them as well.

(pause)

Ordinarily, the inner dialogue and our emotional valuations provide information that we do not objectively evaluate or verify. In fact, we are most often oblivious of its existence as the major portion of perception!

Take a moment now to compare the objective information perceived by your eyes, with the subjective information provided by your emotional reactions and internal dialogue. How much, if at all, have your emotional reactions and inner dialogue distorted, informed or transformed your perception of objective details?

(pause)

What you have just accomplished is intentional-objective perception. You have intentionally perceived the objective details of your object and you have *objectively* perceived the subjectifying responses of your unintentional awareness to those objective details. Even though your perception included a great amount of subjective information from your unintentional awareness, you nonetheless perceived it with your intentional-objective awareness.

Your intentional-objective awareness is, of course, your essential Self.

Next, we will use our intentional-objective awareness to perceive sound. Close your eyes and focus your awareness upon your hearing. Listen for external noises (or ring your bell) and focus intently upon your perception of the sound.

Note its objective details of pitch, loudness, duration, rhythm, etc.

(pause)

And now focus upon how you feel emotionally about this sound. Does it please you or displease you or neither?

(pause)

Note the contents of your accompanying internal dialogue and objectively perceive its relevance.

(pause)

Note that when perceiving sounds whose origins you cannot see, your mind generates its own images to describe the sound's origin. These are closely related to your internal dialogue and emotional reactions and share the same subjective source within your unintentional awareness. With your intentional-objective awareness, observe the images that your mind puts forth to depict the sound's origin or cause.

(pause)

Now compare the differences between the objective details of the sound and the subjective content provided by your unintentional awareness.

(pause)

Next, we will use our intentional-objective awareness to perceive aroma. Close your eyes and focus your awareness upon your sense of smell. Inhale the aroma of your chosen item and focus intently upon your perception of its scent.

Note its objective details and note what parts of your olfactory organ are affected by the aroma.

(pause)

And now focus upon how you feel emotionally about this scent. Does it please you or displease you or neither?

(pause)

Note the contents of your accompanying internal dialogue and objectively perceive its relevance.

(pause)

Note that when perceiving an aroma, your mind immediately tries to define it, tries to name what it is you're smelling through images. These are closely related to your internal dialogue and emotional reactions and share the same subjective source within your unintentional awareness. With your intentional-objective awareness, observe the images that your mind puts forth to define the aroma.

(pause)

Now compare the differences between the objective details of the scent and the subjective content provided by your unintentional awareness.

(pause)

Next, we will use our intentional-objective awareness to perceive flavor. Close your eyes and focus your awareness upon your sense of taste. Lick, sip or take a small bite of your chosen item and focus intently upon your perception of the flavor.

Note the objective details of the flavor you perceive with your tongue.

(pause)

And now focus upon how you feel emotionally about this taste. Does it please you or displease you or neither?

(pause)

Note the contents of your accompanying internal dialogue and objectively perceive its relevance.

(pause)

Now compare the differences between the objective details of the flavor and the subjective content provided by your unintentional awareness.

(pause)

Next we come to our exploration of perception through our sense of touch or physical feeling. There really is no adequate name for this sense – the terms "touch" and "tactile" merely cover one aspect of all that this sense reveals to our awareness. The tactile aspect is geared toward sensing the *external* environment and is reliant upon nerve endings within the layers of skin capable of detecting objective environmental factors such as texture, temperature and pressure. The non-tactile aspect on the other hand, is geared toward sensing our *internal* environment, such as a muscular ache, an itchy patch of skin or intestinal gas, and is likewise reliant upon specialized nerve endings, except that these include sensory nerves spread throughout our body's deeper tissue and bone.

Ultimately, this is the sense that most ties our awareness to our physical body and to physical existence. It also pervades or influences perception through our other four physical senses. For example, if what we are looking at is too bright, we *feel* discomfort in our eyes; if a sound is too loud or too shrill, we likewise *feel* discomfort in our ears; and, with both smell and taste, tactile sensations are involved as you draw air in through the sinuses and take food or drink into the mouth.

Each of these tactile sensations that occur during the ***process*** of perception subtly, or not-so-subtly, influence the resulting perception, especially at an emotional level. For example, if it physically hurts our eyes to look at something, we stop looking at it and form a negative emotional memory that keeps us from looking at similar should we encounter it again. Conversely, if it gives us physical pleasure to look at a thing, then we keep looking and form a positive emotional memory that leads us to seek out the observation of similar things.

The perceptions of physical feeling are normally ***processed*** by the unintentional-subjective awareness before they even register within the intentional awareness. In other words, we create an **immediate** emotional valuation of the sensation. This is a biologically "hard wired" feature of instinctive self-preservation which generates an immediate response to physical threat. For example, when you touch something so hot that it burns your fingertip, your hand immediately withdraws without your having to first think, "Oh, that's too hot, I'd better not leave my finger there while the skin melts."

In spite of this biological imperative of self-preservation, we are quite capable of intentional-objective perception through and with this sense. We cannot, of course, *eliminate* the unintentional-subjective component, but we *can* observe it objectively and without involvement, and take it as a piece of objective information concerning how the sensation affects us.

So, let's get back to our exploration and put these words and ideas into practice.

Close your eyes and sense the air temperature of the room you are in. Is it warm? Cool? Or just right?

(pause)

Note the value judgment inherent to determining the temperature. It is completely based upon the variation of the temperature from your "comfort zone". If the temperature is lower than this zone then you judge it cool; if higher, then you judge it warm. The only *objective* information revealed is the relationship of the actual air temperature to your personal comfort level.

Now let's turn this sense inward and perceive the interior of our own bodies. Notice the sensation of the air entering your sinuses as you inhale, or passing over your tongue, if you are breathing through your mouth. Focus your awareness upon the exact physical location of this sensation and experience it closely.

(pause)

Again, there is the immediate value judgment of relative warmth or coolness of the air and of its relative goodness or badness. But beyond this emotional *reaction* to the physical sensation, there is the objective *experience* of sensation. The objective experience *includes* the unintentional-subjective valuations, but it's more than just how we feel about the sensation -- it's also our actual real-time experience of the sensation as it is occurring.

Focus your intentional awareness upon this experience of the sensation of the inhaled air passing over nerve endings and ignore any emotional value judgments that arise.

(pause)

Now follow this sensation inward. Sense the air as it touches deeper areas of your sinuses and then throat. With each inhalation, follow the sensation deeper and deeper until you actually feel the air filling your lungs.

(pause)

Now expand your focus so that you are sensing your entire chest area as a whole. *Experience* the feeling of your chest expanding with each inhalation and contracting with each exhalation.

(pause)

Now shift your awareness to your right hand and experience all of the sensations present within it.

(pause)

Now expand your awareness so that you experience the sensation of your entire physical body as a whole. Spend a few moments here now, *experiencing* what it feels like to be in your physical body. Freely allow the subjective emotional judgments to arise and let them inform you of your emotional attitudes about your own body.

(longish pause)

Focus again on the sound of my voice and gently return to an awareness of your surroundings.

(pause)

Open your eyes and sit up from your reclining position while I say a few words.

I hope that from this brief exploration you have learned a few important things about physical perception. First among them is the degree to which your unintentional-subjective awareness influences the process of perceiving. And second is the degree to which your intentional-objective awareness can intercede in the process of perception and make of it something much more informative.

When left to the unintentional-subjective awareness, perception informs us mostly about ourselves and about how we relate to the world. But when we intercede with our intentional-objective awareness, perception begins to inform us about the objective reality that exists separate from our emotional reactions to it. It also provides us with an objective perception of our own subjectifying content and its relationship to the objective reality.

Use of our intentional-objective awareness reveals the subjective filter through which we normally perceive the world and ourselves.

I suggest that during the coming days and weeks, you use the faculties of the intentional-objective awareness in your acts of perception. Truly see the things you look at and experience the sensations you encounter. Savor them to their fullest and draw from them their objective meanings hidden among your subjective reactions. Use your senses and your awareness to spend time truly experiencing life within the miracle of your own body!

# KNOW THYSELF MEDITATION TWO
## ASTRAL PERCEPTION

In this meditation exercise, we will explore the nature of our own astral body and perception through our astral senses. Our first task will be to experientially identify our own unique astral body and to accomplish this, I will be introducing a new technique.

Our work this time does not require all of the special environmental arrangements necessary for the first meditation exercise. All you will need is a room where you are assured of privacy and the ability to recline comfortably. Again, the preferred physical posture for this meditation exercise is reclining, with your head slightly elevated above your chest, and your chest slightly elevated above your abdomen.

So, get comfortable in your reclining position and close your eyes . . .

(pause)

To begin, we need to truly connect our intentional-objective awareness with our physical body. The best way to achieve this is by turning our tactile, feeling sense inward and *experiencing* how it feels to be in our body.

Focus your awareness in your left foot and perceive the sensations present within it. Objectively note the subjective content inherent to this perception and focus your attention upon the *experience* of the sensation.

(pause)

Now shift your awareness to your left calf and likewise perceive the sensations present within it. Objectively note the subjective content and focus upon the *experience* of the sensation.

(pause)

Now shift your awareness to your left thigh and repeat the same regimen of perception and experience.

(pause)

Now shift to your left hip and buttocks.

(pause)

Now repeat the same sequence with your right foot, (pause) calf, (pause) thigh, (pause) hip and buttocks (pause).

Now expand your awareness to encompass your entire left and right legs, from hips to feet, simultaneously, and perceive the sensations present within this region. Objectively note the subjective content inherent to this perception and focus your attention upon the *experience* of the sensation.

(pause)

Now expand your awareness to include your left hand, your right hand, and your pelvic region, within your field of perception. Perceive and experience your hands and pelvic region as they are each included.

(pause)

Now expand to include your left forearm, your right forearm and your abdomen, perceiving and experiencing as each is included within your field of perception.

(pause)

Now expand to include your left upper-arm and shoulder, your right upper-arm and shoulder, and your entire chest area.

(pause)

And finally, expand your field of perception to include your neck and head. Perceive and experience your neck and head as they are added.

(pause)

Spread your awareness throughout your entire physical body and truly *experience* what it feels like to be *in* it.

(pause)

Recognize that you – an intentional-objective awareness – an essential Self – are *in* your physical body. You *occupy* your physical body. You *use* your physical body. But you are not *dependant upon* your physical body. *You exist aside from your physical body. You can choose to not be affected by your body, to not experience your body.*

(pause)

Focus your awareness upon the subjective emotional aspect of your perception of your physical body. Perceive the ways that you feel emotionally about your body as a whole and about each of its parts.

(pause)

This body of emotional feelings is the densest, most personalized aspect of your astral body. On average, its content is almost exclusively derived from the unintentional awareness. Which means that the average person has really had little or no hand in shaping how they truly feel about their own bodies, even though these attitudes color so much of how a person expresses themselves through their body.

The next layer of our astral body is composed of this same emotion-substance but of a somewhat more rarified form. Since we are generally so unused to directly perceiving this astral emotion-substance we will need to begin the process of attaining a perception by first *imagining* its presence and in this way, come to *experience* it.

Begin by imagining that this emotion-substance forms a thick, cocoon-like layer surrounding your physical body. Let it be without detail or color for now. It is just raw emotion-substance.

(pause)

Now focus your awareness upon your own personality traits, both positive and negative. Name them to the best of your ability and as you name each one, imagine that it gives form to a portion of the emotion-substance surrounding your physical body.

(long pause)

Eventually, all of the emotion-substance surrounding your body is taken over by your character traits. The result is a very complex shell filled with the symbolic colors and shapes of your specific personality traits.

(pause)

Now focus upon a specific trait-form that exists within this body of emotion-substance. Use your intentional-objective awareness to perceive this character trait and objectively note the subjective content inherent to this perception.

(pause)

Now focus your attention upon the *experience* of this trait. Really place yourself within the experience of what it feels like to **be** this trait.

(pause)

Now shift your focus to an adjacent trait within your emotion-substance body and follow the same perceptual and experiential process in its exploration. Perceive it and note its subjective content, then experience what it feels like to **be** this trait.

(pause)

Continue in this manner, shifting your focus from one trait to the next until you have perceived and experienced all of your personality traits reflected within your emotion-substance body.

(long pause)

Now expand your awareness to include your entire emotion-substance body and all of your character traits simultaneously within your field of perception and truly *experience* what it feels like to be **in** it.

(long pause)

This layer of your astral body represents the form your character gives to, or impresses upon, the astral substance. Normally, the character traits that give form to this aspect of the astral body are the product of unintentional processes and as such, this aspect of the astral body infuses perception and expression with unintentional-subjective content. This astral content acts as one of our main subjectifying filters in perception.

Perception through this aspect of the astral body occurs by a process of emotional emulation in which an external emotional state is compared with the contents of our own character. We then experience either resonance or dissonance in relation with the external emotional state, depending upon whether or not we recognize that state within our own emotional content. Resonance occurs when we find similarity and are able to emulate the state within our own astral body and, conversely, dissonance occurs when there is no recognition and we cannot achieve emulation. Thus the range and quality of the emotions that have been given form within this layer of our astral body determines our astral sensitivity.

When we transform our character from its ordinary state of unintention-ality, into a creation of the intentional-objective awareness, then the nature and quality of our astral body and its powers of perception and expression shift from the unintentional to the intentional. In other words, when the character traits that give form to the emotion-substance of the astral body become a matter of intention and positive purpose, then the astral body itself becomes a **tool** of the essential Self.

Once the character has been transformed into an intentionalized state, it ceases to be restricted by the limitations of its own content and can then achieve resonance with emotional states not present within the scope of its own content. This is when the so called astral senses of clairvoyance, clairaudience and clairsentience become accessible to the intentional awareness. Here, the intentional awareness is able to use the refined astral body to achieve resonance with any emotional states it chooses, thus gaining a direct emotional *experience* of those states.

For now though, we will set aside discussing the attributes of the transformed astral body and return to our exploration of the more basic astral perception available to all.

Once again, focus your awareness upon the perception of your entire emotion-substance body and all of the character traits that give it form. *Experience* what it feels like to be **in** this body.

(pause)

Now gently open your eyes and expand your perceiving awareness to include an external examination of the room you are in. Simultaneously, retain your awareness of your astral body.

Now take note of the ways that your astral body reacts or interacts with the details of the room. Note which details your astral body experiences resonance with and which it experiences dissonance with. Note which details give you emotional comfort and satisfaction, and which elicit a sense of repulsion and emotional discomfort.

(pause)

Focus your awareness **into** your astral body's *experience* of resonance and dissonance as it occurs.

(long pause)

Note the degree to which these astral perceptions of your surroundings inform you primarily of *your reaction to* the objective details you are observing.

(pause)

Aside from your subjective astral reaction, there is also the emotional state of the object itself which is in no way dependant upon your emotional reaction. It is this objective emotional state of the object itself to which *your* astral body reacts. Focus your intentional-objective awareness upon the direct perception of the emotional state that each object itself possesses separate from your astral reaction to it.

(long pause)

Focus again on the sound of my voice and gently return to a more normal perception of your surroundings.

Sit upright and reorient yourself while I say a few words in closing.

The great difficulty in designing this particular meditation exercise of exploring the astral body is the fact that it must be suited to a broad spectrum of personalities. If you have already achieved the transformation of your character as described in the first three Steps of *Initiation Into Hermetics*, then you will naturally be capable of far more precise astral perception than covered by this brief exploration. If that is your situation, then I recommend further exploration and experimentation along those lines. Use the methods I've outlined to deepen your objective perception of the objective emotional states inherent to your surroundings.

If on the other hand, you have not engaged in a disciplined examination and transformation of your personal character, then I highly recommend it to you! Doing so will, among other benefits, open your perceptual faculties to a whole new and far richer view of the world and of yourself.

In any event, I suggest that over the coming days and weeks you use the faculties of your intentional-objective awareness and actively pursue astral perception in your mundane encounters. Truly experience the emotional states you encounter. Savor them to their fullest and draw from them their objective meanings hidden among your subjective reactions. Use your awareness to spend time truly experiencing life within the miracle of your own astral body!

# KNOW THYSELF MEDITATION THREE
## MENTAL PERCEPTION

In this meditation exercise, we will explore the nature of our own mental body and mental perception.

This time you will need to have one simple object close at hand for viewing later. It does not matter what this object is. And as usual, you will need a room where you are assured of privacy and the ability to recline comfortably. The preferred physical posture for this meditation exercise is reclining, with your head slightly elevated above your chest, and your chest slightly elevated above your abdomen.

So, get comfortable in your reclining position and close your eyes . . .

(pause)

To begin, we will need to fully relax our physical body and disengage our awareness from bodily distractions.

Begin by shifting your awareness into both feet simultaneously and relax all the muscles in your feet. Now gently raise your awareness upward through your body and relax the muscles in each area as your awareness passes through it. First will be your ankles, then calves, thighs, hips and hands; then abdomen, lower back and forearms; then chest, upper back, upper arms and shoulders; then neck, jaw, scalp and finally, relax all of the muscles in your face.

(pause)

Now, with your body's muscles fully relaxed, turn your attention away from bodily concerns and focus upon my words.

My first word for your consideration is "warrior".

(pause)

In response to this word, your mind automatically generated a series of images, emotions and thoughts, all somehow related to the concept of "warrior". All of these arose spontaneously from your unintentional awareness and were rooted in your past experiences and in the thoughts you have integrated over the course of your life.

Your response to this word was unique in as much as the content of your own unintentional awareness reflects the unique circumstances of your life. A different person will experience somewhat different images, emotions and thoughts than you did.

Let's try that again but with a new word -- and this time, take note of what transpires _as_ it occurs. The new word is "Elephant".

(pause)

As before, your unintentional awareness will have generated an image, or series of images, related to "Elephant". Using your intentional objective awareness, try to discern where these images came from. Do they come from a personal encounter with an Elephant? Or from a film about Elephants? Or from a book?

(pause)

Now, again using your intentional objective awareness, examine the emotions that accompany these images. How does the image of "Elephant" make you feel? Is this feeling related to your emotional state at the time when the image of "Elephant" was originally formed? For example, if the image comes from when you saw an Elephant at a zoo as a small child and you were having a pleasant day with your parents visiting the zoo, then odds are that the emotions that arise now, carry with them the imprint or flavor of that childhood happiness.

(pause)

Once again using your intentional objective awareness, examine the thoughts and ideas that arise in unison with the images and emotions in response to the word "Elephant". As before, try to discern the origin of these thoughts. Are they your own original thoughts or are they thoughts you've learned or heard from others?

(pause)

Overall, what percentage of your automatic response to the word "Elephant" comes from your own personal interaction with an Elephant and how much of it comes from second-hand sources such as things you've heard or read?

(pause)

In much the same way that the astral emotion-substance condenses around our character traits, thus giving form to the densest layer of our astral body, so too the mental thought-substance condenses around the ideas and thought patterns resident within our unintentional awareness and thus gives form to the densest layer of our mental body. Every thing and idea we encounter and thus perceive, passes through this dense layer of the mental body before affecting our intentional objective awareness.

The domain of the mental body is that of essential meaning. By this I mean the meaning that each thing manifests. This is different than the meaning that we give to things in our process of personalization and sub-jectification. That is a secondary or interpreted meaning, not an ***essential*** meaning.

Essential meaning is the mental materia which constitutes the mental realm itself, and it is ***this*** mental materia that is crystallized by the ideo-logical content of our unintentional awareness into the densest level of our mental body. At its purest level of manifestation however, a human mental body perfectly reflects the essential meaning of its own Individu-ality or essential Self instead of the personalized content of the uninten-tional awareness.

The primary characteristic responsible for the structure and function of our mental body is that in the mental realm ***similarity*** is the basis of at-traction. Opposite essential meanings have no power of attraction be-tween each other, but similar essential meanings are inseparable. Thus the mental materia that is ***similar to*** the ideological content of our unin-tentional awareness crystallizes to form this dense layer of our mental body. And since it is this dense layer through which we perceive, the quality of our unintentional ideology dictates the objective quality of our perceptions. In other words, if the ideas that form the basis of how we perceive the world and ourselves are rife with self-hatred and self-doubt, then our experience of the world itself will be colored with the same bleak hues. Likewise, if they are filled with ideas of self-love and self-confidence, then our experience of the world will be bright and fulfilling.

The types of ideas that crystallize the mental body also dictate the types of essential meaning that our mental body automatically attracts and is attracted to. These are the ideas that are easiest for us to process, under-stand and sympathize with, and which affect us the most immediately. But we also encounter manifestations of essential meaning that we do not share similarity with and these, obviously, are the ideas that we have the most difficulty processing and understanding. Yet once we do process and understand them, these foreign ideas have the greatest power to change us utterly and absolutely by broadening our range of affinities within the mental realm.

The mental body is capable two basic approaches or techniques for the integration of essential meaning. The most common, default mode is ruled by the unintentional awareness and consists of modifying the essential meaning so that *it* fits within our own ideology. This prevents the encounter from significantly altering the ideological content of the unintentional awareness. Your automatic reaction to the words "warrior" and "Elephant" are examples of this mode in action.

You drew content from your unintentional awareness which limited your experience to the predictable and comfortable. You didn't learn anything from your initial reaction and you were not in any way changed by the encounter.

The second mode of approach, ruled by the intentional awareness, is to open *yourself* to change and modification so that *you* achieve greater affinity with the manifest essential meaning you have encountered. This means setting aside your resistance to change and your inclination to subjectify, and instead, exercising your power to truly explore the essential meaning for what *it* is. In other words, to truly open yourself to an experience of its *essential* meaning.

One way we go about this is to *think* about an idea. When we do this with an open mind, free of assumptions and preconceptions, then the idea will exert its attractive force over us and draw illuminating thoughts into our awareness. This can be a long process of looking at the idea from every angle imaginable and letting the mind follow the meanings that reveal themselves. A brief example of this was your objective examination and analysis of your automatic response to the word "Elephant".

The drawback of this method of thinking about something is that the process of thinking is itself influenced by the unintentional awareness. In other words, it occurs within the arena of our basic mind-set, that array of fundamental ideas which shape our every experience. Thus it is incapable of *directly* experiencing the essential meaning.

To *directly* perceive essential meaning is to *experience* it. Direct perception of essential meaning is never achieved through interpretation or through thinking. It is only achieved through *becoming*. By this I mean that you completely open yourself to being affected by the essential meaning. Thinking and interpretation come *after* direct perception and are not in any way a part of the act of *__perceiving__*.

When approached in this way, essential meaning opens itself to your awareness and shares itself with you, creating the deepest sort of mutual affinity or similarity. This *__experience__* of essential meaning increases your scope of affinities within the mental plane and grants you easy access to a broader variety of essential meaning than before the experience. In other words, it increases your objective Understanding.

To illustrate, I will now guide you through a technique for experiencing the essential meaning contained within an abstract idea. The first step is best described by one of my favorite poets as "resting with the question". This is a time during which you simply let the words which describe the idea float in your mind. You just sort of sit with them quietly and let them crystallize in your awareness. So, rest with the following words for a few moments:

**"The Universe is infinite."**

(pause)

In order for a thing to be infinite, it must encompass all space, all time and all meaning. Imagine now that space stretches without end in all directions from where you are reclining.

(pause)

You are at the exact center point of this infinite expanse. No matter where you move, space still stretches infinitely in all directions from where *__you__* are.

(pause)

Now feel how time stretches infinitely behind you and ahead of you.

(pause)

You exist at the exact center point of time in a bubble of now-ness and time always stretches infinitely in both directions.

(pause)

And now feel the infinite variety of essential meaning that fills this infinite space and time. There is no end to the variety.

(pause)

Your own essential meaning exists in context with all of the infinite variety of essential meaning that surrounds you and no matter how you change, you are always surrounded by an infinite variety.

(pause)

Within this infinite Universe, no matter how much or how little space, time and meaning you yourself encompass, you are always at the exact center of space, time and meaning.

(pause)

This is true for each and every point in space, each and every moment of time and each and every bit of meaning, not just those that _**you**_ occupy. There are an infinite number of centers in an infinite Universe.

(pause)

Now spread your awareness outward infinitely and _**become**_ the whole. _**Feel**_ yourself spatially infinite. _**Feel**_ yourself temporally infinite. _**Feel**_ yourself manifesting an infinite variety of essential meaning. _**BE**_ the infinite Universe.

(long pause)

Now gently refocus on my voice and listen to my words. Even though I just _**led**_ you through a series of conclusions rooted in the simple phrase "the Universe is infinite", all of these conclusions are nonetheless inherent to the idea itself and naturally arise in your awareness when you open yourself to this idea without the inclusion of thinking and interpreting. In other words, given sufficient time and openness, you would have had much the same experience of the essential meaning on your own had I not been guiding you through its layers. Only in introducing you to the technique was my guidance necessary.

Essential meaning is manifest in _**all**_ things, ideas being just one type of thing. To illustrate, I will now guide you through a technique for experiencing the essential meaning contained within an object. Specifically, the essential meaning manifest within the object you chose at the beginning of this meditation.

Please note that just by my mentioning your object, a series of events were initiated in your mind. In a flash of less than a second, you most likely pictured your object, experienced your usual emotional feelings about the object, and named or described your object.

However, in order to _**directly**_ perceive your object's essential meaning, you must now leave all of that behind and use only your intentional objective awareness. If you start thinking about your object then you are not _**perceiving**_. Instead, you are thinking and interpreting and trying to shape its essential meaning. So keep this in mind as we proceed.

Now open your eyes and fix your gaze upon your chosen object. Set aside all of your thinking and feeling about the object and just observe objectively for a moment. Rest with it for a moment and let its objective details crystallize in your awareness.

(pause)

Now open your awareness to the object itself and objectively perceive how it affects your awareness.

(pause)

If you find your internal dialogue thinking about the object then let your go of your thinking and refocus your awareness upon simply perceiving.

(long pause)

Try to experience for a moment what it would feel like to _**be**_ your object.

(pause)

Now let your mind think about your object and objectively observe the meaning that those thoughts express.

(pause)

To what degree and in what way do your thoughts express your _**experience**_ of the object's essential meaning?

(pause)

Now objectively perceive your emotional responses to your object and ask yourself to what degree and in what way they express your ***experience*** of the object's essential meaning.

(pause)

Now objectively examine the physical details of your object and observe how they manifest and communicate the object's essential meaning.

(pause)

Now close your eyes again and turn your awareness inward. Take a few moments to review your direct encounters with essential meaning and examine the unique qualities of your experience with essential meaning that make its direct perception different than any other form of perception. Try to fix this difference in your mind so that you can recall how it feels in the future.

(long pause)

Focus again on the sound of my voice and gently return to a more normal state of awareness. Gently open your eyes, sit upright and reorient yourself while I say a few words in closing.

Our temporal mental body is the clothing of ideas and thought patterns through which we manifest our own essential meaning. When their formation is left to the whims of the unintentional awareness, they allow us only a partial or clouded expression of our essential meaning and a skewed perception of the objective Universe. On the other hand, when these foundational ideas and habits of thinking are examined and transformed by the intentional objective awareness, our self-expression then becomes clearer and more sure, and our perceptions begin to truly reveal the objective Universe to our understanding.

By intentionalizing our mental body we also gain the power to open our awareness to an infinite range of essential meaning. This is important because it is through the incorporation of ever-new types of essential meaning that the essential Self evolves and expands and ultimately comes to encompass the whole infinite Universe.

I suggest that over the coming days and weeks you use the faculties of your intentional-objective awareness and actively pursue the direct perception of essential meaning in your mundane life. Truly experience the essential meanings you encounter and savor each to its fullest. Use your awareness to spend time truly experiencing life within the miracle of your own mental body!

# APPENDIX

# SOWANTHA

A Mystical Journey

By Rawn Clark

1996

I stepped again through the gazing glass and encountered the Greaters. I don't know what else to call them. My friend, the single Greater who welcomed me, has a name, but also a sense of self that utterly defies the limitations implied by "name". I call my friend Sowantha, only because that was the name I was told, not because I think I can somehow sum this entity up with a single word. Sowantha is neither male nor female in any sense that I can perceive, yet there is an overall femaleness to the world of the Greaters....a context in which my understanding and experience of gender quickly became useless.

Sowantha has no "body" in any way we conceive of. Being a completely mental creature, Sowantha assumes Individual shapes only as needed. That, in fact, is Sowantha's modus operandi, if you will. When I first encountered Sowantha and the world of the Greater's, I perceived myself standing on the surface of a dark planet where I was soon greeted by a darkly dressed, androgynous humanoid, sporting long black hair and aquiline features. I came to understand that both the planet beneath my feet and the humanoid speaking to me, were Individual manifestations of Sowantha, projected solely for the purpose of communication with me.

I've visited Sowantha and the world of the Greaters many times in the past year and a half. With each visit, Sowantha's planetoid and humanoid become brighter, more filled with light. It is absolutely clear to me that the brightness of Sowantha's projections is directly related to my level of understanding. Each thing I learn from the Greaters, brightens my perception of Sowantha, and what began as a very dark world, is fast becoming a luminous, detail filled gray.

Let me tell you about the world of the Greaters, or at least what I currently do and don't know of it. One thing I don't know, is exactly how many Greaters there are. Number, in this realm, is less relevant somehow, involving as it does "infinities" which are treated as closed Individuals. So, in our human terms, there could be anywhere from an infinite number of Greaters to only a small few. I can't tell yet, but I know intuitively that eventually I'll understand enough to figure it out.

I do know for certain that the Greaters have only one focus...the Work. They always capitalize this word when they speak it. I've seen the Work (perhaps I should say, *T*he Work) and I am awed, overwhelmed, and humbled beyond words by its grand scope and sheer Beauty. The Greaters were kind enough to project a visual image of The Work for me, so that I could more easily learn about It. Their visual projection displayed a very sculptural work of art, composed of several modules. These modules are the Greaters themselves, and their Work is their Ultimate Unity (yes, they capitalize these words too). I won't go into any real detail of the image itself (and believe me, I could write thousands of pages, it was so detailed!) because the image was specific to my particular understanding. Its symbols might mean something entirely different to you (in which case you'd be presented with a different image), so I've only ventured to outline its essential meaning.

As I said earlier, their modus operandi is the projection of Individuals. This bit is hard to explain, so bear with me. Sowantha, as a Greater, somehow condenses and then projects its awareness, manifesting autonomous Individuals. Sowantha's Individuals have a greater density than Sowantha does. It appears that the whole process of the Greaters condensing and projecting their awareness', creates a special Universe. This Universe seems infinite from within, but closed and finite from the external perspective of the Greaters. Inside, there are things like time and space, which are foreign to the Greaters. Yet it is inside of this Universe that the Greaters project their Individuals. These Individuals inhabit physical bodies and have their own projections, which they wear like masks, called Personas. At the Persona level, there is usually no awareness of the Greater self, and only vague intimations of the Individual, so dense is its level of manifestation and so dim the penetration of light.

The Greaters perform their Work with, through, and for their projected Individuals. In a time-space sense, their "goal" is for their Individuals to become aware of their true nature, and for each of them to reach a state of conscious connection with their Greater selves. From the perspective of their Individuals within their time-space Universe, The Work is something "to be done", something that has beginning, middle and end. To the Greaters though, The Work simply "is". Their Ultimate Unity is a thing of which they constantly partake, while simultaneously they strive to create it. Since we have time-space words and language, the Greater's perspective is hard to translate. It seems filled with contradictions, but these are only contradictions in space-time...opposites which neatly resolve themselves in the world of the Greaters.

The Greaters very much see themselves as intermediary creatures. They bridge two realms, that of physical time-space and that of undifferentiated Unity. Their realm has three perspectives: From within the Universe, their *Individuals* assume that they are the creators of their world, and that the world exists for their benefit alone. The *Greaters'* perspective is that they are the ultimate creators of the Universe and of Individuals, but also the humble servants of the Ultimate Unity. Of course the *Ultimate Unity* knows with absolute certainty that It is all there really is, and that all other speculations of creatorship are irrelevant (and probably irreverent).

I guess the Greaters could even be said to be the projections of the Ultimate Unity, and that the whole shebang is just a single entity manifesting across a broad spectrum of self-projected "reality". So much depends upon one's perspective.

Truly, perspective is why I write this at all. You see, it has become quite clear to me that I am one of Sowantha's projected Individuals! When I rise to the realm of the Greaters, my proper place is Sowantha.

In that rising, my pathway is through the core of my Individual self. I withdraw from my physical life, as if I viewed it from above, detached from its alluring and consuming drama. I stand in my Tiphareth, my Individual Solar being, my Center. It is through this small Center that I encompass the whole infinite Universe by traveling both inward towards the infinitely finite, and outward towards the illimitable. Then, in looking down with my encompassing vision, my perspective shifts, by direct act of will, to that of the Greater's realm. My awareness explodes with a trumpeting of many-colored lights, to encompass several Individual perspectives, simultaneously. My ability to focus and choose amongst the various Individual awarenesses, comes from a grandly inclusive and completely self-assured consciousness. And this is Sowantha, whom I know as only self can know self.

Each visit with Sowantha, each brightening of the Greater's world to my vision, brings me closer to the full perspective of my Greater self. I am becoming more consciously a part of The Work as with each visit I bring my Greater self's perspective and understanding, back with me to my Individual perspective. The once solid barriers between these perspectives are melting away and my Greater self finds more and more direct expression through my Individual self.

When I am with my Sowantha now, I explore other Individuals that I manifest throughout the stream of time-space, returning down "their" avenues instead of "my" rawn-Individual one. Some of these Individuals are familiar to my rawn-memory. A few of them/us/me even exist in the same time frame as my/our rawn-Individual. In this way, I-rawn am learning the Individual manifestations of my Greater part in The Work.

Each time that I merge with my Sowantha self, there is a moment in which I experience a sort of instinctual panic. It is expressly the fear of death, experienced by my rawn-Individual, as if I might get lost and not find my way back to rawn. At first this was a barrier, surmounted eventually by an act of faith and will. Conversely, when returning to my rawn-Individual, I am faced with an opposite panic of constriction, and a confusion over so great an abundance of choices within which to find rawn. This too was a temporary barrier, for it had the effect of making my search for the rawn-avenue, rather frantic, and precluded investigating other of the Individual-avenues available. With time, I have learned that these small panics are helpful guides that do not bar one's way when they are recognized as such. They naturally regulate the flow of consciousness from one focus to another.

Once these barriers became my friends and guides, I began randomly exploring some of the other Individuals which Sowantha manifests.

I have used the word "avenues" in this connection, because it seems the most poetically descriptive. When I shift my Sowantha focus to that point where I can view all my Sowantha-Individuals arrayed before me, my connection to each of them feels/looks like an avenue. I have the option of traveling down any one of these avenues from this point of focus. With the act of choosing a single avenue, I find my Sowantha awareness focused into an Individual form, though at first nondescript, standing upon said avenue. As I walk forward and down, the Individual-life I am exploring makes itself known to me through the scenery surrounding the avenue. This progresses and transforms, both itself and me, and I become steadily more involved in this Individual. Following this avenue ultimately leads to a fully conscious, real-time experience of this particular Individual perspective. But my Sowantha awareness is not bound by such a descent, and easily arises from involvement with the Individual chosen. At each step along this avenue, a specific focus upon this Individual's life is achieved. The further I travel into the Individual, the more narrow the viewable time frame, but the more intimate my experience. But from the beginning of each avenue, I can glimpse, albeit less intimately, the entire lifetime of my/this Individual, and pick from it what I want to know, sifting through scenes of an entire life experience.

With another shift of focus, all my Sowantha-Individuals are experienced simultaneously, and with varying degrees of intimacy depending entirely upon my-Sowantha will.

Sound confusing with the me/us/them/my/our/we? Indeed, shifting from any one of these perspectives to another, with any fluidity, has taken practice. My first experiences where very abrupt and disorienting, but now I smoothly and willfully move from perspective to perspective. And to do this is very blissful...no other English, time-space word comes as close to an accurate description. I know that eventually there will be no separation between these perspectives and that "my" perspective will come to encompass them all as a Unity.

Three days ago, in my rawn-Individual experience of things, I was approached "physically" for the first time, by Sowantha. I say "physically" in quotes, because while I experienced it from the perspective of my physical body, it was with my more subtle senses that I actually did the perceiving. At any rate, three days ago, just before noon, I turned a corner in my small house and was confronted with the translucent, yet visually solid, appearance of a person very familiar to me. This Individual was a teacher of mine once, and is a person for whom I hold a deep love and respect. The apparition was very strong, and likewise, it affected me very strongly. My friend was mute yet he spoke volumes with the poetry of his blissful smile.

I simply did not know what to make of this apparition. It wasn't till later that night, when I journeyed to Sowantha in my nightly meditation, that I discovered the meaning of my friend's visit. The humanoid who greeted me upon Sowantha's brightening planetoid was not the same Individual I had come to associate with Sowantha, but was instead the visage of my former teacher. I came to understand that this Individual is/ was also a manifestation of Sowantha Greater self.

The implications as to the complexity of The Work and its interweavings revealed to me by this simple statement were mind-boggling! Sowantha-memory passages were opened to me that showed in intricate detail, how for countless millennia, Sowantha has woven its Individuals together. One teaching the next in an unbroken chain of succession. And here and there, another Greater's string weaves in, revealing the richly textured fabric of The Work. Suddenly I see the Greaters as THE Weavers, and their Work appears as a grand tapestry.

The minutiae of the Ultimate Unity shines with a mind-numbing complexity. Looking at it closely is like shrinking down to sub-atomic size and glimpsing the endless rhapsody of universe-within-universe, hidden within absolutely everything, layer upon endless layer. In this looking, my Sowantha senses encompass the whole scene, offering the perspective of each and every one of its Individuals, strewn throughout the whole of time. To perceive as Sowantha is to also perceive, to some degree, as the Ultimate Unity, and so my focus shifts back and forth, from Individual to Greater to Unity, and back and forth.

This pendulum swing mixes my perspectives, broadening and contextualizing each to the point of radiant luminescence. I see my rawn-Individual part in The Work quite clearly, and from literally countless perspectives. Oh but that sounds so misleading when carved in these stone-like words! It sounds like everything is pre-destined...like we are locked into a mere, will-less enactment of some grand plan or something. This is assuredly NOT the case, but how to explain???

In their natural state, the Greaters do not have either space or time. In space-time terms (which are all we've got to work with here), I think the closest description would be that they experience ONLY a present moment, a "now". In time-space, we have "now" stretched out and divided into sequential moments, like an endless chain. The Greaters though, have only one "now", and encompassed by their "now" as a universe-within-universe, is the eternal time-chain of their Individual's Universe. No matter how I wrap my words around this concept, I still stumble over the fact that non-space/time just doesn't translate into space/time language.

Space-time is only truly experienced by Individuals. The magic in Individual perceptions is that they do not encompass all of time, and so each moment is experienced as spontaneous and filled with a multitude of choices. Individuals experience time-space as a living, evolving thing. I think this is a consequence of the Individual's short chain of moments called a lifetime. If we broaden our perspective to a hundred year span, we can see entire life cycles of Individuals and some part of the ripples of consequence their lives stir up, all encompassed by our singular view. Multiply this by infinity, add to it the perceptions of each of the countless Individuals involved, and then multiply again by the power-filled knowledge that you're essentially responsible for the whole thing, and you'll have a mere glimmer of an idea of a Greater's perspective.

From the midst of my immersion in the Greaters' perspective, I glimpse my Sowantha-self speaking to my rawn-Individual-self through the medium of my former-teacher-Individual-self. From some aspects of my multifaceted perspective, there seems a confusion of self-dialogue, of self telling self what self already knows. Yet at the more inclusive levels of my perception, this is quite clearly the natural mode of Greater communication with their Individuals. For my rawn-Individual to achieve a genuine understanding, I must needs receive information decipherable by, and relevant to, my Individual experience. It seems that this can only be accomplished one Individual to another, and so I-Sowantha speaks with me-rawn through the Individual of my former teacher.

I-rawn learn many things from my old friend, and when I look upon his face and hear his words, it is like conversing with completely familiar kin, so intimate is our knowledge of each other. We are like two mirrors reflecting each other, amplifying our Individual differences infinitely, yet by that very infinity we reveal our commonality. We revel in our commonality, and with equal élan, celebrate our differences. We are kin not by blood but by that inner spark which we share, whose relatedness is revealed only just now, here in the Greaters' realm.

I come to understand that a Greater translates those of its Individuals which achieve the level of their Greater self's awareness, into an existence external of the space-time Universe. Hence my former teacher, who assuredly reached at least this stage of self-realization during his Individual lifetime, has been translated to the Greaters' realm, his particular Individuality becoming an ambassador of Sowantha, for purposes of consistent and specific communication with Sowantha's self-realizing Individuals. This is yet another aspect of The Work's mind-boggling complexity of minute interdependencies and interweavings, as self raises self from within.

Individuals such as my old friend work together, seeking always to raise their fellow Individuals and move The Work forward through time-space. They are somehow an essential part of the Greaters' communication between Greater and Individual aspects of self. They seem to be a self-revealing veil that both separates, yet translates between, the realms of space-time and non-space-time...self-consciously Individualizing their Greater self.

These Individuals share the perspective of their Greater self, but not yet fully that of the Ultimate Unity. At some point in their eternal moment, they will choose to dissolve their Individual pattern and merge still further into their self. Again, this happens outside the realm of time-space and so these time-space words give only a small part of the picture. Suffice it to say, that these Individuals serve The Work, and most especially their Greater part in the Ultimate Unity.

Generally, Individuals like my former teacher act in the capacity typified by his contact with me. Here, he is the mouth-piece of Sowantha, communicating with me at an Individual level. It is important that his meaning be communicated to me at this specific level, instead of at the level of a direct merging with my Sowantha Greater self. For here at the Individual level, I have directly time-space involved experiences and learn things in ways that allow for a further communication on my part as an Individual to other Individuals. At the encompassing level of a Greater awareness, my rawn-Individual does not learn in the same way, and so translating these ephemeral perceptions into terms communicable to other Individuals would be made all the more difficult. The Greaters seem ever so considerate of their Individuals!

As my friend speaks his Sowantha words into our mirrored, infinite ears, I experience what I already know, and in so experiencing, come to know it differently, more viscerally. I am invited forward and offered conscious inclusion in Sowantha's part of The Work. This is not presented as an honor, for surely there are no rewards in accepting, nor any loss in refusing. What is offered is no different from what I-rawn am already doing and have no other desire but to do. But somehow this phrasing of it by Sowantha changes the context of my work, placing it in aspect to The Work, and I am deeply humbled. I must shake my Individual-rawn self to its foundation to first see if I am capable of such a task... I must ask my self and answer so many questions before answering my Sowantha's call. Oddly, this challenge is inherent in Sowantha's communication, but seems a benign, natural mechanism of self-proving internal communication between Greater and Individual levels of self. I-rawn do not feel questioned nor doubted, it is simply most appropriate to now make sure that all is in order and that the foundation is firm.

Each self-question is answered in its asking, and so I turn and answer my Sowantha with the only answer I have ever answered with..."yes". This changed nothing and changes everything at once! Sowantha opens to me-rawn and I-rawn melt, merging inexorably with Sowantha Greater self. It is very like I-rawn am a stream of water, entering the vast and seemingly infinite Ocean, connecting instantly with all the other molecules of water and becoming self aware as Ocean. As Ocean, I can easily distinguish between my Individual streams and see that it is their very multitude of differences that make me an Ocean at all...yet I, in my

Ocean-ness, am what is common throughout. No longer need I communicate with my self through the medium of another Individual, for now I can communicate with the Universe directly through my rawn-Individual.

As all Individual time-space experiences must, this experience ended. I, Rawn Clark, an Individual Human being, re-inhabited with excruciating awareness of its cramped state, my very familiar physical body. My physical body is unchanged, only in need of movement after so long a stasis, but my conscious awareness is quite changed indeed. There is no barrier remaining between Greater and Individual levels of my self awareness, though my contact with the Ultimate Unity is still quite limited. I am still quite clearly Rawn Clark, with all my Individual foibles and strengths, only now more clearly so, more inclusively so.

Made in the USA
Middletown, DE
21 December 2024

68051507R00135